Bloom's Literary Themes

DEATH AND DYING

Bloom's Literary Themes

DEATH AND DYING

Edited and with an introduction by
Harold Bloom
Sterling Professor of the Humanities
Yale University

Volume Editor
Blake Hobby

BLOOM'S
LITERARY CRITICISM
An imprint of Infobase Publishing

Bloom's Literary Themes: Death and Dying

Bloom's Literary Criticism
An imprint of Infobase Publishing
132 West 31st Street
New York NY 10001

Library of Congress Cataloging-in-Publication Data
Death and dying / edited and with an introduction by Harold Bloom ; volume editor, Blake Hobby.
    p. cm. — (Bloom's literary themes)
  Includes bibliographical references and index.
  ISBN 978-0-7910-9799-1 (hc : alk. paper) 1. Death in literature. I. Bloom, Harold.
II. Hobby, Blake.
  PN56.D4D395 2009
  809'.93548—dc22   2008042989

Bloom's Literary Criticism books are available at special discounts when purchased in bulk quantities for businesses, associations, institutions, or sales promotions. Please call our Special Sales Department in New York at (212) 967-8800 or (800) 322-8755.

You can find Bloom's Literary Criticism on the World Wide Web at
http://www.chelseahouse.com

Text design by Kerry Casey
Cover design by Takeshi Takahashi

Printed in the United States of America

IBT EJB 10 9 8 7 6 5 4 3 2 1

This book is printed on acid-free paper and contains 30 percent postconsumer recycled content.

Contents

Series Introduction by Harold Bloom: Themes and Metaphors

1. TOPOS AND TROPE

What we now call a theme or topic or subject initially was named a *topos*, ancient Greek for "place." Literary *topoi* are commonplaces, but also arguments or assertions. A topos can be regarded as literal when opposed to a trope or turning which is figurative and which can be a metaphor or some related departure from the literal: ironies, synecdoches (part for whole), metonymies (representations by contiguity) or hyperboles (overstatements). Themes and metaphors engender one another in all significant literary compositions.

As a theoretician of the relation between the matter and the rhetoric of high literature, I tend to define metaphor as a figure of desire rather than a figure of knowledge. We welcome literary metaphor because it enables fictions to persuade us of beautiful untrue things, as Oscar Wilde phrased it. Literary *topoi* can be regarded as places where we store information, in order to amplify the themes that interest us.

This series of volumes, *Bloom's Literary Themes*, offers students and general readers helpful essays on such perpetually crucial topics as the Hero's Journey, the Labyrinth, the Sublime, Death and Dying, the Taboo, the Trickster and many more. These subjects are chosen for their prevalence yet also for their centrality. They express the whole concern of human existence now in the twenty-first century of the Common Era. Some of the topics would have seemed odd at another time, another land: the American Dream, Enslavement and Emancipation, Civil Disobedience.

I suspect though that our current preoccupations would have existed always and everywhere, under other names. Tropes change across the centuries: the irony of one age is rarely the irony of another. But the themes of great literature, though immensely varied, undergo transmemberment and show up barely disguised in different contexts. The power of imaginative literature relies upon three constants: aesthetic splendor, cognitive power, wisdom. These are not bound by societal constraints or resentments, and ultimately are universals, and so not culture-bound. Shakespeare, except for the world's scriptures, is the one universal author, whether he is read and played in Bulgaria or Indonesia or wherever. His supremacy at creating human beings breaks through even the barrier of language and puts everyone on his stage. This means that the matter of his work has migrated everywhere, reinforcing the common places we all inhabit in his themes.

2. Contest as both Theme and Trope

Great writing or the Sublime rarely emanates directly from themes since all authors are mediated by forerunners and by contemporary rivals. Nietzsche enhanced our awareness of the agonistic foundations of ancient Greek literature and culture, from Hesiod's contest with Homer on to the Hellenistic critic Longinus in his treatise *On the Sublime*. Even Shakespeare had to begin by overcoming Christopher Marlowe, only a few months his senior. William Faulkner stemmed from the Polish-English novelist Joseph Conrad, and our best living author of prose fiction, Philip Roth, is inconceivable without his descent from the major Jewish literary phenomenon of the twentieth century, Franz Kafka of Prague, who wrote the most lucid German since Goethe.

The contest with past achievement is the hidden theme of all major canonical literature in Western tradition. Literary influence is both an overwhelming metaphor for literature itself, and a common topic for all criticism, whether or not the critic knows her immersion in the incessant flood.

Every theme in this series touches upon a contest with anteriority, whether with the presence of death, the hero's quest, the overcoming of taboos, or all of the other concerns, volume by volume. From Monteverdi through Bach to Stravinsky, or from the Italian Renaissance through the agon of Matisse and Picasso, the history of all the arts demonstrates the same patterns as literature's thematic struggle with itself. Our country's great original art, jazz, is illuminated by what the great creators called "cutting contests," from Louis Armstrong and

Duke Ellington on to the emergence of Charlie Parker's Bop or revisionist jazz.

A literary theme, however authentic, would come to nothing without rhetorical eloquence or mastery of metaphor. But to experience the study of the common places of invention is an apt training in the apprehension of aesthetic value in poetry and in prose.

Volume Introduction by Harold Bloom

I

To call "death and dying" a literary *topos* or commonplace can induce a momentary startlement, if only because learning to live with one's own mortality is the most universal of educations in reality. At 78, still recovering from a catastrophic year of illnesses and a near-fatal accident, I approach this introduction with an ironic wariness.

All literary tragedy depends upon delayed recognition, since in a tragic context to recognize fully indeed is to die. Hamlet, in my judgment, accepts death in the play's foreground. His spiritual father, the royal jester Yorick, died when the prince was seven, as we learn from the gravedigger in Act V. We thus know, again with the aid of the gravedigger, that Hamlet is thirty, an age irreconcilable with his undergraduate status at Wittenberg, but Shakespeare does not care about such details and so we need not either.

In my interpretation of *The Tragedy of Hamlet, Prince of Denmark*, it is not the murder of King Hamlet by his brother Claudius that has appointed the play's protagonist as death's ambassador to us. The loss of Yorick, who as playfellow had been mother and father to the prince, began the grand death-march of Hamlet's consciousness. All of Shakespeare's most famous drama is its protagonist's meditation upon death and dying.

Hamlet delays revenge because he does not know whether King Hamlet or King Claudius actually was what Freud calls his "phallic father". Nor do we know, because this most elliptical of all Shakespeare's masterworks gives us no intimation of how far back the fierce sexual passion of Gertrude and Claudius began. Hamlet is freed to kill Claudius only when the prince realizes that both he and his mother are dying. The rest is silence.

The tragedy, *Hamlet*, cannot be interpreted with any confidence, because everything that constitutes it is profoundly questionable. A drama that turns upon unanswerable questions deserves G. Wilson Knight's characterization, "The Embassy of Death." Literary and pictorial traditions have made the play's emblem Hamlet contemplating the skull of Yorick in the graveyard.

II

A very few great writers—Goethe, Tolstoy, Victor Hugo, Ibsen among them—have dallied with the fantastic surmise that literal immortality somehow might be possible for prodigies of nature such as themselves. The strongest of Renaissance Western authors—Shakespeare, Montaigne, Cervantes—entertained no such fiction, nor did the most magnificent of the ancients: the Yahwist, Homer, Virgil, and their son, Dante.

Norman Mailer once assured me that he himself believed in his weird fiction of a literal immortality, *Ancient Evenings*, after I had reviewed (with affection) that gorgeous compendium of humbuggery and bumbuggery. Perhaps he did.

One of the greatest of Western tropes is the fiction of the leaves in Isaiah, Homer, Pindar, Virgil, Spenser, Milton, Coleridge, Shelley, Whitman, Wallace Stevens. I trudge about New Haven in this golden October, and my cane kicks up the scarlet leaves of the maple, reminding me of my own impending mortality. The tale of any individual life in a mellow autumn of the body too easily can become a study of the nostalgias. Is it perhaps the final use of high imaginative literature to tint one's own fading with the color of the Sublime?

Can there be a power of the mind *over* a universe of death? Sometimes I think that is the unifying theme holding together the Western canon. We tell ourselves the saving lie that Whitman's great fourfold trope of night, death, the mother, and the sea is not the inevitable representation of our universal fate. Set against the abyss, the literary mind is hardly adequate to cope, yet what mode of mind is? Religion, particularly in the United States, is the poetry of the people but its force also is illusory in confronting death, your own death.

A persuasive fiction, literary *or* religious, turns back from natural limit to celebrate the will to live. The strongest Western authors—the Yahwist, Homer, Dante, Montaigne, Shakespeare, Cervantes, Milton, Goethe, Whitman—ultimately teach us that Spinoza was accurate in saying that wisdom is meditation upon life rather than upon death. Even in Shakespeare, the Sublime of literature, the greatest figures testify to the power of the mind over the sorrow of their fates: Falstaff, Hamlet, Cleopatra. Falstaff dies broken-hearted, yet his wit abides. Supreme intelligence never abandons Hamlet, and Cleopatra's high style, at the end, achieves its own sublimity.

ALL QUIET ON THE WESTERN FRONT (ERICH MARIA REMARQUE)

"Erich Maria Remarque's
All Quiet on the Western Front"
by Merritt Moseley,
University of North Carolina at Asheville

The First World War lasted four years and caused the deaths of millions of men, the mutilation of millions more, the widowing of millions of women, and the orphaning of millions of children. It led to the fall of well-established imperial regimes in Germany, Austria-Hungary, and Russia, the dissolution of the Ottoman Empire, the rise of the world's first Bolshevik state, the creation of new countries, and the redrawing of national boundaries between old ones. John Mueller's study of changing attitudes toward war acknowledges the excessive destructiveness of the First World War—in France the decade 1910-1919 saw 5.63 percent of the population killed or wounded in battle, while the highest previous percentage was 1.54 percent in the decade that included the Napoleonic wars—but Mueller doubts that the First World War contained an unprecedented destruction of human lives (14). Instead, he contends that the conflict seemed so destructive because it followed a long period of unprecedented peace. And it is the seeming that is most important; as Mueller explains:

> The experience of the First World War clearly changed attitudes toward war in the developed world. In an area where war had been accepted as a fixture for thousands of years, the

> idea now gained substantial currency that war was no longer an
> inevitable fact of life and that major efforts should be made to
> abandon it. (1)

Though the First World War involved many millions of combatants, most people did not experience it in the usual sense of the word. If their attitudes toward war changed, then the experience that changed them was secondhand. Moreover, the likelihood is that it came through reading.

The poems and novels of World War I had a powerful impact on people's thoughts about war. Perhaps none had so much influence as Erich Maria Remarque's novel *Im Westen Nichts Neues,* serialized in the German newspaper *Vossiche Zeitung* in 1928, then published in book form in January 1929. It created an immediate sensation, meeting with astonishing success. Within three months it sold 640,000 copies. An English translation was published in March, an American one in May, a French one in June (note the fervor with which the countries that had been at war against Germany, and provided troops for the Western Front, took to the novel). It was a Book-of-the-Month selection in the United States. The already great impact of the novel was multiplied when Hollywood produced a film version in 1930, itself described as "a document of staggering force" (Jones 273). It won the Academy Award for best film.

And the success of *All Quiet* was not simply popular; the novel (and film) were critical favorites, particularly on first appearance. Remarque's supposedly frank portrayal of human responses to war and the depiction of a pitiful dignity under suffering were praised with gusto. "The greatest of all war books" was a phrase that appeared in numerous reviews. Its "holy sobriety" would bring about "the rehabilitation of our generation," predicted German writer Axel Eggebrecht. Herbert Read—an English critic, Great War combat veteran and author of a war memoir himself—heralded Remarque's account as "the Bible of the common soldier" and struck a religious note that would recur frequently. "... [It] has swept like a gospel over Germany," wrote Read, "and must sweep over the whole world, because it is the first completely satisfying expression in literature of the greatest event of our time." In the initial reviews, then, there was rarely a note of vigorous criticism, and there was near unanimity that the book presented "the truth about the war."

It did not take long for doubts to arise, at first about Remarque's own military experience (it seems to have been very slight, hardly the years suggested by the publicity accompanying the book) and then—since a novel's quality is really independent of the author's own firsthand knowledge of its materials—about what "truth" it told about the war and, more broadly, what sort of effect the book had on readers' morale.

Remarque's popular success surprised many observers who thought that war books would not sell. There had been earlier books about the war, some of them distinguished novels and memoirs, such as Henry Barbusse's angry, antiwar *Le Feu* (*Under Fire*) in 1916, Ernst Jünger's *In Stahlgewittern* (usually translated *Storm of Steel*) in 1920, and John Dos Passos' *Three Soldiers* in 1921. But the best-known Great War novels and memoirs weren't published until about a decade after the war ended. Edmund Blunden's *Undertones of War* appeared in 1928; Robert Graves's *Goodbye to All That*, Ernest Hemingway's *A Farewell to Arms*, and Richard Aldington's *Death of a Hero*, like *All Quiet*, were all published in 1929. Frederic Manning's *Her Privates We* and Siegfried Sassoon's *Memoirs of an Infantry Officer* came out in 1930. All these books were by trench veterans, except for Hemingway's (he was in the ambulance corps); all, again excepting Hemingway's, were about the Western Front. All made their impact on readers by at least giving the impression that they were *telling the truth*. The early reactions to *All Quiet* testify to this. Likewise, Aldington included a note to his readers promising, "I have recorded nothing which I have not observed in human life, said nothing I do not believe to be true" (Willis 467).

What was that truth? It could not have been the kind of truths obvious to anyone who thinks about war: that men kill and die, that wounds are painful, that the private soldier knows little of the geopolitical aims for which he is supposedly fighting. The "truths" these novels revealed were unsettling ones, far beyond the mere facts of death and destruction.

One such category of truth had to do with the behavior of the soldiers and the way in which the veneer of "civilization"—for which, ironically, all sides claimed to be battling—fell away. As Willis explains:

> The problem facing the young war novelists in the 1920s was how to be faithful to the bitter, life-changing experience

of modern warfare in a realistic depiction of both action and dialogue. The war had altered forever the perceptions of soldier-writers, and when the novelists finally found their voices almost 10 years after the armistice, they were determined to depict accurately and unblushingly the sexual behavior of men at war and the four-letter language they used with regularity. (470–71)

This proved impossible. Aldington, Hemingway, and Remarque all had to submit to some editing, usually of the language their soldiers spoke. The American edition of *All Quiet* went beyond modifying language to the removal of two scenes: one a tender scene of sexual reconciliation between a wounded soldier and his wife, assisted by his comrades at arms, and the other a lighthearted account of men using the latrine (472). These scenes were not restored for American readers until 1975, though the censored translation is still the most widely used American version (Tighe 48). It is hardly likely that the publishers at Little, Brown thought it *untrue* that soldiers defecate, so truthfulness was less the problem than general decorum of the times.

The larger issue of truthfulness had to do with the nature of the war itself. Among the "truths" that readers of World War I stories stood to learn were that:

- Young men enlisted in idealism, often encouraged by their elders, whose promises of quick glory were false, even if not knowingly so;
- Life at the front was dreary and uncomfortable (lice and rats are usually mentioned), always dangerous, and dangerous to no particular purpose, since the war seemed to accomplish nothing; charges were always repelled, sooner or later, the men remained in their trenches, and the only thing that happened to them was getting wounded or killed;
- The officers, at least above about the rank of lieutenant, were out of touch, callous about loss of life, and simple-minded in their plans for the soldiers;
- The only positive value for men at the front was comradeship, or love for one another;

- The civilians back home were willfully ignorant of the facts of the war, and soldiers found themselves unable to communicate and in some cases (Barbusse's novel and Sassoon's poetry are particularly good examples) unable to prevent themselves from hating politicians, journalists, and civilians generally, often specifically the women;
- Alienation from the world beyond the battlefield often left men feeling more benevolence for the "enemy" than others—again, this might include officers, civilians, women—on their own side.

All Quiet on the Western Front is a central repository for all these war ideas. It is narrated by Paul Bäumer, who enlists right out of school, urged on by his schoolmaster. Bäumer goes to the front and forms a cohesive emotional group with some of his schoolmates who joined up with him, other men including some from unfamiliar (lower) classes, and their leader, an older veteran called Kat. Throughout the war Paul sees his friends wounded and killed. The monotony of charges and countercharges and the passive endurance of shelling demoralize him. He is wounded and hospitalized. He goes home on leave and is amazed at how estranged he is from his family and everything behind the front lines. He knifes a Frenchman and spends the night in a shell hole, watching him die. Finally, Paul loses Kat, and, shortly afterward he is killed, near the end of the war, on a day when so little happened (except, probably, several thousand men lost their lives), it was "so quiet and still on the whole front, that the army report confined itself to the single sentence: All quiet on the Western Front" (291).

For the most part, Paul's war activity is narrated in an impressionistic way. For instance, during an attack:

> We have become wild beasts. We do not fight, we defend ourselves against annihilation. It is not against men that we fling our bombs, what do we know of men in this moment when Death is hunting us down—now, for the first time in three days we can see his face, now for the first time in three days we can oppose him; we feel a mad anger. No longer do we lie helpless [under the preliminary bombardment that preceded the enemy attack], waiting on the scaffold, we can

destroy and kill, to save ourselves, to save ourselves and to be revenged. (113)

A more detailed narrative style is reserved for peaceful episodes, including conversations among the comrades, a touching sexual interlude with some French women, and visits to the hospital.

But perhaps the most powerful passages are those of commentary and reflection, strongly philosophical moments that vividly express the novel's main themes: for instance, the idealism that would be followed by cruel disillusionment:

> When we went to the district commandant to enlist, we were a class of twenty young men, many of whom proudly shaved for the first time before going to the barracks. We had no definite plans for our future. Our thoughts of a career and occupation were as yet of too unpractical a character to furnish any scheme of life. We were still crammed full of vague ideas which gave to life, and to the war also an ideal and almost romantic character. (20)

Remarque also particularly highlights the gulf between the young and the old. At first, it is schoolmasters and other authority figures:

> For us lads of eighteen they ought to have been mediators and guides to the world of maturity, the world of work, of duty, of culture, of progress—to the future. We often made fun of them and played jokes on them, but in our hearts we trusted them. The idea of authority, which they represented, was associated in our minds with a greater insight and a more humane wisdom. But the first death we saw shattered this belief. We had to recognize that our generation was more to be trusted than theirs. . . . While they continued to write and talk, we saw the wounded and dying. While they taught that duty to one's country is the greatest thing, we already knew that death-throes are stronger. . . . We loved our country as much as they; we went courageously into every action; but also we distinguished the false from true, we had suddenly learned to see. (11–12)

Later, when Paul goes home on leave, he finds that the gulf divides him from his father and mother as well. As Evelyn Cobley writes, in the "mildest form, fathers are guilty of perpetuating war by wanting to experience it vicariously" (82).

Remarque also focuses on the dehumanization of the civilized German youth (and presumably the French youth as well). At one point, he observes that "man is essentially a beast, only he butters it over like a slice of bread with a little decorum" (43). The ability to regress to animalism is the key to survival; shedding the decorum that is useful at home is a necessity at the front. Once the men hear approaching artillery shells and somehow, instinctively, save themselves, Paul comments:

> By the animal instinct that is awakened in us we are led and protected. It is not conscious; it is far quicker, much more sure, less fallible, than consciousness. . . . It is this other, this second sight in us, that has thrown us to the ground and saved us, without our knowing how. If it were not so, there would not be one man alive from Flanders to the Vosges. We march up, moody or good-tempered soldiers—we reach the zone where the front begins and become on the instant human animals. (556)

Though the reversion to an animal state is a successful adaptive technique for frontline troops, it also has its drawbacks. Paul is saddened when he realizes he can no longer enjoy his books, and he worries about what will become of the dehumanized men when the war is over. It is this worry that underlies his frequent plaint that they are lost and forlorn. His death, of course, obviates answering the question in his case, but it resonates for the survivors. Perhaps this notion of animal behavior is a convenient excuse, because man is the only animal that actually assembles armies and goes to war. Cobley comments: "Even when First World War narratives depict scenes of frenzied killing, soldiers are generally exempted from responsibility. Such scenes tend to suggest that the conditions of war strip men of their humanity, to reveal the primitive animal instincts we suspect are lurking in all of us" (85).

What positive values can be set off against the misery of life at the front, the pain of loss, the futility of military action, the likelihood of one's own death? In war novels possible consolations might be the hope of victory, or the thought of loved ones. Paul lacks these comforts. His mother is dying, the rest of his family are strangers to him, and he has enlisted in the army too young to have any romantic ties. Furthermore, Paul sees the war as lost, an important distinction from English war novels: At least the English *won*.

The most important positive value (aside from continued life itself) that *All Quiet on the Western Front* presents is comradeship. Paul's life is made tolerable by his small group (a group that gets smaller by attrition, of course) of good friends and comrades and his wise companion Kat. There has been considerable treatment of this theme in recent criticism. Santanu Das vividly insists that close quarters and bodily contact foster loyalty, and "Such intimacy must also be understood to exist as a triumph over death; it must be seen as a celebration of life, of young men huddled against long winter nights, rotting corpses, and falling shells" (55). Paul gives eloquent testimony to the value of what he calls "the finest thing that arose out of the war—comradeship" (27). Paul's love for his friend Kemmerich, who loses his leg and then his life, is part of the evidence that Paul is not in fact the animal he—sometimes shamefully, sometimes proudly—declares himself. Toward the end of the novel (which is also toward the end of the war, as Paul dies in its last month) Paul interrupts a passage of melancholy reflection on war and death with this:

> It is a great brotherhood, which adds something of the good-fellowship of the folk-song, of the feeling of solidarity of convicts, and of the desperate loyalty to one another of men condemned to death, to a condition of life arising out of the midst of danger, out of the tension and forlornness of death—seeking in a wholly unpathetic way a fleeting enjoyment of the hours as they come. If one wants to appraise it, it is at once heroic and banal—but who wants to do that? (269)

It is but one step further to find companionship with the enemy, and one of the most powerful scenes in *All Quiet* is when Paul, during a charge, slides into a shell hole and resolves to kill anyone who joins him there. He duly knifes a French soldier, then spends hours with him, in enforced intimacy, while he slowly dies. He feels guilty, then tries to help the Frenchman, calling him "'Comrade, *camerade,*

camerade, camerade'—eagerly repeating the word, to make him understand" (223). When he dies, Paul addresses him with:

> Forgive me, comrade. We always see it too late. Why do they never tell us that you are poor devils like us, that your mothers are just as anxious as ours, and that we have the same fear of death, and the same dying and the same agony—Forgive me, comrade; how could you be my enemy? If we threw away these rifles and this uniform you could be my brother just like Kat and Albert. (226)

This is a moving passage. It is also the sort of sentiment that undoubtedly led to condemnation of *All Quiet* by those worried that it would undermine martial spirit. There is little doubt that Remarque *wanted* to undermine enthusiasm for war; he has Paul say to his dead Frenchman, "If I come out of it, comrade, I will fight against this, that has struck us both down; from you, taken life—and from me—? Life also. I promise you, comrade. It shall never happen again" (229). Of course, Paul did not come out of it. But Remarque did.

After the first largely enthusiastic reception of the novel, voices of dissent began to be heard, including critics on both the left and the right. Ecksteins points out how "Traditionalists were incensed by what they saw as a completely one-sided portrait of the war experience. They objected to the language in the novel, to the horrifying images, to the frequent references to bodily functions, and, especially, to a scene involving a jovial group perched on field latrines" (355). The decades after 1918 involved a controversy over what the war meant and particularly over who owned the war.

Despite its enormous popularity, *All Quiet on the Western Front* did not turn the tide of popular opinion. It was less a cause of postwar disenchantment than a symptom; it caught a mood that thoughtful people had already begun to feel. John Mueller sums up the change in language that Paul would understand:

> ... before 1914 the institution of war still carried with it much of the glamour and the sense of inevitability it had acquired over the millennia. Despite the remarkable and unprecedented century of semi-peace in Europe, war still appealed not only to woolly militarists, but also to popular

opinion and to romantic intellectuals as something that was sometimes desirable and ennobling, often useful and progressive, and always thrilling. . . . The First World War may not have been all that much worse than some earlier wars, but it destroyed the comforting notion that wars in Europe would necessarily be long on dashing derring-do and short on bloodshed, and it reminded Europeans of how bad wars on their continent could become. (24–25)

Yuval Noah Harari concurs: "[T]he twentieth-century martial experience of disillusionment is the product of prewar cultural expectations more than of any new military realities" (69). But attempts to minimize the change in expectations—the war was *not* deadlier than any other wars; it *did* serve a purpose; some men actually felt most fully alive and jolly at the front; people had always known what war was like—are beside the point. For the first time, the revulsion against a war was widespread among all sorts of people and, more remarkably, among the victors as well as (maybe even more than) among the vanquished. That mood was both the condition that permitted, and was the fruit of, a set of remarkable World War I narratives, of which one of the most famous continues to be Remarque's *All Quiet on the Western Front.*

WORKS CITED

Cobley, Evelyn. "Violence and Sacrifice in Modern War Narratives." *SubStance* 23 (1994): 75–99.

Cole, Sarah. "Modernism, Male Intimacy, and the Great War." *ELH* 68 (Summer 2001): 469–500.

Das, Santanu. "'Kiss me, Hardy': Intimacy, Gender, and Gesture in World War I Trench Literature." *Modernism-Modernity* 9 (January 2002): 51–74.

Harari, Yuval Noah. "Martial Illusions: War and Disillusionment in Twentieth-Century and Renaissance Military Memoirs." *The Journal of Military History* 69 (January 2005): 43–72.

Jones, Dorothy B. "War Without Glory." *The Quarterly of Film, Radio, and Television* 8 (Spring 1954): 273–289.

Mueller, John. "Changing Attitudes Towards War: The Impact of the First World War." *British Journal of Political Science* 21 (January 1991): 1–28.

Remarque, Erich Maria. *All Quiet on the Western Front.* Trans. A.W. Wheen. Boston: Little, Brown, 1929.

Tighe, Joseph A. "*All Quiet on the Western Front*: A Phenomenological Investigation of War." *Critical Survey* 16 (2004): 48–61.

Willis, J.H., Jr. "The Censored Language of War: Richard Aldington's *Death of a Hero* and Three Other War Novels of 1929." *Twentieth Century Literature* 45 (Winter 1999): 467–487.

"Because I Could Not Stop for Death" (Emily Dickinson)

"Toward Eternity: The Final Journey in Emily Dickinson's 'Because I could not stop for Death'"
by Robert C. Evans, Auburn University at Montgomery

"Death is the mother of beauty."
　　　　　　——Wallace Stevens, "Sunday Morning"

Most animals are aware of death, but perhaps only humans are aware of its personal inevitability. A common synonym for human beings is, appropriately enough, "mortals"—creatures who are not only fated to die but who are also fated to be aware, throughout most of their lives, of the unceasing approach of death. Death may arrive abruptly or gradually, but its coming is certain and inescapable. Despite its certainty, death remains perhaps the most mysterious of all aspects of existence. We have no idea how to prevent it, nor do we have any certainty about what, precisely, it involves. Is there any kind of survival after death? Is death merely a transition to a new state of conscious being, or is it the final cessation both of consciousness and of being altogether? And, if consciousness does somehow survive death, what might such survival involve? Is the "afterlife" (if one exists) full of pleasure or of pain? Or is it full of pleasure for some and pain for others? Or is it, perhaps, a kind of existence we simply cannot comprehend or describe using the language and ways

13

of thinking to which we are normally accustomed? In all these many ways death remains mysterious—and, for that reason, it also remains endlessly fascinating and intriguing.

Few works of literature manage to convey the mysteriousness of this compelling topic more effectively than Emily Dickinson's brief lyric "Because I could not stop for Death," which is deservedly one of its author's most widely read and highly praised poems. Interpretations of the purpose, meanings, and final significance of the work vary widely, yet almost everyone who reads it concedes its force and power. Paradoxically, this poem in which Dickinson confronts death most directly is one of her most immortal works. Thus a poem in which she imagines her speaker's expiration has allowed Dickinson herself to attain a kind of everlasting literary life. The poem explores one of the most common and basic concerns of existence in ways that never seem trite or predictable. It is a poem that seems to have been born of deep meditation, and one that in turn provokes further meditation in its readers.

Only a very close reading can even begin to do justice to the complexities of this lyric and its subtly ambiguous treatment of death. The anonymous, unidentified speaker (who is later revealed to be a female) begins with a word—"Because"—that suggests a rational, logical mind—yet the rest of line 1 is illogical to the point of being humorous: "Because I could not stop for Death." The joke, of course, is that eventually and inevitably, every single person living *must* "stop for Death" (or be stopped *by* death). Yet the joke is not merely at the expense of the preoccupied speaker but at the expense of all of us who tend to take our lives, and our mundane preoccupations, for granted. The fact that the speaker is willing to mock herself already suggests the wisdom and maturity the ensuing poem will repeatedly demonstrate. The speaker is, for the most part, unafraid of death; for much of the poem, her tone is calm, reasonable, and even wryly amused. Certainly the tone is never morbid, neurotic, or excessively fearful, nor does the speaker ever really seem narcissistic or excessively self-absorbed. In some respects, the poem is oddly gothic—as if we are hearing a voice from beyond the grave—yet the effect is not (for the most part) creepy or bizarre. Dickinson could easily have written a far more disturbing poem, but instead she presents us with a mostly calm speaker whose opening emphasis on comic self-absurdity sets a mood that seems both witty and wise. This poem avoids the mawkish pitfalls of much funereal verse. It is never moralizing, never sentimental, and never heavy-handed.

Humor in the face of death continues in line 2: because the speaker could not stop for Death, "He kindly stopped for me." If we cannot make time for Death (the speaker implies), then he will courteously make time (while also, of course, ending time) for us. By this point in the poem, it becomes clear that in this work "Death" is not an abstract concept but a personification. Paradoxically, Death is described as if he were a living being. Yet he is not at all a clichéd grim reaper, nor a malevolent, almost sadistic figure of the sort who appear in so many other literary works. Instead, Death in Dickinson's poem is a "kindly" figure—almost a direct ancestor of that "gentleman in a dustcoat" who would later appear in John Crowe Ransom's somewhat similar poem titled "Piazza Piece." The young woman in Ransom's poem, however, threatens to scream when approached by Death, whereas the woman in Dickinson's poem remains calm and self-controlled. Perhaps the tone of the word "kindly," then, is not entirely (or even at all) sardonic or paradoxical. Perhaps the speaker feels that Death really *has*, in fact, done her a kindness by having "stopped" to pick her up in his carriage. Christians, after all, believe that death could be the door to an eternally happy life, and if the ensuing poem is read with this assumption in mind, then the tone of the opening stanza is not only partly humorous but also reassuringly comic. The initial stanza implies an ultimately happy ending to this strange (but also completely common) encounter between an individual and Death. If the speaker assumes that Death will finally escort her into a joyous eternal life, then the word "kindly" loses much of its initial sense of apparent irony.

The assumption that Death is being genuinely kind helps explain the readiness with which the speaker enters Death's "Carriage" (l. 3), which is often read as a symbolic hearse. No sooner is Death mentioned than the speaker has joined him on a drive. Although resistance would (by definition) be futile, literature is full of examples of characters who have refused (in Dylan Thomas's famous phrasing) to "go gentle into that good night" but instead have chosen to "Rage, rage against the dying of the light." The fact that the speaker of the poem is later revealed to be a woman is significant because the apparent passivity—or trust, or faith—she demonstrates in this opening stanza was thought, at the time of the poem's writing, to be typical of her sex. Yet all people, of whatever gender, are necessarily passive when facing death: All people must ultimately submit when Death and his carriage arrive. Dickinson's speaker, when confronting Death, shows none of the frantic desperation or even hysteria that might have been expected of a stereotypically emotional woman of her day. She immediately and quietly acquiesces, but her acquiescence seems not a sign of weakness but of strength, trust, and calm rationality.

Readers may feel more troubled by her entrance into the carriage than she herself feels, especially when the third line suggests that the woman is apparently alone with Death. Yet Dickinson plays another subtle joke on us by unexpectedly revealing, in line 4, that this odd couple is attended by a chaperone: Immortality. However, Immortality is in some ways as shadowy and mysterious a figure as Death. Should the speaker (and the poem's readers) feel reassured by Immortality's presence? What, exactly, does Immortality's presence imply? Immortality could just as easily be associated with immortal pain as with immortal happiness. The tone of the poem suggests that the speaker associates Immortality with the latter fate rather than the former, but the ultimate significance of the figure (who is mentioned just once) is by no means clear. Like so much else in this poem—a poem, incidentally, that is full of simple diction, direct images, and a relatively straightforward structure—the presence of Immortality is ultimately mysterious. Neither he, nor Death, nor the speaker herself ever engages in conversation; their ride together is intimate but silent, and the fact that they never talk is just one of many aspects of this poem that leaves its readers largely in the dark.

Having opened the poem with a stanza guaranteed to create interest and suspense, in the second stanza Dickinson now launches her speaker on both a literal and figurative rite of passage. The poem is constructed as a leisurely ride, a metaphorical movement through space as well as through time, thereby implying that if life itself is conventionally viewed as a journey, then the same also is true of the movement toward death. The poem moves with the same unhurried, deliberate pace as Death's "Carriage": "We slowly drove—He [Death] knew no haste" (l. 5). The very slowness of the ride creates suspense, especially since we are given no clear sense of the underlying purpose of the journey or its ultimate destination. Yet the speaker's attitude remains unperturbed. She describes how she "put away" both her "labor" and her "leisure too" (ll. 6-7): everything that had once seemed so important and distracting (everything that had once made her think she "could not" take the time to "stop for Death") now recedes in importance. She has acquiesced in this journey (after all, what choice did she have?), and her attitude toward Death reflects the same kind of "Civility" she attributes to Death himself (l. 8). So far the poem demonstrates none of the fears normally associated with thoughts of death, including the fear of mortality, the fear of the process of actually dying, or the fear of what comes afterward. Death, here and throughout the poem, is not depicted in conventional fashion as either a punishment or a reward. There is no emphasis on its ugliness, grue-someness, or pain. No threats are stated or even strongly implied, and the personified Death remains an oddly abstract, colorless figure who is not described in any elaborate or eerie detail. His lack of color or character is perfectly appropriate to his role; he is, after all, the very extinction of personality. What little we learn of him concerns the speaker's perceptions rather than any vivid depiction of him per se.

The focus of the work is less on Death the personified, alle-gorical figure than on the journey he and the speaker undertake, and Dickinson shows her skill in using a "metaphysical conceit" (that is, an analogy that is pursued at length over several stanzas). Here the "conceit" (or comparison) implies that death is a slow, steady move-ment outward and away from the routine and familiar, and in the brilliantly organized third stanza this emphasis on the journey—as Death and the speaker pass through (and away from) life—becomes especially conspicuous. Dickinson uses "anaphora" (repetition of a word or words at the beginnings of lines) to emphasize the idea of movement through time and especially through space: "We passed . . . / We passed . . . / We passed" (ll. 9, 11-12). The repetitions mark the stages of movement of both the carriage and the poem, but they also help reinforce the sense of leisurely progression. If this is a journey toward death, it involves no quick or hasty rushing. The lady passenger is given time to notice and comment on the sights and neglects to protest at all. She merely observes. She notices "the School, where Children strove / At Recess—in the Ring" (ll. 9-10); she notices "the Fields of Gazing Grain" (l. 11). And finally she notices "the Setting Sun" (l. 12). It has become a critical commonplace to associate each of these details with the stages of life: the children symbolize care-free youth; the "Gazing Grain" symbolizes the attainment of physical maturity; the "Setting Sun" symbolizes the onset of old age. This standard interpretation is persuasive, and the stanza also seems to be organized not only as a movement away from the populated town (associated with the school) and toward the unpopulated countryside (associated with the grain) but also as a progress from noon or thereabouts (presumably the time of a schoolyard "Recess") toward later in the day.

However all the sense of regular, steady movement is abruptly disrupted at the beginning of stanza four. The speaker suddenly concedes that it is not she, Death, and Immortality who "passed the Setting Sun" (l. 12); "rather—He passed Us" (l. 13). This shift in perspective is accompanied by a shift in imagery: The focus is no longer on the details of the external scenery but on the speaker's own discomfort. She realizes that she is dressed in inappropriately light clothing now that darkness and cold are coming on, and she notes (with effective assonance) that "The Dews drew quivering and chill" (l. 14). For the first time in the poem, the tone is somewhat ominous or uncomfortable, and for the first time the whole experience takes on some of the more familiar connotations conventionally associated with death. Dickinson, however, still has the power to surprise, as when she says that the carriage "paused before a House that seemed / A Swelling in the Ground" (ll. 17-18). The decision to describe a grave (associated with the dead) as a "House" (associated with the living) is typical of the paradox and ambiguity that are strong features of this entire poem. Equally memorable are the ensuing lines: "The Roof was scarcely visible—/ The Cornice—in the Ground" (ll. 19-20). The repetition and rhyming of the word "Ground" emphasizes the brute fact and finality of the grave. However, it is also typical of the unpredictable nature of this entire work to speak of the grave's "Roof" or "Cornice," and the inclusion of these kinds of unexpected and somewhat puzzling details adds to the sense of mystery and strangeness evoked by this entire lyric. It is a poem that treats Death as if it were alive; a poem that depicts a speaker who is weirdly calm in the face of her own demise; a poem that speaks of "Grain" as "Gazing"; and a poem that makes the grave seem almost reassuringly domestic. Dickinson also leaves it unclear whether the journey continues past the grave or whether the grave is indeed the final destination. The carriage is said to have "paused before" the grave (l. 17), but is this pause permanent or merely temporary? Like so much else in this thought-provoking work, the answer is unclear. Dickinson seems in no hurry to provide simple or easy answers to any of the mysteries this poem evokes; like death itself, her poem is shrouded in uncertainties.

This is especially true of the peculiar final stanza. "Since then," the stanza begins (l. 21)—but when, precisely, is "then"? Does "then" refer to the pause at the grave? Or does it refer to the beginning of the whole initial encounter with Death? Does "then" imply that the speaker has already died and that she is speaking to us literally from beyond (or within) the grave? Or is she still living, and was the whole experience of the carriage ride simply an eye-opening daydream that has nonetheless radically altered her perspective on life? The speaker says that it is "Centuries" (l. 22) since "then," but is the reference to "Centuries" literal or metaphorical? Is this time reference, in other words, reasonably precise or wildly exaggerated? As usual (and as befits its subject), the poem raises far more questions than it clearly answers. The speaker concludes by saying that she "surmised" that the "Horses' Heads / Were toward Eternity" (ll. 23-24), but this statement is at least as puzzling as anything else in the poem. For instance, does the statement imply that she has already reached "Eternity" or that she is still merely headed in that direction? And what, precisely, does "Eternity" mean (or refer to) in this poem? Is it synonymous with "Immortality," or is it somehow distinct? Is "Eternity" a comforting prospect, or is it something that should (or might) seem troubling? Does the verb "surmised" imply a strong degree of certainty, or does it suggest mere conjecture—a conclusion, in other words, that is merely a guess? The effect of these final lines would be much different if Dickinson had used the verb "realized" rather than "surmised." Instead, in a final gesture of open-ended ambiguity, she leaves it to *us* to "surmise" for ourselves the answers to such important questions as the final fate of the speaker and the final tone of the poem. Should we find this poem consoling or disturbing? Should we trust or question the speaker's responses to her experiences? What, precisely, *did* she experience? At the very end of the poem, is she alive or dead?

The poem concludes, appropriately enough, with a word— "Eternity"—that, almost by definition, is tantalizingly open-ended and lacking in closure. The decision to end with a word suggesting endlessness is just the last in a series of paradoxes typical of the entire work. The poem remains inscrutable. It is a poem about the speaker's personal death that suggests—especially through its references to the playing children and the "Gazing Grain"—that the larger cycle of life will go on. It is a poem that uses a journey through space and time to describe the annihilation of both. It is a poem in which the grave seems almost a welcoming, decorated home, and it is a lyric in which the final status of the speaker is left in ultimate doubt. Finally, it is a poem that seems at once highly personal, though it deals with perhaps *the* most common of all experiences endured by all living things (aside from birth itself). It is not a poem that makes a simple point and then is easily forgotten; it is a poem that stirs our deepest thoughts and curiosity.

In part, Dickinson's lyric has this effect precisely because of its central theme. What other topic provokes more serious thought (or anxiety, for that matter) than death? What topic seems more pressingly or personally relevant to every single reader? Yet Dickinson refuses to offer the kinds of easy, clear consolations or certainties readers might seek from such a poem. She never mentions God, and she never gives us any clear sense of the nature of the afterlife. She never makes clear that any "afterlife" (in the reassuringly conventional sense) even exists. The poem does imply the existence of "Immortality" and "Eternity," but their precise characteristics are never spelled out, nor can we even be sure that they exist for all people. The poem plays with and exploits one of the most basic of all human concerns (how, precisely, will each one of us face death? How will each of us react to the moment of our passing?) and is, in its general calmness and serenity, perhaps a model of behavior worthy of emulation. Yet the poem ends as quietly and unassumingly as it began; it offers no grandly affirmative (or even darkly disturbing) conclusion. It leaves us, quite simply and quite literally, with a surmise—which is, perhaps, all that we had any right to hope for or expect.

BELOVED
(TONI MORRISON)

"Death and Dying in *Beloved*"
by Deborah James,
University of North Carolina at Asheville

In some ways, *Beloved* reads like a classic ghost story. The haunting of 124 Bluestone Road by a vengeful baby ghost sets up the story as a mystery. How did the baby die? Why is it angry? On whom does it seek vengeance and why? These are important questions. Readers learn quickly (or begin to suspect early on) that the ghost is the two-year-old baby slave girl who, with her two brothers, had been sent to freedom with their grandmother in Cincinnati, while their mother made her own arduous escape from the Sweet Home plantation. But twenty-eight days later, because of the Fugitive Slave Act, their former owner and his men arrive to take them back. Sethe, her mother, attempts to kill them all but only succeeds at cutting the baby's throat before she is apprehended. This part of the story is based on the 1854 case of Margaret Garner, a woman enslaved in Kentucky who likewise killed her baby when faced with recapture. But Toni Morrison's work is often concerned with the deeper truths than historical facts. Readers, therefore, must probe the details of the novel to discern what these truths might be. They must consider what Sethe's (and Margaret Garner's) choices mean about slavery as well as death. Morrison challenges readers to consider the physical and psychic cost of living enslaved, as well as the actual price of "freedom." She also raises questions about the various types of death—*Beloved* illustrates some of the many ways a person can be killed or die. By the time readers arrive at the actual scene in which Sethe slits the baby's throat, they are already aware of a number of equally horrific scenes of individual mutilation through the mechanism of slavery.

The novel requires that readers "remember" slavery, in more than just its outlines and statistics. For example, many sources document the facts: how many people were enslaved, where, and for how long, when it ended and its general conditions. Instead, *Beloved* endeavors to supply information about the specific individuals' lived experiences of slavery. Morrison has deliberately set this tale on a "good" plantation, Sweet Home, where Mr. Garner, much against local custom, treats his male slaves as "men." However, even before Garner's death and the coming of his brutal replacement, Schoolteacher, Morrison confronts the reader with the constant, daily assault on the spirit, mind, and body caused by enslavement. From the Garners' refusal to allow Halle and Sethe to marry (marriage is not possible for slaves; no legal tie can be honored for persons not deemed human), to Sixo's quest to be with the Thirty-Mile Woman and live as a "natural" man, Morrison makes clear that even under benevolent rule, slavery violates life. Examining its specific effects on Stamp Paid, Baby Suggs, Paul D., and Sethe illustrates the ways in which body and soul, mind and heart die in slavery.

Stamp Paid, a secondary character, provides one glimpse of death and dying in the novel. His self-chosen name refers to the experience he and his wife share when she submits for more than a year to her master's lust. She elicits a promise from Stamp not to make trouble. They both know that should he object or even openly acknowledge his awareness of this liaison, he endangers them both. From the moment her master begins pressing her to have an affair, she has few choices. She could try to make her mistress aware of his advances, but that could easily result in her being sold or punished for lying. She could try to run away (with or without Stamp), but that could result in her death or capture (and consequent return to face some greater punishment). She chooses what she thinks will be the safest way—eliciting Stamp's promise. Living out that promise, however, nearly kills him psychologically. He cannot protect the woman he loves from this predator; he cannot protect himself.

When he can endure no longer, Stamp goes to the mistress of the house under the pretext of looking for his wife. He subtly communicates her husband's treachery to her. Having made that choice, he must have been prepared to escape. Though we do not know the particulars immediately following this revelation, we do know two important outcomes. First, after what Stamp endured during that year (let alone what his wife endured), he declares that he has paid in full for whatever else he does in life, and second, he focuses the rest of his life on rescuing others from slavery.

Stamp's story is one of several in *Beloved* that focuses on the degradation of the bodies, souls, and spirits of the enslaved. These stories also cast light on the degradation and dehumanization of the enslavers. Harriet Jacobs (*Incidents in the Life of a Slave Girl*) and Frederick Douglass (*Narrative of the Life of Frederick Douglass*) each escaped slavery and published memoirs that call attention to how slavery as an institution corrupts all of its participants. *Incidents in the Life of a Slave Girl* includes an example of a white woman in a position similar to the house mistress's in *Beloved*. In Jacobs's case, the mistress becomes part of the affliction. She seems to believe Jacobs but is still angry and vengeful toward her and powerless to prevent her husband's advances. Both women are miserable, but the white woman does not see in her slave a potential ally against their joint oppression. Douglass joins Jacobs in creating a view of such women driven nearly mad by their husband's infidelity and their own racist recoil at the idea that their husband—their social, racial, and economic equal—has "lowered himself," and thereby lowered his wife, by engaging in sex with a black woman. As for the deadly effect of slavery on the masters, Jacobs's, Douglass's, and many others' works document the corroding of morals, emotions, thinking, and even the bodies of the master. From slave ship captains and crew, to the plantation owners, overseers, and bounty hunters who participate in slavery, death is dealt all round.

Beloved, however, focuses on more deep insights into the particular, personal deaths experienced by the enslaved themselves. Morrison most fully accomplishes this as she directs our gaze to the Sweet Home characters. The life of Baby Suggs provides a distinct view of the insidiousness of slavery.

Baby Suggs is Sethe's mother-in-law, freed by her son's labor; she is the one to whom Sethe and her children flee from Sweet Home.

Within this free black community, she is hailed as "Baby Suggs, holy" because she has found her calling in sharing her great heart with her people, helping them to new life in freedom. She is a healer.

But first Morrison reveals what Baby Suggs is trying to heal from:

> ... in all of Baby's life, as well as Sethe's own, men and women were moved around like checkers. Anybody Baby Suggs knew, let alone loved, who hadn't run off or been hanged, got rented out, loaned out, bought up, brought back, stored up, mortgaged, won, stolen or seized. What she called the nastiness of life was the shock she received upon learning that nobody stopped playing checkers just because the pieces included her children. Halle she was able to keep the longest. Twenty years. A lifetime. Given to her, no doubt, to make up for *hearing* that her two girls, neither of whom had their adult teeth, were sold and gone and she had not been able to wave goodbye. To make up for coupling with a straw boss for four months in exchange for keeping her third child, a boy, with her—only to have him traded for lumber in the spring of the next year and to find herself pregnant by the man who promised not to and did. That child she could not love and the rest she would not. "God take what He would," she said. And He did, and He did, and He did and then gave her Halle who gave her freedom when it didn't mean a thing. (23)

Baby Suggs terms these circumstances, "the nastiness of life." Morrison's style here forces readers to sort through this accumulation of facts to get at the truths revealed within them. In this case, the facts reveal the layers of injury visited on body and soul through slavery.

Baby Suggs's own "cure" for this condition is powerfully illustrated by the call-to-healing scene in the Clearing. She instructs those who have been assaulted by "the nastiness of life" on how to rid themselves of it, how to reclaim their own beating hearts. Her sermon instructs them, group by group (men, women, children) and part by part (body, mind, heart), how to bring themselves individually and collectively back to wholeness. She articulates a way to experience resurrection even after the multiple traumas, the death experiences, of slavery. The antidote she preaches, for each individual and the community as a whole, is love. So what goes wrong?

Apparently loving one's self is insufficient.

Baby Suggs's case suggests the difficulty and perhaps the impossibility of achieving permanent recovery from these traumas. She had come back to life in freedom and claimed herself as a whole person for the first time. However, when she witnesses Schoolteacher's attempt to re-enslave Sethe and the children, with its awful aftermath, she loses faith in her own doctrine. Not even love itself seems to provide protection from the continual invasion of this "nastiness." It is then that Baby Suggs takes to her bed, unable to condemn her daughter-in-law and unable to figure out *how* to live in the face of so much death. Although she has lived through some of the same horrors as Sethe, her actual death occurs only after her spirit has lain down. The dying presented here is more painful and seems much worse than physical death: the death of the spirit—the death of hope. Baby Suggs suffers and eventually dies from a broken heart.

Paul D.'s life provides another demonstration of the soul death that slavery causes. His physical, sexual, and mental abuse in the Alabama prison to which he is delivered after his failed attempt to escape Sweet Home graphically illustrate how this dying progresses. But the variety and intensity of ways that slavery can kill are vividly captured in the image of this man, chained and bit in mouth, mutely, miserably aware of the crippled rooster (Mister) as it struts freely by him. Hearing this part of his story, Sethe thinks

> He wants me to ask him about what it was like for him—about how offended the tongue is, held down by iron, how the need to spit is so deep you cry for it. . . . The wildness that shot in the eye the moment the lips were yanked back. Days after it was taken out, goose fat . . . rubbed on the corners of the mouth but nothing to soothe the tongue or take the wildness out of the eye. (71)

At the moment Paul D. is being hauled off in chains, he is not only physically unable to speak but emotionally disabled as well. He has witnessed Sixo's fiery death and Halle covering himself with clabber, mind broken. Years later, as Paul D. remembers these events, the questions these memories raise for him about manhood reveal the extent and continuation of the psychological damage he endured. He defended Halle's inability to save Sethe from assault by Schoolteacher and his nephews by reminding her that "A man ain't a goddamn ax. Chopping, hacking, busting every goddamn minute of the day. Things get to him. Things he can't chop down because they're inside" (69). Yet pondering his own situation, he is profoundly troubled by his uncertainty about whether the Sweet Home men were only men because Garner said so. Could they be men, he asks himself, without Garner's or some other white man's permission or definition? He is especially concerned about whether or not *he* could have been a man without that permission. For him the question of Halle's manhood is answered because Halle is husband to Sethe, father to their children. But even more definitively, he frees his mother through his own labor. Likewise, Sixo's manhood is much clearer to Paul D. than his own, from Sixo's alignment with the Thirty-Mile Woman to his defiant death. Sixo, as Paul D. remembers him, was never diminished by his enslavement. What Paul D. experiences first through his own enslavement and again as he examines his behavior within that enslavement, is an assault on his sense of self. As he questions his manhood, what he is really questioning, for himself and for readers, is what can it mean to be human if one's human experience is enslavement? His life illustrates that under the best of conditions (i.e., Sweet Home under Garner's rule) slavery still kills something in the enslaved. And even when it doesn't kill outright, it stunts growth so that relationships become distorted, sometimes twisted within its confines. That, too, is death.

That distortion of relationships forms the centerpiece of the novel in Sethe's relationships with everyone around her, especially her children. She literally loves them to death. Paul D. describes hers as "too thick love," a love he castigates her for by saying, "Sethe you have two feet, not four." Besides the horrific death of the baby girl, now an avenging ghost, the novel details how Sethe's "too thick love" results in near suffocation of the living, particularly Denver, who grows up isolated and alienated from all the humans around her and afraid to "go out the yard." Learning about her mother's successful murder of her sister and attempted murder of herself and her brothers is news that "stops sound" for Denver for several years. Sethe replies to Paul D. that "Love is or it ain't. Thin love ain't no love at all"(164).

One of the complicated truths beyond the facts that Morrison calls attention to is that there is something fierce and heroic about Sethe's way of loving, something admirable yet frightening about her single-mindedness and dedication. If agency or the willingness to make choices and live by their consequences is one way to define being human, then even before she arrives in freedom, Sethe has lived as a human being. She has never accepted the slave owners' right to define her. She steals the materials for her own wedding garment when Mrs. Garner and the social mores of the time ignore her longing for ceremony with Halle as her husband. She takes sprigs of flowers to attach to the iron when she is working even as a slave so that she can do her work with something to lighten her heart. That these actions seem so small reflects one kind of distortion caused by slavery.

However, given her response under even the best of conditions, it seems quite natural that her reaction to learning how Schoolteacher and his nephews are literally defining her and her children (human characteristics on one side, animal on the other) propels her into the action that culminates in Beloved's death. She refuses to accept what other people—even others in the black community—say should be her reaction. She refuses to enact even her grief in prescribed ways. When Sethe decides that the baby's grave will have a marker, she prostitutes herself for the headstone engraved with the seven letters "Beloved." She may be enslaved, but she is not truly a slave from her own viewpoint. And once she realizes that under Schoolteacher's domination she will have to accept the conditions of slavery with no more room for any expression of her own agency, she sets out for freedom—pregnant, beaten, and alone. But, first, she has sent her children (her best things) to safety.

Sethe instinctively recoils from being dictated to in any form. This instinctive recoil, however, sometimes contributes to the distortion of her relationships. From the moment of Paul D.'s arrival, she maintains her right to conduct her life as she sees fit, perfectly willing to pay whatever price. He asks why she doesn't leave the house, haunted as it is, isolating as it seems to be. She replies, with heat, that there will be no more running for her. She has taken her stand at 124 and does not intend to be moved again. Running physically did not prevent Schoolteacher from coming for her and hers. Only her action—slitting the baby's throat, knocking out her two small sons, and trying to bash the other baby's brains out, stopped the slave catchers. But she has not foreseen the way her action will distort her relationship with her community, Baby Suggs, and especially with her children. Even if she had, from her view there was no other choice. That is the way Sethe responds to the death threat of slavery. Thus, she announces her intention to face whatever else comes right where she is. And so she does.

In a sense, Sethe's real offense against society, both the black and white communities she lives in, is this insistence on choosing and acting on those choices even within the severe limitations her status imposes. Even Paul D. and Stamp, who know firsthand the horrors of slavery, judge Sethe as too proud. But her refusal to accept outside limitations also creates another way of killing her (and those who live with and love her)—death through isolation.

Sethe's and Denver's isolation from the community is a consequence of Sethe's distorted view of herself. Her slave experience causes her to value only her children. In fact, there is little evidence that she values herself at all. In her own eyes, she is valuable because she is the only one who has the milk her crawling baby needs, because she is the womb/eggshell for the unborn daughter. Baby Suggs did not have enough time to teach Sethe that she might have an obligation to love, value, and claim herself. Sethe had only twenty-eight days to experience freedom within the small community before Schoolteacher's incursion. What had she missed? Sethe claims responsibility for protecting the lives of her children; she is willing to take their lives rather than have them be victims of the soul-killing enslavement she has witnessed. What she has not foreseen is the living death that her isolation from the community causes and possibly the effect of that isolation on Baby Suggs as well. And while Sethe is willing to accept whatever consequences attend her actions, she has not understood entirely the weight of her own anguish and guilt. Thus, her next death threat is Beloved herself.

The real threat to Stamp Paid, Baby Suggs, Paul D., Sethe and most of the other characters in this tale is that their experience in slavery will have left them heartbroken and numbed, unable to respond to life, unwilling to risk feeling—true death. The community, which with the inspiration and vision of Baby Suggs has begun to craft its own identity and to live out individual and community values, might have provided Sethe with some new way to consider herself, something else to take into account before making her drastic decision. In her hour of great need, the community fails Sethe; it fails Baby Suggs; and it fails itself. Its members refuse to honor their commitment to one another out of petty jealousy. To build and maintain itself as a sanctuary where the disregarded, traumatized, and mutilated could heal required constant vigilance from the internal as well as the external threats to their safety. But, in the end, the struggle to create such a place, to continue to heal and grow, continues. Amy Denver, the white girl who ministered to Sethe during her escape, said, "Anything dead coming back to life hurts." (35) Although the novel graphically depicts death and dying, its ultimate message is about the anguish involved as life returns.

WORKS CITED AND CONSULTED

Baum, Carol. "Teacher and Student." *The Humanist* 55 (1995): 46–47.

Berila, Beth. "Unsettling Calls for Unity: The Pedagogy of Experimental Multiethnic Literatures." *MELUS* 30.2 (2005): 31–47.

Cottle, Thomas J. "The Reflections of Values: A Response to Toni Morrison." *Michigan Quarterly Review* 40.2 (2001): 279–287.

Denard, Carol C. "Beyond the Bitterness of History: Teaching *Beloved.*" *Approaches to Teaching the Novels of Toni Morrison.* Ed. Nellie McKay and Kathryn Earle. New York: The Modern Language Association, 1997. 40–47.

Holland, Sharon P. and Michael Awkward. "Marginality and Community in *Beloved.*" *Approaches to Teaching the Novels of Toni Morrison.* Ed. Nellie McKay and Kathryn Earle. New York: The Modern Language Association., 1997. 48–55.

Joyner, Louisa (with Margaret Reynolds and Jonathan Noakes). *Toni Morrison: The Essential Guide.* Vintage Living Texts: Contemporary Literature in Close Up. London: Random House, 2003.

Kang, Nancy. "To Love and Be Loved." *Callaloo* 26:3 (2003): 836–854.

McCoy, Beth A. and Jacqueline M. Jones. "Between Spaces: Meditations on Toni Morrison and Whiteness in the Classroom." *College English* 68 (2005): 42–71.

McKay, Nellie Y. and Kathryn Earle eds. *Approaches to Teaching the Novels of Toni Morrison.* New York: The Modern Language Association of America, 1997.

Reed, Roxanne. "The Restorative Power of Sound: A Case for Communal Catharsis in Toni Morrison's *Beloved*." *Journal of Feminist Studies in Religion* 23 (2007): 55–71.

CATCH-22
(JOSEPH HELLER)

"Joseph Heller's *Catch-22*"
by Merritt Moseley,
University of North Carolina at Asheville

With very few exceptions, novels about war are about death and dying. The threat of violence provides a crucible for the testing of character, which is why it is at the heart of many classic narratives both ancient and modern (*The Epic of Gilgamesh, The Iliad, The Mahabharata, The Song of Roland, War and Peace, All Quiet on the Western Front*). Some wars are only remembered because they figure in great literature: The Trojan War, if it even took place, is known only because of Homer, and whatever engagement the Franks may have fought with the Moors at the valley of Roncesvalles, it survives only because someone made *The Song of Roland* about it. Catharine Savage Brosman comments that this is not just a Western phenomenon:

> To note a similar association between much of the oral tradition of non-Western peoples, as it is now known, and their armed conflicts with surrounding tribes is then to affirm the near-universality of war as a subject for—and doubtless often an impetus to—song, drama, and narrative, oral and written. (85)

Brosman makes the important point that "crucial with respect to the vital themes of self and manhood are the encounter with fear and the question of conduct under fire," and this is as true of *Catch-22* as it is of more traditional war novels (88).

War novels can glorify war—that is, assert that killing the enemy is worthwhile, that the sacrifice men make (or at least risk) is worth whatever the war is designed to accomplish. Such novels often present their warriors as heroes, larger-than-life men capable of almost unheard-of acts of endurance, slaughter, and self-sacrifice. In an interview, Joseph Heller commented that his protagonist, Yossarian, "has heroic qualities but he acts anti-heroically as well. I don't know if I say it in the book or if I've ever said in any other interviews, but military heroes of antiquity are kind of oafish—Samson in the Bible, even Don Quixote" (Vosevich 94). Don Quixote is an unconventional example to mention, since he is a deluded blunderer rather than a military hero. Nevertheless, it is true that the uncomplicated war hero is easier to find the further back a reader looks.

But *Catch-22*, according to Eric Solomon:

> culminates a tradition of bitterly ironic war fiction. In *Catch-22* the major elements common to nearly all war fiction are presented and mocked. Like the Fabrizio of Stendhal's *The Charterhouse of Parma*, Heller's Yossarian loses his innocence through attempts to comprehend the madness of battle; like the Pierre of Tolstoy's *War and Peace*, Heller's protagonist discovers the cruelty of death in battle, and like the Frederic Henry of Hemingway's *A Farewell to Arms*, Yossarian makes his separate peace. What makes *Catch-22* differ from its twentieth-century predecessors, with the possible exception of *The Good Soldier Schweik*, is its coruscating humor. (94)

What is odd about Heller's book as a "bitterly ironic war fiction" is that it is about the Second World War. Heller does not write from a position of pacifism. The American forces in 1941-1945 were fighting against the powerful, threatening imperial strengths of Germany and Japan; the Japanese had invited war by the attack on Pearl Harbor, and the Germans had, after overrunning most of Europe, declared war on the United States. Adolf Hitler, the dangerous madman who seemed to credibly threaten civilization, was seemingly unstoppable. With these events in mind, World War II is harder to satirize. Even though contemporary observers were unaware of the full dimensions of the Holocaust, enough was known to place Hitler among the evil forces of history, and Heller was writing with the benefit of retrospective knowledge. The result is that, at least in the United States, World War II has been seen as "The Good War" and the generation that fought it as "The Greatest Generation." One commentator assures us that it was "assuredly the most justifiable war in recent history" (Stern 209).

For wars more suitable for ironic presentation, one should look a couple of decades earlier or later—that is, at the First World War or the war in Vietnam. Evelyn Cobley's discussion of "an often unacknowledged anxiety about the contradiction of war as 'legalized murder'" regards only World War I and Vietnam. She explains that "First World War writers rationalize their participation in acts of aggression by constructing the soldier as a sacrificial victim of forces beyond his power," while in Vietnam narratives the soldier is often constructed as a 'crazed killer'" (75). In between, in the Good War (at least in American narratives), the soldier is most likely to be shown as doing a grim job, perhaps without enthusiasm, and often in the face of obstruction and nonsense from the officers (he is usually a noncommissioned infantryman). Heller's is an unusual World War II novel in positioning its protagonist, Yossarian, and his fellows as sacrificial victims of forces beyond their power, much like the literary representation of Great War trench soldiers, mechanically fighting a war without purpose other than to bleed the enemy white.

Though the success of *Catch-22* is often attributed to the war with Vietnam that followed several years after the novel's publication, Heller does not represent his characters as having been dehumanized into crazed killers. They *are* killers, of course; Yossarian is a bombardier, and his bombs undoubtedly bring death to some of those on whom they fall; but the men are, for the most part, reluctant warriors, who sometimes drop their bombs in the sea and who object to unnecessary bomb runs. Even their commanders, crazy and dangerous as they are, do not seem very interested in killing Germans, much less Italian civilians. Instead, they want to achieve "glory" by making their crews fly more missions than anyone else in the war (glory is defined as getting featured in a story in the *Saturday Evening Post*) or meet a fictitious military aim—the tight bomb pattern explained by scheming General Peckem: "A bomb pattern is a term I dreamed up just several weeks ago. It means nothing, but you'd be surprised at how rapidly it's caught on. Why, I've got all sorts of people convinced I think it's important for the bombs to explode close together and make a neat aerial photograph" (Heller 335).

One can only hope that no American general ever chuckled quite so irresponsibly over pointless but still deadly missions. Antiwar novels often proceed from the premise that a true or realistic presentation of what war is really like is necessarily an antiwar statement. People glorify war, this reasoning goes, only because they are ignorant of what it is really like. Insisting that civilians ought to know what actually happens is the burden of literary works like Mark Twain's "The War Prayer," Wilfred Owen's "Dulce et Decorum Est," and Paul Fussell's *Wartime*. Fussell, a veteran, writes that "What annoyed the troops [while they were fighting the war] and augmented their sardonic, contemptuous attitude toward those who viewed them from afar was in large part this public innocence about the bizarre damage suffered by the human body in modern war" (270). Michael C. Scoggins has usefully compared some of the details of *Catch-22* to what is known of the air war in the Mediterranean and judged it accurate on such matters as number of missions flown, the day-to-day details of the base, and "the attrition of high ranking officers" (224). *Catch-22* is a satirical comedy, not a documentary; but its verisimilitude has been challenged in the process of questioning Heller's politics and ethics.

J.P. Stern, for instance, writes on anachronisms ("Chief among them are the IBM machines and the daily and even hourly signing of the loyalty oath by all flying members of the squadron" and concludes that "its realism is a means to an end. Mr. Heller uses the Second World War in order to show the impact of war—any war—on the privacy of a human being" (209). From that realistic beginning, he explains, Heller proceeds to "the heights of humorous and satirical exaggeration" in the novel's succeeding chapters, though "their humor is never disconnected from their realism" (203). This is a matter of judgment; Andrew Rutherford puts the case against Heller when he writes that Heller's abandonment of realism

> raises further problems which remain unsolved: firstly the extent to which grotesque caricatures are offered by the author or accepted by the reader not just as vehicles but as images of truth; secondly, the extremely partial nature of the

truth involved, whether our criteria are historical or ethical; and thirdly, the incongruity of the modes of fantasy and realism. (196)

On the one hand, Rome, indeed, is like Rome, the bombers are like real U.S. aircraft, bombs fall downward, men are blown up or shot into the ocean. On the other hand, the machinations of ex-PFC Wintergreen, who runs the Mediterranean theater of war, or of Milo Minderbinder, the mess officer who contracts with the Germans to bomb his own base and steals the CO_2 cartridges from life jackets to power sodas for the base, or the superhuman powers of Nately's whore to transcend time and space, are unrealistic, exaggerated beyond all possibility—certainly exaggerated beyond the point where a sensible reader could accept them as images of truth.

That is, they are exaggerated for satirical effect.

Now the question is whether Heller's aim is to satirize war, to satirize World War II, or to satirize some other target—the army, large organizations, human folly, the plight of the individual in a mass society—and whether satire is the end of his objectives. Certainly the novel has been taken as antiwar, though even Heller seems uncertain about this. In a 1997 interview, when asked if he considered the novel antiwar, he answered:

> It is more anti-traditional establishment than antiwar. To say it's antiwar doesn't say much to differentiate it from other stories about the war. I used the military organization as a construct, as a metaphor for business relationships and institutional structures. Of course it was antiwar. I can't think of any good American fiction that is not antiwar. But I don't think anyone in *Catch-22* raises the question whether we should be fighting the war. (Vosevich 94).

But *does* it raise the question of whether the war should be fought? Certainly its protagonist (never offered as a "hero") decides that, even if it should be fought, he no longer wants to be the one to fight it. He has flown many missions; at the beginning of the war "he was as patriotic as anybody else" (Scoggins 215). Now, worn down by the war, filled with dread after the Avignon mission, persuaded that he is surrounded by enemies—and an enemy is anybody who is trying to kill him, including Americans just as surely as Germans—he chooses a separate peace, taking off in a life raft for Sweden.

This is the crux of the criticism of Heller's novel as unpatriotic or even un-American. John Bodnar writes that *Catch-22*'s "cynical view of the American military in World War II Italy completely debunked not only the integrity of military leadership but any effort to look at the war in heroic or sentimental terms" (816), and Norman Podhoretz's protest was that

> its vision of war leaves no room for courage or noble sacrifice, much less for old-fashioned patriotism. Quite to the contrary, the novel 'justified draft evasion and even desertion as morally superior to military service. After all, if the hero of *Catch-22*, fighting in the best of all possible wars, was right to desert and run off to Sweden (as Yossarian does at the end), how much more justified were his Vietnam-era disciples in following the trail he had so prophetically blazed?' (Pinsker 606)

This is not a negligible point. Heller is careful to locate Yossarian's desertion near the end of the war, when the Nazis are essentially defeated. Yossarian has flown many more missions than originally expected (and many more than the 25 required of crews elsewhere in Europe [Scoggins 216]); in other words, his actions cannot really threaten the likelihood that the U.S. will prevail in the war, nor are they motivated by simple cowardice or unwillingness to do his part. Yet, he does desert.

To examine the meaning of this point it is necessary to consider one of the most striking features of *Catch-22*: its nonlinear plot. It begins *in medias res*, with the absurd lines, "It was love at first sight. The first time Yossarian saw the chaplain he fell madly in love with him. Yossarian was in the hospital with a pain in his liver" (15). It takes the reader some time to sort out what is happening at this point and to discover that the time is near the end of Yossarian's war; it is July 1944, and the number of missions has just been raised to forty-five. Six months later, December 1944, when Yossarian leaves the U.S. Army, the required missions are at 80. He has been in the Army since 1941 and on the island of Pianosa since 1943 (for a chronology of the novel, see Burhans, 245-247). The novel not only does not start at "the beginning" and move forward; its patterns of flashback and foreshadowing never become predictable or orderly. The ending of *Catch-22* is indeed the latest event it chronicles; but the beginning is not the earliest, and the ones in between are not in chronological order. Instead, the linkages that connect one piece of the narrative to another are, at least on their face, personal (the chapters almost all bear the name of one of the characters) and associated through shaky logic or emotion. A typical example comes early in the novel when Yossarian has asked Hungry Joe if it is normal to have nightmares every night:

> "Why not every night? Hungry Joe demanded.
>
> And suddenly it all made sense. Why not every night, indeed? It made sense to cry out in pain every night. It made more sense than Appleby, who was a stickler for regulations and had ordered Kraft to order Yossarian to take his Atabrine tablets on the flight overseas after Yossarian and Appleby had stopped talking to each other. Hungry Joe made more sense than Kraft, too, who was dead, dumped unceremoniously into doom over Ferrara by an exploding engine after Yossarian took his flight of six planes in over the target a second time. The group had missed the bridge at Ferrara again for the seventh straight day with the bombsight that could put bombs into a pickle barrel at forty thousand feet, and one whole week had already passed since Colonel Cathcart had volunteered to have his men destroy the bridge in twenty-four hours. Kraft was a skinny, harmless kid from Pennsylvania who wanted only to be liked, and was destined to be disappointed in even so humble and degrading an ambition. Instead of being liked, he was dead, a bleeding cinder on the barbarous pile whom nobody had heard in those last precious moments while the plane with one wing plummeted. (63–64)

The "Splendid Atabrine Insurrection" had taken place in 1943 as the men were being shipped to the front; Kraft was killed in May 1944. The connection the narrator supplies between these two events and Hungry Joe's nightmares is that they make less sense. A second example of this arrangement:

> Dobbs was in even worse shape than Hungry Joe, who could at least fly missions when he was not having nightmares.

> Dobbs was almost as bad as Orr, who seemed happy as an undersized, grinning lark with his deranged and galvanic giggle and shivering warped buck teeth and who was sent along for a rest leave with Milo and Yossarian on the trip to Cairo for eggs when Milo bought cotton instead and took off at dawn for Istanbul with his plane packed to the gun turrets with exotic spiders and unripened red bananas. (238–239)

Dobbs's bad shape, so bad that he would kill Colonel Cathcart if Yossarian approved, is a result of the missions having been raised to sixty. Milo's flight to Cairo is earlier, with the missions at forty; the connection is that Orr, who was on the trip to Cairo, is even worse (though he actually turns out to be better, as Orr is one of the very few survivors) than Dobbs.

The other striking structural feature of Heller's narrative is the repetition, either of the same thing happening twice, or of the same thing being narrated at least twice and often many more times. Is this violation of the conventional expectation of narratives—events presented in chronological order and narrated the same number of times that they occurred—an example of the kind of formless-ness reviewers complained of in 1961 as "undisciplined," "boring," "repetitive and monotonous," "no novel" and even "not really a book"? (Solomon, "Structure" 46). Or, if it is not simple carelessness or incompetence (and the power of the novel and its success—even its success as a bad example, in the view of its detractors—suggest that incompetence is not to blame), why would Heller write the book this way?

One answer is that it is part of his satiric plan. The refusal of chro-nology, the disdain for economy in the use of incidents, the movements from one section to another by such apparently loose connectives as "X was nothing like Y," are ways of insisting that everything is absurd. A man named Major Major Major is absurd; so is the attack on the bridge at Ferrara. A good pilot motivated by patriotism (Nately) is as absurd as Hungry Joe, who likes to fly because he suffers nightmares when grounded. It is absurd that Aarfy, who kills an unoffending maid to cover up a rape, is ignored by MPs, who instead arrest Yossarian for being AWOL. It is absurd, or, to use the word much employed by the book's characters, "crazy," to pray for a tight bomb pattern, to moan at a briefing, to fly missions that get men killed.

Nevertheless, this is not what the novel says. To reduce every-thing to the same level of absurdity is to produce moral incoherence. *Catch-22* actually has an ethical point to make. It is driven home by two important passages near the end. One is the long and powerful chapter called "The Eternal City," in which Yossarian wanders around Rome at night witnessing horrors—soldiers being beaten, soldiers raping, terribly disfigured civilians, a street full of teeth:

> The night was full of horrors, and he thought he knew how Christ must have felt as he walked through the world, like a psychiatrist through a ward full of nuts, like a victim through a prison full of thieves. What a welcome sight a leper must have been! At the next corner a man was beating a small boy brutally in the midst of an immobile crowd of adult spectators who made no effort to intervene. . . . On squishing straw sandals, a young woman materialized with her whole face disfigured by a God-awful pink and piebald burn that started on her neck and stretched in a raw, corrugated mass up both cheeks past her eyes! Yossarian could not bear to look, and shuddered. No one would ever love her. His spirit was sick; he longed to lie down with some girl he could love who would soothe and excite him and put him to sleep. (425–427)

Yossarian is like a visitor to hell, and he recognizes his own complicity in what he calls a "lousy earth!" (422).

After being arrested and wounded, Yossarian (in the hospital again, where the book began) has a recollection of the death of Snowden, the most important repeated or déjà vu event in the novel. Reliving the horror of Snowden's evisceration and suffering, Yossarian realizes the lesson of this death, above all others: "Man was matter, that was Snowden's secret. Drop him out a window and he'll fall. Set fire to him and he'll burn. Bury him and he'll rot like other kinds of garbage. *The spirit gone*, man is garbage" (450; emphasis added). The final chapter follows, significantly called "Yossarian," and in it he leaves, headed (absurdly and implausibly, setting off from a military base on an island in the Mediterranean Sea) for Sweden, which seems to represent not only peacefulness, as it is a neutral country, but also socialism and love. Throughout the novel, love (actually sex, which Yossarian calls love) has been one countervailing value to death and dying. In "The Eternal

City" even the reliable whores have been dispersed, and that no longer seems a solution to despair; only flight will do.

Earlier Yossarian has reflected on Nately's whore, who keeps trying to kill him in revenge for Nately's death:

> Why the hell shouldn't she? It was a man's world, and she and everyone younger had every right to blame him and everyone older for every unnatural tragedy that befell them; just as she, in her grief, was to blame for every man-made misery that landed on her kid sister and on all other children behind her. Someone had to do something sometime. Every victim was a culprit, every culprit a victim, and somebody had to stand up sometime to try to break the lousy chain of inherited habit that was imperiling them all. (415–416)

Yossarian tries to save Nately's kid sister, ineffectually. He has even tried to stop the bombing, ineffectually. Somebody had to do something sometime, and his removal from the war zone, though it will do almost nothing to slow down the death and dying, will at least remove him as one link in the chain of killing and being killed, hurting and being hurt, being victimized and making victims of others.

WORKS CITED

Bodnar, John. "*Saving Private Ryan* and Postwar Memory in America." *The American Historical Review* 106 (June 2001): 805–17.

Brosman, Catharine Savage. "The Functions of War Literature." *South Central Review* 9 (Spring 1992): 85–98.

Burhans, Clinton, Jr. "Spindrift and the Sea: Structural Patterns and Unifying Elements in Catch-22," *Twentieth Century Literature* 19 (October 1973): 239–250.

Cobley, Evelyn. "Violence and Sacrifice in Modern War Narratives." *SubStance* 23 (1994): 75–99.

Fussell, Paul. *Wartime: Understanding and Behavior in the Second World War.* New York: Oxford University Press, 1989.

Heller, Joseph. *Catch-22.* New York: Simon & Schuster, 1961.

Pinsker, Sanford. "Reassessing Catch-22." *The Sewanee Review* 108 (Fall 2000): 602–610.

Rutherford, Andrew. "Realism and the Heroic: Some Reflections on War Novels." *The Yearbook of English Studies* 12 (1982): 194–207.

Scoggins, Michael C. "Joseph Heller's Combat Experiences in *Catch–22*." *War, Literature and the Arts: An International Journal of the Humanities* 15 (2003): 213–227.

Solomon, Eric. "From Christ in Flanders to 'Catch-22': An Approach to War Fiction." *Texas Studies in Language and Literature* 11 (Spring 1969): 851–866; rpt. in Frederick Kiley and Walter McDonald, *A 'Catch-22' Casebook.* New York: Thomas Y. Crowell, 1973: 94–101.

Solomon, Jan. "The Structure of Joseph Heller's *Catch-22*." *Critique* 9 (1967): 46-57.

Stern, J.P. "War and the Comic Mode: *The Good Soldier Schweik* and *Catch-22*." *Comparative Literature* 20 (Summer 1968): 193–216.

Vosevich, Kathi A. "Conversations with Joseph Heller." *War, Literature and the Arts: An International Journal of the Humanities* 11 (Fall-Winter 1999): 91–102.

CHRONICLE OF A DEATH FORETOLD
(GABRIEL GARCÍA MÁRQUEZ)

"More Deaths Than One:
Chronicle of a Death Foretold"
by William Gass, in *New York Magazine* (1983)

INTRODUCTION

Focusing on Santiago Nasar, the novel's murder victim, William H. Gass sees *Chronicle of a Death Foretold* as "a rather gruesome catalogue of the many deaths—in dream, in allegory, and by actual count—that Santiago Nasar is compelled to suffer." Gass details both the literal and figurative meanings of death and dying in the novel; as Gass argues, Nasar is the victim of the many characters who foretell his murder and also a victim of the author, who picks up the pieces of Nasar's life and resurrects them in the story he tells. For Gass, the murder is "simply a late symptom of an illness that had already wasted everyone." He focuses on the way that death and dying form a central theme and enable Márquez to weave a fantastical tale that is also a commentary on the diseased Latin American world: "The inertias of custom, the cruelties of a decaying society, daily indignities, hourly poverties, animosities so ancient they seem to have been put in our private parts during a prehistoric time,

---

Gass, William. "More Deaths Than One: *Chronicle of a Death Foretold*." *New York Magazine* Vol. 16, No. 15 (11 April 1983): 83–84.

the sullen passivity of the powerless, the feckless behavior of the ignorant, the uselessness of beliefs," which "combine in this remarkable, graphic, and grisly fable to create a kind of slow and creeping fate."

❧

Chronicle of a Death Foretold does not tell, but literally pieces together, the torn-apart body of a story: that of the multiple murder of a young, handsome, wealthy, womanizing Arab, Santiago Nasar, who lived in the town where Gabriel García Márquez grew up. The novel is not, however, the chronicle of a young and vain man's death, for that event is fed to us in the bits it comes in. It is instead the chronicle of the author's discovery and determination of the story and simultaneously a rather gruesome catalogue of the many deaths—in dream, in allegory, and by actual count—that Santiago Nasar is compelled to suffer. Had he had a cat's lives, it would not have saved him.

It is his author who kills him first, foretelling his death in the first (and in that sense final) sentence of the novel: "On the day they were going to kill him ..." We are reminded immediately of García Márquez's habit of beginning his books in an arresting way, perhaps a by-product of his long journalistic practice. "Many years later, as he faced the firing squad ..." *One Hundred Years of Solitude* commences, and *The Autumn of the Patriarch* is no less redolent with death or its threats: "Over the weekend the vultures got into the presidential palace by pecking through the screens on the balcony windows." Santiago Nasar's death is first foretold in the way any fictional fact is, for the fact, of whatever kind, is already there in the ensuing pages, awaiting our arrival like a bus station.

Santiago Nasar also dies in his dreams—dreams that could have been seen to foretell it, had not his mother, an accomplished seer of such things, unaccountably missed "the ominous augury." Before the day is out, his mother will murder him again. Unwittingly, and with the easy fatality we associate with Greek tragedy, Santiago dons a sacrificial suit of unstarched white linen, believing that he is putting it on to honor the visit of a bishop, just as he has celebrated the day before, along with the entire town, the wedding that will be his undoing. So attired, he stands before his mother with glass and aspirin and tells her of the dreams she will misunderstand. Santiago Nasar is then symbolically slain and gutted by the cook as he takes a cup of coffee in her kitchen and has another aspirin for his hangover. His father has mounted this woman, and she is remembering Santiago's father as she disembowels two rabbits (foretelling his disembowelment) and feeds their guts, still steaming, to the dogs.

The cook's daughter does not tell Santiago that she has heard a rumor that two men are looking to kill him, for he continually manhandles her, and she wishes him dead; the town, it seems, knows too, and participates in the foretelling. Attempts to warn Santiago are halfhearted: People pretend that the threats are empty; that the twin brothers bent on his death are drunk, incapable, unwilling; that it is all a joke. But Orpheus has his enemies in every age. Dionysus was also torn to pieces once, Osiris as well. The women whose bodies Santiago Nasar has abused (the metaphor that follows him throughout, and that appears just following the title page, is that of the falcon or sparrow hawk) await their moment. They will use the duplicities of the male code to entrap him. The girl whose wedding has just been celebrated goes to her bridegroom with a punctured maidenhead, and he sends her home in disgrace, where she is beaten until she confesses (although we don't know what the real truth is) that Santiago Nasar was her "perpetrator." And had not her twin brothers believed that the honor of their family required revenge, Nasar would not have been stabbed fatally, not once but seven times, at the front door of his house, a door his mother, believing him already inside, had barred.

The coroner is out of town, but the law requires an autopsy—the blood has begun to smell—so Santiago Nasar is butchered again, this time while dead. The intestines he held so tenderly in his hands as he walked almost primly around his house to find a back door he might enter in order to complete the symbolism of his life by dying in the kitchen he had his morning aspirin in—those insides of the self of which the phallus is only an outer tip—are tossed into a trash can; the dogs who wanted them, and would have enjoyed them, are now dead, too.

Santiago Nasar's mother's last sight of her son, which she says was of him standing in her bedroom doorway, water glass in hand and the first aspirin to his lips, is not, we learn, her last. Her final vision, which she has on the balcony of her bedroom, is of her son "face down in the dust, trying to rise up out of his own blood."

One man is dead, and hundreds have murdered him. The consequences of the crime spread like a disease through the village. Or, rather, the crime is simply a late symptom of an illness that had already wasted everyone. Now houses will decay, too, in sympathy. Those people—lovers, enemies, friends, family—who were unable to act now act with bitter, impulsive, self-punishing foolishness, becoming old maids and worn whores, alcoholics and stupid recruits, not quite indiscriminately. The inertias of custom, the cruelties of a decaying society, daily indignities, hourly poverties, animosities so ancient they seem to have been put in our private parts during a prehistoric time, the sullen passivity of the powerless, the feckless behavior of the ignorant, the uselessness of beliefs, all these combine in this remarkable, graphic, and grisly fable to create a kind of slow and creeping fate—not glacial, for that would not do for these regions, but more, perhaps, like the almost imperceptible flow of molasses, sticky, insistent, sweet, and bearing everywhere it goes the sick, digested color of the bowel.

Gregory Rabassa has rendered García Márquez's rapturous reportorial style into poignant, precise, and stabbing English. *Chronicle of a Death Foretold*, like Faulkner's *Sanctuary*, is about the impotent revenges of the impotent; it is about misdirected rage; it is about the heart blowing to bits from the burden of its own beat; yet the author, Santiago Nasar's first murderer, goes patiently about his business, too, putting the pieces back together, restoring, through his magnificent art, his own anger and compassion, this forlorn, unevil, little vegetation god, to a new and brilliant life.

"THE DEAD"
(JAMES JOYCE)

"The Dead"
by Bernard Benstock,
in *James Joyce's* Dubliners: *Critical Essays* (1969)

INTRODUCTION

Bernard Benstock, one of the great Joyce critics of the late twentieth century, focuses on "the motif of death" in the final story of *Dubliners*: "The Dead." Noting the paradoxical relationship of the joyous feast of the Epiphany being celebrated in the story and the reality of death and dying depicted there, Benstock argues that "three levels of these dead become apparent upon close examination: the deceased, the moribund, and the living-dead, the composition of the last group expanding with the progression of the story." Benstock sees Gabriel Conroy, the story's protagonist, as a mockery of the wise men who journey to Bethlehem to see the Christ child. Arguing that Gabriel is both a lost magi and also someone who sets out for a kind of new frontier, Benstock rounds out his essay by comparing Joyce's vision of death and dying in the story with W.B. Yeats' vision of the beast that "slouches toward Bethlehem to be born" in his poem "Second Coming." For Benstock, "The Dead" simultaneously depicts the many

Benstock, Bernard. "The Dead." *James Joyce's Dubliners: Critical Essays*. Ed. Clive Hart. New York: Faber and Faber, 1969. 153–170.

deceptions that round our lives and also our potential to rise
above the mortality that haunts us and to discover ourselves.

∽⌒∾

The motif of death is solidly established in the coda story of *Dubliners*,
not only with Joyce's succinct title, but with the various rhetorical
devices embedded in the terse opening sentence: "Lily, the caretaker's
daughter, was literally run off her feet." Lily's tag-name, that of the
funereal flower, serves as a symbol of death—as well as an ironic
allusion to purity; the connotation of "caretaker" is mere innuendo,
since we later realize that he is custodian of the estate, rather than of
a cemetery, but by then the effect is unalterable, and the smell of the
graveyard is in our nostrils; and the hyperbolic figure of speech ("run
off her feet"), which although figurative, is offered to the reader to be
accepted "literally." Yet this early impregnation of death symbolism is
soon belied, ostensibly by the Christmas setting, the musical enter-
tainment, the sentimental speech, the 'gourmeterring and gourman-
dising'—the *élan vital* of the story's surface. The hostesses bubble
and flitter about; Freddy is hilariously drunk; Browne lecherously
enthusiastic; and Gabriel Conroy himself seems the embodiment of
contented self-importance. The dead appear far removed from the
celebration of the Nativity.

The dead are very much in evidence, however, and death hovers
over the feast at all times, emerging triumphant by the end. Three
levels of these dead become apparent upon close examination: the
deceased, the moribund, and the living-dead, the composition of the
last group expanding with the progression of the story. Four of the
"dear departed" remembered and acknowledged during the course of
the evening's activities are: Gabriel's mother, whose "last long illness"
he recalls in conjunction with her "sullen opposition to his marriage"
to Gretta ("Some slighting phrases she had used still rankled in his
memory; she had once spoken of Gretta as being country cute"); the
two Patrick Morkans, "brother Pat" (Mary Jane's father, whose death
terminated the residence of his sisters in Stoney Batter) and "the old
gentleman" (whose horse Johnny had circled the equestrian statue of
King Billy in mesmerized paralysis); and finally Michael Furey, whose
spectre takes possession of the tale in a way comparable to Parnell's
domination of "Ivy Day in the Committee Room." These in turn are

represented by the array of opera singers conjured up during dinner (dating back to the Parkinson remembered only by the oldest participant) and even by the snow-covered statue of Daniel O'Connell.

Those obviously close to death are the three old women, Aunts Kate and Julia and Mrs. Malins. Aunt Julia, whose "flaccid" face is grey with "darker shadows," has the "appearance of a woman who did not know where she was or where she was going." Aunt Kate, whose face is healthier, nonetheless has a face "like a shrivelled red apple," and is "too feeble to go about much." And Mrs. Malins is "a stout feeble old woman with white hair." There is enough evidence, therefore, from Joyce's capsule descriptions of them, for the reader to realize, even before Gabriel's awareness late in "The Dead" of the imminence of Julia's death, that these old and sickly women are reminders of the final gasp of life. Their totems are the monks of Mount Melleray who sleep in their coffins "to remind them of their last end."

But old age is not the only requisite for inclusion among the moribund, as Gabriel also comes to realize, since time brings all men towards death: "One by one they were all becoming shades. Better pass boldly into that other world, in the full glory of some passion, than fade and wither dismally with age." Such passionate glory is denied to the living-dead, those who remain alive, but fail to live: the disillusioned, the self-destructive, the blighted and wasted lives. It is with these that "The Dead" is most concerned. First there is the servant girl Lily, just out of school and already cynically world-weary, presumably because of a prematurely unpleasant experience with a man. The mature and proper Gabriel is actually shocked at her assertion that "The men that is now is only all palaver and what they can get out of you." And although we are informed that "she got on well with her three mistresses," a change is mirrored in Kate's recent disappointment: "I'm sure I don't know what has come over her lately. She's not the girl she was at all." (No longer a girl, Lily has been initiated into womanhood, and it is not difficult to speculate about what has come over her lately.) Less serious reminders are seen in Mary Jane, in her thirties and unmarried, who plays "Academy pieces" on the piano that no one listens to; Freddy Malins and Browne have their obvious vices; and Bartell D'Arcy, the much-praised tenor, is hoarse and consequently rather grouchy. Most important of course is the revelation that Gretta has been living a dead life in contrast to the remembered and cherished romance of her youth, a revelation that destroys the bubble of her husband's unreal existence, permanently deflating the self-assurance of his artificially bolstered world.

Even for those who are quick to perceive "the skull beneath the skin" of most of the characters in "The Dead," the Conroys at first seem to be a healthy contrast. Had there not been so much dynamic spontaneity associated with them, as they came in out of the snow much anticipated and warmly welcomed (Gabriel scrapes the snow from his shoes "vigorously;" his clothes emit "a cold fragrant air from out-of-doors," while Gretta goes upstairs with the aunts "laughing"), perhaps we might have been more suspicious of their poses. Surely the opening conversation contains enough indications that all is not sound as Gretta good-naturedly belittles her husband's prissy solicitousness: Gabriel is worried that his country wife will catch cold and has therefore engaged a hotel room in order to avoid the return home to Monkstown late at night. Gretta ridicules his insistence upon goloshes ("Guttapercha things," she calls them), and doubles her scorn by crediting his faith in them as both conformity and affectation: "Gabriel says everyone wears them on the continent." (Buck Mulligan sneers at Stephen: "O, damn you and your Paris fads.") Worse still, Gretta compounds his faults almost maliciously: "He's really an awful bother," she reports to his aunts in his presence, "what with green shades for Tom's eyes at night and making him do the dumb-bells, and forcing Eva to eat the stirabout." And finally she boasts of her successful rebellion against him, that on this particular evening she refused to wear her goloshes despite the snowfall. None of this, however, is as heavy as it might sound, extrapolated this way, but an important barometer of Gretta's effect on her husband's sensitivity can be seen from the changes in his attitudes as she babbles away: at first he answers his wife's glance with "admiring and happy eyes," and we learn that "Gabriel's solicitude was a standing joke" with the aunts, but the goloshes prove too sore a point ("Gabriel knitted his brows . . . as if he were slightly angered")—it takes Aunt Kate's tact to change the subject. Beneath Gretta's delightful banter, therefore, can be seen a slight but significant rift in the marital lute, and Mrs. Conroy's objection to Gretta's country-cuteness might suggest a disparity in social levels, that her good looks have netted her the climb through marriage into the solid middle class.

Class distinctions are not irrelevant in "The Dead." Next to the son of a merchant-prince butcher in "After the Race," this last story gives the reader a glimpse into the best of the middle class in a volume whose range includes every aspect of the bourgeois spectrum. (There is almost a touch of Dickens when Gabriel thinks, "People, perhaps, were standing in the snow on the quay outside, gazing up at the lighted windows and listening to the waltz music.") But economic decline, an important factor in the depiction of the Dedalus family of *A Portrait*, is in evidence. The Morkans delight in living well, as attested by their annual fête and their general insistence upon the best in food ("diamond-bone sirloins, three-shilling tea and the best bottled stout"), but their rented floors in the "dark gaunt house" on Usher's Island represent a significant change from the house in Stoney Batter, and their zeal in preventing Mary Jane's pupils, who came from "the better-class families on the Kingstown and Dalkey line," from being discomfited by Freddy's drunkenness mirrors an attitude of social subservience. (Mary Jane personally serves as waitress for these pupils, offering them the best.) The three Graces have been reduced to selling their talents while nurturing their bourgeois assumptions that music is not a commodity like corn, the source of income for the Mr. Fulham who owns their house and conducts his business on its ground floor. Ironically they also disclose their middle-class snobbery by insisting that the "old gentleman," their father, had owned a starch mill rather than a glue factory. ("Well, glue or starch," says Gabriel democratically, his intellectual snobbery sparing him the necessity of the snobbery of his class.) From affluent mill-owner to shabby-genteel music teachers indicates another Joycean irony. Yet the cause of the financial decline is somewhat unusual: it can be assumed that with the death of Brother Pat no male was left to run the business—the masculine line had run out, leaving only women. Pat's only child (at least from internal evidence) is also female, and only one of his sisters married, producing two sons, neither one of whom she groomed to soil his hands boiling starch (or glue). The priest and the teacher fulfill the family ideals of their class, rising above its mercantile level, but leaving the Morkans unable to reproduce themselves.

The musical Morkans by their very talent contain the seed of their own destruction. We have seen from "A Mother" the extent to which music is a dead end in Dublin; in a nation which considers vocal music its principal art form, a concert like the four-part series scheduled for the Antient Concert Rooms proves to be an acid test of the state of art in general in Ireland's capital city. Joyce has indicated that the trio of stories preceding "The Dead" ("Ivy Day," "A Mother," "Grace") concentrate on the public life of the city, isolating politics, art, and religion as areas of focus. The closing story summarizes this concentration as well as all themes inherent throughout *Dubliners*. Joe Hynes' sincere if ineptly expressed Parnellism is in healthy contrast to the betrayers in the Committee Room, but emerges as the narrow nationalism of Molly Ivors in "The Dead." The cash-register Catholicism of Father Purdon's sermon for businessmen is reduced to Gabriel's Christmas gratuity to Lily and Freddy Malins' Christmas-card shop, while the vestiges of Tom Kernan's Protestant objection to candles can be seen in Protestant Browne at the Morkans' party, in front of whom the Catholics fear that they are "giving scandal." In general, religion as a dead end is personified by the Mount Melleray monks in their coffins. And the failure of the concert series is prolonged in the reaction to Mary Jane's piano piece (which bores Gabriel and causes the four topers to slink away to the bar, returning only at the conclusion to offer the "most vigorous clapping"). D'Arcy's singing of "The Lass of Aughrim" receives a better response, although he himself proves irritable because of his hoarseness, but Gretta's reaction of intent rapture is due to personal nostalgia rather than critical appreciation. In contrast to these "failures," however, we seem to have the very substantial success of Aunt Julia's rendition of "Arrayed for the Bridal," where even the performer is moved by the applause which "sounded so genuine." Apparently a genuine response is a rarity (which in itself should make us suspicious), but Julia's triumph is tinged with irony. She is many years past her prime and in the process of being replaced by boy sopranos in the choir at Adam and Eve's Church. When Gabriel, who "applauded loudly with all the others" at the time, later realizes that he "caught that haggard look upon her face for a moment when she was singing," the full horror of the phenomenon should become apparent. "Arrayed for the Bridal," as incongruous a selection for the ageing spinster as "I dreamt that I Dwelt" was for Maria in "Clay," is Julia's beautifully executed Swan Song.

Joyce's comment that he might have been "unnecessarily harsh" in his treatment of the moral state of affairs in Ireland (made after the first fourteen stories had gone to the publisher but before he wrote "The Dead"), may indicate that the added *novella* was in some way intended to offset the effect of the preceding epiphanies. Yet in dozens of small correspondences "The Dead" serves as a summation of the entire volume. The religion-art-politics of the immediate predecessors re-emerge here, while the breakdown of family relationships in those stories is paralleled as well: father-son in "Ivy Day" (not only the caretaker, Jack, and his profligate son, but the contrast established by Henchy between Joe Hynes and his father), mother-daughter in "A Mother" (although Mrs. Kearney's domination of her husband is also important), and husband-wife in "Grace" (if Tom Kernan is a cross for his wife to bear, Martin Cunningham has one in his wife). The destruction of the superficial harmony of the married Conroys is well anticipated. And what are we to assume about the names Tom and Eva for the Conroy children? In "Counterparts" Farrington has a son named Tom whom he beats for letting the fire go out; by way of contrast, Gabriel, a very different sort of father, is concerned about his son's muscles and eyes. (Two adults are also named Thomas: Chandler and Kernan.) And is Eva to remind us of Eveline Hill? Her relationship with her father has certainly soured. With the reference to Kathleen Kearney in "The Dead" we find the first instance in which a previous *Dubliners* character is mentioned, the beginning of a process that Joyce went on to exploit fully, as both Kathleen and Gretta figure in Molly Bloom's thoughts.

The key words of the first paragraph of the first *Dubliners* tale (paralysis, simony, gnomon) are significant in varying degrees for every one of the fifteen stories, and reach their culmination in "The Dead." The whole process of the Morkans' soirée is a repeated one, so that even the reader (for whom this is a fresh experience) soon begins to feel an aura of *déjà vu* (Gretta caught cold after last year's party; Freddy can be expected to be drunk again). The participants themselves know the formula, as can be seen when Bartell D'Arcy, apparently a newcomer, at first refuses to allow his glass to be filled, until "one of his neighbours nudged him and whispered something at him"—the ceremonial toast is next on the programme. The "never-to-be-forgotten Johnny" is almost a parody of the theme of paralysis, and one might suspect that Daniel O'Connell, frozen in stone and covered with snow, is still another. The instances of simony are perhaps subtler, but the birth that took place in a manger among shepherds is being celebrated here in high style with the best of everything among the comfortable bourgeoisie, while irresponsible Freddy pays his debts after having cashed in on the Nativity by way of a Christmas-card shop. Even Gabriel is guilty of simony when, unnerved by his awkward conversation with Lily, he gives her a coin in order to cover his embarrassment, and when her attempt at refusal further discomfits him, he credits Christ as a precedent: "—Christmas-time! Christmas-time! said Gabriel, almost trotting to the stairs and waving his hand to her in deprecation."

[...]

There has been some speculation about the Christmas setting for "The Dead," but little of it has been germane to this central idea of betrayal and self-awareness. There is no mistaking the yule season in the story, and a precise placement of the significance of this setting is vital to an understanding of it. We know that it is "Christmas-time! Christmas-time!" from Gabriel's gratuity to Lily; Freddy Malins has sold Christmas cards and Mr. Browne has been "laid on here like the gas ... all during the Christmas." Yet it is neither Christmas Eve nor Christmas night, nor is it Boxing Day nor New Year's Eve nor New Year's Day. Florence Walzl[1] is quite correct in announcing that the Morkan party is taking place on January 6, the Day of the Epiphany, but she has neglected the one piece of evidence that makes that choice of date almost conclusive: Freddy Malins is drunk despite the fact that "his poor mother made him take the pledge on New Year's Eve." This could hardly refer to *last* New Year's Eve—no one would be shocked that he violated a pledge taken a year ago. A mere six days have elapsed since New Year's Eve and it is still Christmas-time. The Day of the Epiphany is a perfect Joycean choice for the final story of a volume in which climactic situations give way instead to a technique Joyce labeled "epiphanies."

What should disturb us about "The Dead" is the total absence of Christianity from the Christmas festivities. Only money earned and offered are reminders of Christmas, unless monks sleeping in their coffins will satisfy a demand for Christian seriousness during the occasion. No grace is said before dining; the dinner oration conjures up pagan Graces instead, but no mention of Christ. No single clergyman is among the guests, and surely Dublin is not short of priests to participate in a Christmas-time party. One such priest comes easily to mind, Father Constantine Conroy, Gabriel's brother and as much a nephew of the old aunts as Gabriel. We learn that Gabriel was "their favourite nephew," but surely his brother should have been invited too.

Gabriel came into town from Monkstown, and is staying the night in Dublin to avoid the trip back; Constantine is at this time "senior curate in Balbriggan," a mere twenty-two miles away, and could have made the journey almost as easily to the Morkans' fest. Joyce tells us just enough about Father Conroy for us to be aware of his existence and conscious of his conspicuous absence. Not only are priests absent, but Father Healey of Adam and Eve's Church is disparaged by Aunt Kate: "if I were in Julia's place I'd tell that Father Healey straight up to his face ..." When discouraged from maligning the Pope in the presence of a Protestant, she directs her attack against the priest instead.

The irreverence of Joyce's depiction of Epiphany Day nineteen centuries later is the crucial element of "The Dead," a reminder that throughout the work of James Joyce it is spiritual death that is at the core of the paralytic condition, the hemiplegia of the will, the death of the heart. And it is the Church in Joyce's Ireland that is primarily responsible for this spiritual annihilation. The conflict of Gabriel and Michael, archangels who were never intended to be antagonists but in harmony with each other, again indicates that there is a serious disjunction, and Gabriel Conroy is no more able than Hamlet to "set it right"—much less so. But he has it in his power to understand the situation, one which he has conveniently ignored until this epiphanic evening. If we allow the suggestion that there is a reduplication of the original Epiphany here, we become aware of an incomplete but interesting pattern. It is true that during the course of the story three arrivals take place at the Morkan House, Gabriel, Gretta and Freddy Malins—all the other guests are already there before the story begins, or at least we never learn of any new arrival other than these three. But they do not come at the same time, and they certainly do not have equal value as individuals—they are hardly kings or magicians. If Joyce is obliquely paralleling the journey of the Magi to the crèche of the Christ child, he has probably meant that Gabriel Conroy should represent all three kings—his name Conroy has already attracted attention as containing *roi*, the French for king.

That Gabriel, a single magus, should be pressed into service to represent all three Magi seems as commonplace as St. Patrick's shamrock, but Joyce probably had a more esoteric source for his whimsical condensation. Joyce was probably well aware that the tradition of a trio of Magi comes from an Irish source. Ludwig Bieler, in *Ireland, Harbinger of the Middle Ages*, notes that "Irish Biblical expositors are responsible for the fact that the unnamed and unnumbered magi from the East who came to adore the newly born Christ became, in western legend, the three holy kings, Caspar, Melchior, and Balthasar. Among the several 'trilingual' sets of names of the magi in the Irish commentaries on St. Matthew we find Melchio, Aspar, Patisara."[2] These stem from the reverence for the three "sacred" languages, Hebrew, Greek, and Latin. Joyce's magus has only two names, Gabriel Conroy, which metrically scan like Melchior and Caspar, but Lily's low Dublin accent gives him a third: "Gabriel smiled at the three syllables she had given his surname"—so that Con-o-roy parallels Balthasar.

Gabriel arrives on this cold night, having traveled a long distance (so far, in fact, that he does not intend making the journey home that night). He comes from the east, or at least from the south-east (it would have been impossible to make a long journey from due east, and the Conroys could not be expected to live in Dublin Bay or in either the Poolbeg or North Bull lighthouses), and his town has a fine ecclesiastical name, Monkstown, a second reference to monks in "The Dead"—that important reminder that the elaborately spread board is in sharp contrast with vows of poverty, with Christian austerity, with the economic conditions of the original manger scene. (Note that Gretta left her "grandmother's house in Nuns' Island" to go to the convent, and now lives in Monkstown.) Does he bring gifts? The offer of gold is mirrored in the coin he gives to Lily (although it probably was not gold), but nowhere do we find myrrh or frankincense, or any fragrance or incense, unless the following is intended to be relevant: as Gabriel is taking off his coat, "the buttons of his overcoat slipped with a squeaking noise through the snow-stiffened frieze, a cold fragrant air from out-of-doors escaped from crevices and folds."

Such parallels, if actually intended at all, are certainly sardonic and tangential, although the Joycean method allows for this sort of speculation, particularly at this point in his development, when the approach was becoming highly refined and was still quite unself-conscious. But are we then to conclude that the Christ child that the magus beholds is the roast goose? that Gabriel, a tame goose at best, aware of the tradition of the Wild Geese who had fled Ireland, sees himself as the cooked goose? More germane and far more serious is the revelation of Michael Furey that is brought to Gabriel during the later part of the evening, a Christ figure who sacrifices himself for his ideal. It would certainly be concomitant with Joyce's oft-quoted criticism of Christ as having shirked the major burden of life by not living with a woman, so that manly Gabriel, who has accepted that burden but is embarrassingly naive in his contact with women, is again a parodic figure. The important point of such an investigation of "The Dead" is that Joyce is holding up Irish religious practices and theory for scrutiny, that he chooses to pit his latter-day archangels Gabriel and Michael against each other, revealing Michael as the traditional victor—though belated and retroactive—and Gabriel much deflated. Even the structure of the story is suspect from this point of approach. We have been informed that Joyce intended that "Grace," the penultimate story and originally the last one in *Dubliners*, parallel the three sections of Dante's *Commedia*. The horizontal structure of "Grace" conforms to that of a triptych, with the central segment of *Purgatorio* as the major section. This three-part structure is also available in "Clay," with the *Dublin by Lamplight* laundry as the *Inferno*, the Dublin streets as *Purgatorio*, and the Donnellys' home as an ironic *Paradiso*—as ironic as the Gardiner Street Jesuit Church of "Grace." If "The Dead" follows this pattern—and there are definite space breaks indicated in the text—the Morkan household at Christmas-time is Hell indeed for Gabriel, while the carriage trip to the Gresham serves as a period of purgations, and the hotel scene of revelation is a third ironic paradise. The three portions in this case diminish in size as the story progresses.

In viewing "The Dead" as a tale of the Epiphany, we see Joyce at an interestingly close juncture with Yeats's attitude in "The Second Coming." Christianity as a dynamic force has dwindled to a mockery of itself: self-contradictory, as Gabriel belatedly and effetely opposes Michael, and self-betrayed, as simoniac symptoms of the commercialization of Christmas become apparent. Its priests die of paralytic strokes, demented and disillusioned; they leave behind them rusty bicycle-pumps and suspect books with yellowed pages, or have gone off to Melbourne or are responsible for evicting spinster sopranos from their choirs in favour of boys. Gabriel as king considers himself above the common paralytic situation, and as magician he has his magical books and his quotations from Browning to keep him uninvolved. But on the Night of the Epiphany Gabriel Conroy follows his star to the Morkans' house on Usher's Island—not a new star, but the same one that has brought him there so often-expecting in his reconquest of Gretta to renew himself and sharpen the distinction and privilege which keep him safe from the doomed, the unbaptized, the unanointed. But on this night he comes face to face with his predecessor and with his own self, with the past that has claimed all the others and the future that he has betrayed in order to maintain his comfortable position on the outside. The enigmatic sentence that has bothered so many readers of "The Dead" ("The time had come for him to set out on his journey westward") indicates his awareness of his new responsibility: Gabriel must begin the quest of self-discovery to arrive at the real epiphany, to follow his star. After many false starts of self-deception, the "rough beast, its hour come round at last, slouches toward Bethlehem to be born."

NOTES

1. Florence L. Walzl, "The Liturgy of the Epiphany Season and the Epiphanies of Joyce", *PMLA*, LXXX, Sept. 1965, p. 449.
2. Ludwig Bieler, *Ireland, Harbinger of the Middle Ages*, London, 1963, p. 14.

DEATH BE NOT PROUD
(JOHN GUNTHER)

"Death Be Not Proud:
Children, Families and Cancer
in Postwar America"
by Gretchen Krueger, in *Bulletin of the History of Medicine* (2004)

INTRODUCTION

In her article on the seminal memoir dealing with death and dying, John Gunther's *Death Be Not Proud*, Gretchen Krueger comments upon both the structure of the book and its enormous societal impact. Tracing both the book's many influences and American society's view of death and dying as it has been informed by cancer research since the late 1940s, Krueger notes how the memoir raised awareness, especially regarding young sufferers. Commenting upon the book's reception and influence, Krueger shows how the response from the book's many readers—often in the form of letters written from parents—revealed the powerful way this private story affected American society. In the end, Krueger finds that "The inclusion of Johnny's voice and experiences both alerted a broad audience to cancer's effects on young sufferers and makes *Death Be Not Proud* an exceptional

---

Krueger, Gretchen. "*Death Be Not Proud*: Children, Families and Cancer in Postwar America." *Bulletin of The History of Medicine.* 78 (2004): 836–863.

historical source," one that dispels postwar American ideals in its depiction of an increasingly disillusioned family while rallying the country to find a cure for the illness that claimed Johnny Gunther's life.

ͽﻭ

In 1947, Johnny Gunther, a seventeen-year-old boy, died of cancer. *Death Be Not Proud*, a best-selling memoir written by his parents, recorded his fifteen-month illness and death. Excerpts in the *Ladies' Home Journal* and *Reader's Digest* gave readers a brief glimpse into the increasing medical management of children's cancers in the 1940s. When medical specialists assigned to Johnny's case admitted to knowing little about the boy's rare, fast-growing brain tumor, its course, or effective therapies, his father, John, and his mother, Frances, carried out a relentless and ultimately fruitless search for new information and treatments. The Gunthers consulted more than thirty physicians in their desperate quest. In this memoir of Johnny's illness, his story and his parents' experiences reached millions of Americans. As with the experiences shared through personal polio stories, private illness entered the public realm.

Death Be Not Proud exerted a profound effect on readers' awareness of cancer in young people through its poignant content and wide audience. In the book's opening pages John Gunther described the book as "a story of what happened to Johnny's brain."[1] His detailed chronological record of his son's fifteen-month illness documented Johnny's diagnosis, the rapid progression of the disease, the repeated hospitalizations and procedures, and the family's search for effective cancer therapies. It focused on the family's protracted struggle to continue living while Johnny hovered so close to death. As John Gunther noted:

> I write it because many children are afflicted by disease, though few ever have to endure what Johnny had, and perhaps they and their parents may derive some modicum of succor from the unflinching fortitude and detachment with which he rode through his ordeal to the end. (p. 3)

In short, he told the intimate story of a "long, courageous struggle between a child and Death" (p. 3) by placing his son at the center of the narrative and including the voices and daily activities of each family member. Gunther's book, and particularly the inclusion of Johnny's experiences, demonstrated that the plight of one boy and his family could heighten the public's awareness of cancer's menace to all ages. I argue that the memoir created an unprecedented outlet for parents to examine their personal feelings about rarely discussed topics—the fragility of life, and the reality of illness, loss, and grief—especially with regard to children. Moreover, the Gunthers' story had a larger impact. At a time when postwar America embraced the promise of conquering disease though scientific and medical methods and championed the child-centered family, the extraordinary volume of readers' responses to *Death Be Not Proud* suggested that cancer and other debilitating diseases threatened these values. For many writers, letter writing granted the sufferers solace during an uncertain time—in their personal lives, in their family circle, and in the nation.

DYING YOUNG

Death Be Not Proud was published at a time when cancer in children was beginning to garner the attention of the American Cancer Society (ACS), physicians, and parents. In the 1940s, the ACS had begun to utilize new educational and fund-raising methods to transform the public face of cancer in America and to raise cancer awareness.[2] By raising funds and spreading their messages of cancer control through modern advertising concepts, the organization emulated the March of Dimes campaigns led by the National Foundation for Infantile Paralysis. The ACS campaign—the "Seven Warning Signals of Cancer"— encouraged adults not to fear cancer, but to actively fight the "dread disease" on both a national scale and a personal level. Focusing on early detection, the campaign urged Americans to seek prompt treatment from orthodox physicians if they observed any suspicious signs. Few ACS educational materials addressed cancer in children directly, but the fund-raising campaigns frequently used photographs and stories of young cancer sufferers and survivors ("poster children") to encourage donations to the organization's annual drives.[3] Like the March of Dimes campaigns led by the National Foundation for

Infantile Paralysis, the ACS used children suffering from cancer to raise funds for education and research.

In the 1940s and early 1950s, ACS campaigns pictured children wielding the ACS sword and collecting pennies to support the organization's activities, but it was polio epidemics, not childhood cancer cases, that incited the greatest amount of concern in American parents. Poliomyelitis affected thousands of children across the country as improvements in hygiene and sanitation made children more susceptible.[4] Leg braces, crutches, and iron lungs became common symbols of polio's drastic effects. Children also feared the disease: historian William Tuttle found that many children had witnessed the effects of the disease firsthand in their classmates and feared polio and the paralysis that often followed more than they feared war.[5] By the late 1940s, Harvard virologist John F. Enders, working with a team at Boston Children's Hospital, had completed preliminary experiments to grow and maintain poliovirus in human tissue cells.[6] As scientists attempted to translate these results into an effective immunization, researchers at Boston Children's Hospital and at Memorial Hospital in New York City investigated a set of lesser-known killers—childhood cancers.

The rarity of cancer in children contributed to the virtual silence regarding childhood cancers in medical literature. Beginning in the late 1930s, the nation's leading cancer hospital, Memorial Hospital, founded as New York Cancer Hospital in 1884, took an active role in identifying, documenting, and treating childhood cancers. In 1937, at a landmark symposium on childhood tumor cases sponsored by the Pediatric Section of the New York Academy of Medicine, physicians from Memorial presented childhood cancer cases. In *Cancer in Childhood*, the published conference proceedings, Harold Dargeon, consulting pediatrician at Memorial, and James Ewing, director of Memorial and a leading cancer specialist, compared the institution's cases with earlier medical publications on childhood cancers. Ewing concluded that previous researchers had relied on improper age divisions, incorrect tumor classifications, and small sample sizes when studying childhood cancers. Both physicians concluded that cancer primarily afflicted those in old age, but affected children as well—albeit on a smaller scale—and argued that directed research into childhood cancers would ensure improved survival rates.[7]

Memorial therefore devoted new spaces and services to childhood cancer. In 1939, an expansion included a seventeen-bed Children's Pavilion, the first clinic in the United States designed especially to house children with cancer.[8] The new ward provided cribs and beds, a slide and a carousel on an outdoor terrace, and classroom facilities for patients who felt well enough to attend classes. In 1946, a major construction project that erected the Sloan-Kettering Institute also included the Helena Woolworth McCann Children's Pavilion. In the hospital's quadrennial report covering the years 1947–51, the section devoted to the Pediatric Service noted that "cancer and allied diseases now constitute a major child health problem," and claimed that Memorial was the first institution in the United States to "accept responsibility for all aspects of the control of childhood neoplasm" including "demands for diagnosis, therapy, and rehabilitation of the patients, for research and for education on all lay and medical levels."[9] According to U.S. Vital Statistics records, New York City health statistics, and data from a new childhood tumor registry established at Memorial, as mortality rates from common infectious diseases of childhood declined due to improvements in sanitation, nutrition, and medicine, cancer had become the second most common cause of child death, behind only accidents.[10]

In the late 1940s, popular magazine articles proclaimed "Cancer Kills Children Too!" and "Cancer, the Child Killer."[11] Cancer—long considered a danger solely for adults and the elderly by the ACS, physicians, and laypersons—became publicized as a rare but menacing disease of childhood. Although often less visible than polio, it was as much to be feared. Writing primarily in women's magazines, authors alerted parents—especially mothers—to cancer's threat. They counseled mothers to schedule regular physical examinations for their children and to be watchful for cancer's symptoms. As one physician wrote:

> The best hope for preventing needless deaths lies with mothers everywhere who must recognize that there is such a thing as cancer in children and that it isn't something to be frightened of or fatalistic about. The signs of cancer in children are so often those which any observant mother cannot help but notice.[12]

Because cancer's symptoms—such as persistent cough, headache, vomiting, pain, or fatigue—often mimicked those of common childhood ailments, such advice may have needlessly induced unwarranted anxiety and blame. Mother-blaming reached its peak, argued historians Molly Ladd-Taylor and Lauri Umansky, during World War II and the postwar years when mothers were targeted for seeking wage work, for contributing to the decline of the home, for creating juvenile delinquents, and for neglecting children's physical health.[13] Women had been expected to prevent infectious disease in the early twentieth century, when experts endorsed measures such as proper feeding and sanitation techniques for reducing mortality.[14] As childhood diseases shifted from acute to chronic in the mid-twentieth century, mothers were still held responsible for maintaining child health. Ladd-Taylor and Umansky noted: "Death serves as 'evidence' of failed motherhood; the refusal (or inability) to protect one's children from danger, or even from disease."[15] Cancer placed a grave burden on mothers—both the loss of their child and societal blame. By employing the rhetoric of maternal responsibility in childhood cancer articles, authors blamed mothers for their child's death during a period when a timely diagnosis did little to improve the dismal mortality rates for most childhood cancers.

Few therapies were available for cancer in the 1940s. Physicians offered radiation and surgery as treatments for solid tumors, but a diagnosis of acute leukemia, the most common childhood cancer, was an inevitable death sentence. In 1948 Sidney Farber, a pathologist at Boston Children's Hospital, announced that aminopterin, a chemotherapeutic agent that acted as an antagonist against folic acid, induced temporary remissions in acute leukemia patients.[16] This discovery stimulated hope that additional, effective chemotherapeutic agents would be identified. In the late 1940s, hope and despair both characterized scientific literature and public portrayals of childhood cancer. These conflicting themes pervade *Death Be Not Proud*—the Gunthers' initial shock over Johnny's diagnosis, and their untiring faith that a medical breakthrough would preserve their son's life in the face of his shattering illness.

JOHN, FRANCES, AND JOHNNY GUNTHER

Like the polio narratives studied by Amy Fairchild, Daniel J. Wilson, and Kathryn Black, *Death Be Not Proud* serves as a way to gain insight into one patient's and one family's experience of illness in the 1940s, and to begin studying childhood cancer narratives published from 1949 through the 1990s.[17] While many historians have explored topics related to children and childhood, child health, and childhood diseases, few have captured the experiences of children themselves.[18] Russell Viner and Janet Golden have argued that the limited number of sources produced by children has restricted medical historians who have attempted to analyze the views of young patients.[19] However, illness narratives—autobiographical or biographical accounts that enable patients or caregivers to document and derive meaning from their experiences of illness, treatment, or recovery and rehabilitation—have aided historians in examining the patient perspective of those suffering from childhood diseases.[20] The inclusion in *Death Be Not Proud* of the voices of John, Frances, and Johnny Gunther expanded the book's audience, but most important, it provided three different perspectives on the family's experience of the debilitating disease.

In part, *Death Be Not Proud* received widespread attention because of the literary reputation of John Gunther. Gunther graduated from the University of Chicago in 1922 and began working as a foreign correspondent for the *Chicago Daily News*. Reporting on events in Central Europe, he did not like to investigate breaking news stories; he preferred to provide "human rather than purely political portraits" of current events.[21] Cass Canfield, an editor at Harper and Brothers publishing house, persuaded Gunther to apply his approach to an extended examination of the European continent.[22] In 1936, Gunther published *Inside Europe*, the first of his best-selling "Inside" series that described the economic and political climate of various countries and continents; following the success of this volume, he continued the series by publishing *Inside Asia* (1939) and *Inside Latin America* (1941). While some critics dismissed his writing style as "superficial," his work was praised by reviewers and widely translated.

From 1944 to 1947, Gunther researched and wrote *Inside U.S.A.* Employing a research method similar to that of his previous books, he undertook a state-by-state survey of the country. He later recalled: "Harper's advance sale was, I was told, the largest in its history for a trade book, and one piquant detail is that Macy's in New York did 90 percent of its book business with this single title on one day shortly after publication."[23] The book topped the best-seller list by the summer and became one of the biggest nonfiction best-sellers in the history of

American publishing up to that time.[24] Gunther had worked months past his publisher's deadline to complete the book by March 1947; in his short autobiography, he recalled: "Most of the writing had to be done under the pressure of acutely difficult and painful circumstances: my son Johnny's long illness."[25]

In *Death Be Not Proud*, Gunther revealed the in-depth research he had single-mindedly pursued to find a treatment or cure for his son. The book's title, the first words of a "Holy Sonnet" composed by poet John Donne, suggested his motivation for publicly sharing these personal events: in Donne's poem, death lost its power, concluding, "One short sleepe past, wee wake eternally, And death shall be no more; Death, thou shalt die."[26] Gunther hoped to lessen death's power over himself, his family, and other cancer sufferers. Through the book, he both immortalized his son and contributed to a cancer cure by raising awareness of the disease. Further, the publisher's profits and his own royalties were donated to cancer research.[27]

John Gunther's name appeared on the title page, but *Death Be Not Proud* was a collaboration between John and Frances Gunther, his ex-wife and Johnny's mother. A short section titled "A Word from Frances" followed John's detailed chronology. Frances contributed a personal view of Johnny's illness and her family. After their marriage in 1927, she had joined her husband in the professional world of journalism and politics by assisting him with the first two "Inside" books, covering Central Europe and the Balkans for the *London News Chronicle*, and publishing a collection of writings about India. While pursuing her professional career, Frances became pregnant with their first child, Judy, who died suddenly in infancy from a condition called "thymic death."[28] Johnny was born in 1930, while the couple was living and working in Paris. Frances and John divorced in 1944, but they shared responsibility for Johnny's care before and during his illness.

In "A Word From Frances," Frances, like John, selectively documented aspects of her son's last months. She recounted the time she and Johnny had spent together at her home in Madison, Connecticut, and addressed Johnny's death and her sense of loss that followed. Frances's personal papers recorded her private sorrow. About six months after Johnny died, a diary entry revealed her intense feelings of self-blame for her children's untimely deaths: "Oh, I let Johnny die and I let Judy die—your great gifts to me, O God, I let them die—How could I let them die?"[29] Frances concealed her private writings from public view, but her essay shared her intimate anxieties about the responsibilities of parenthood and the anguish of losing a child. She directly addressed other parents, both those who still had their children and those who had lost children to illness or war. Despite John's claim that his ex-wife's section was too personal to be published, it was included in the volume and added another perspective to the story of Johnny's illness.[30]

The Gunthers' writing made Johnny's voice virtually audible to readers of *Death Be Not Proud*. John's constant note-taking, together with Johnny's letters and diary entries, enabled him to insert Johnny's lively dialogue throughout the account; for example, Johnny exclaimed "I am quite a guinea pig" when faced with the initial onslaught of diagnostic tests and medical procedures (p. 32). John also included his son's constant demands to be told about the dire nature of his condition and prognosis despite his physicians', nurses', and parents' attempts to hide the truth. Frances's words animated him in readers' minds:

> An open fire with a broiling steak, a pancake tossed in the air, fresh nectarines, black-red cherries—the science columns in the papers and magazines, the fascinating new technical developments—the Berkshire music festival coming in over the air, as we lay in the moonlight on our wide open beach, listening—how he loved all these! (p. 254)

Excerpts from Johnny's brief diary entries told the reader about his daily activities. Letters sent to friends and teachers revealed his concerns about his schoolwork and his progressing illness. The inclusion of Johnny's voice and experiences both alerted a broad audience to cancer's effects on young sufferers and makes *Death Be Not Proud* an exceptional historical source.

NOTES

1. John Gunther, *Death Be Not Proud: A Memoir* (New York: Harper, 1949), p. 3. (Further references to this work will be given parenthetically in the text.)

2. See James Patterson, *The Dread Disease: Cancer and Modern American Culture* (Cambridge: Harvard University Press, 1987), for a history of cancer and ACS activities.

3. For a brief discussion of children as fund-raising tools, see Jane S. Smith, *Patenting the Sun: Polio and the Salk Vaccine* (New York: Anchor Books, 1990), pp. 82–83. Smith wrote: "Cute little kids on crutches, kids from your hometown, were what opened the wallets and the coin purses" (p. 83). The *ACS Bulletin*, a fund-raising publication, pictured seven-year-old cancer survivor Leroy Curtis in multiple issues: "Prize Story Depicts Fight for Survival: Quick Action Meant Life to Doomed Boy," *ACS Bull.*, 13 July 1953, 2/23: 4; "White House Ceremony Opens Cancer Crusade," ibid., 11 April 1955, 4/16: 1; "Leroy Curtis on New York Visit Wins Attention for Crusade," ibid., 18 April 1955, 4/17: 4; "Ed Sullivan Has Whirlwind Day at Cincinnati," ibid., 5 March 1956, 5/9: 3.

4. Smith, *Patenting the Sun* (n. 3), p. 35.

5. William M. Tuttle, *"Daddy's Gone to War": The Second World War in the Lives of America's Children* (New York: Oxford University Press, 1993), p. 191.

6. For the history of polio research and the development of vaccines, see Smith, *Patenting the Sun* (n. 3); John R. Paul, *A History of Poliomyelitis* (New Haven: Yale University Press, 1971).

7. Harold Dargeon, ed., *Cancer in Childhood and a Discussion of Certain Benign Tumors* (St. Louis: Mosby, 1940), p. 25.

8. "First Child-Cancer Ward Functioning in New York," *Newsweek*, 15 January 1940, p. 29.

9. Memorial Center for Cancer and Allied Diseases, *Quadrennial Report 1947–51* (New York: The Center, 1951), p. 67. The Children's Tumor Registry, a record-keeping service sponsored by the American Academy of Pediatrics, was also housed at Memorial; begun in 1942, it tallied cases and gathered qualitative descriptions of the common childhood tumor types.

10. Harold W. Dargeon, "Cancer in Children from Birth to Fourteen Years of Age," *JAMA*, 1948, 136: 459–68.

11. Frank Rector, "Cancer Kills Children Too!" *Women's Home Companion*, March 1947, pp. 36–37; Lawrence Galton, "Cancer, the Child Killer," *Collier's*, 15 May 1948, pp. 64–66.

12. Galton, "Cancer, the Child Killer" (n. 11), p. 66.

13. Molly Ladd-Taylor and Lauri Umansky, *"Bad" Mothers: The Politics of Blame in Twentieth-Century America* (New York: New York University Press, 1998).

14. Nancy Tomes, *The Gospel of Germs: Men, Women, and the Microbe in American Life* (Cambridge: Harvard University Press, 1998).

15. Ladd-Taylor and Umansky, *"Bad" Mothers* (n. 13), p. 4.

16. Sidney Farber et al., "Temporary Remissions in Acute Leukemia in Children Produced by Folic Acid Antagonist 4-Aminopteroyl-Glutamic Acid (Aminopterin)," *New England J. Med.*, 1948, 238: 787–93. See also Ilana Löwy, *Between Bench and Bedside: Science, Healing, and Interleukin-2 in a Cancer Ward* (Cambridge: Harvard University Press, 1996), pp. 39–63. Löwy contextualized Farber's work within developments in chemotherapy research and the organization of cancer clinical trials from the mid-1940s through the 1980s.

17. Rather than focusing on national events such as the March of Dimes, Wilson drew upon published polio narratives, interview transcripts, and letters sent to President Roosevelt to gain insight into patients' daily physical and psychological struggles, their financial concerns, and their hope for recovery: see Daniel J. Wilson, "A Crippling Fear: Experiencing Polio in the Era of FDR," *Bull. Hist. Med.*, 1998, 72: 464–95; idem, "Crippled Manhood: Infantile Paralysis and the Construction of Masculinity," *Med. Hum. Rev.*, 1998, 12: 9–28. Adopting a literary perspective, Wilson also studied patients' uses of this genre: idem, "Covenants of Work and Grace: Themes of Recovery and Redemption in Polio Narratives," *Lit. & Med.*, 1994, 13: 22–41. Amy Fairchild considered two distinct groups of published illness narratives that created a dialogue with the story of Franklin Delano Roosevelt's recovery from polio: Amy L. Fairchild, "The Polio Narratives: Dialogues with FDR," *Bull. Hist. Med.*, 2001, 75: 488–534, esp. p. 491. Black drew directly from young polio survivors and their relatives to supplement descriptions of the hospital regulations and daily routines and to gain insight into the disease's emotional and psychological effects on the patients and their families: see Kathryn Black,

In the Shadow of Polio: A Personal and Social History (Reading, Mass.: Addison-Wesley, 1996).

18. For a comprehensive overview of the field, see two recent collections on child health and welfare: Alexandra Minna Stern and Howard Markel, eds., *Formative Years: Children's Health in the United States, 1880–2000* (Ann Arbor: University of Michigan Press, 2002); Roger Cooter, ed., *In the Name of the Child: Health and Welfare, 1880–1940* (London: Routledge, 1992). The first provides a concise overview of the field, including medical specialties, technologies, adolescent health, and changing definitions of childhood diseases. The authors in the latter volume examined topics such as children's bodies, childhood diseases, child abuse, child labor, and child guidance in comparative articles that crossed geographical boundaries.

19. Janet Golden and Russell M. Viner, "Children's Experiences of Illness," in *The History of Twentieth-Century Medicine*, ed. Roger Cooter and John Pickstone (Amsterdam: Harwood International Press, 2000), pp. 575–87.

20. For analyses of this literary genre, see Arthur Kleinman, *Illness Narratives: Suffering, Healing, and the Human Condition* (New York: Basic Books, 1988); Howard Brody, *Stories of Sickness* (New Haven: Yale University Press, 1987); Anne Hunsaker Hawkins, *Reconstructing Illness: Studies in Pathography* (Lafayette, Ind.: Purdue University Press, 1993). Other major works on illness narratives include Arthur W. Frank, "The Rhetoric of Self-Change: Illness Experience as Narrative," *Sociol. Quart.*, 1993, 34: 39–52; G. Thomas Couser, *Recovering Bodies: Illness, Disability, and Life Writing* (Madison: University of Wisconsin Press, 1997); and "Illness, Disability, and Lifewriting," *a/b Auto/Biography Studies*, special issue, Spring 1991, 6/1. For a comprehensive and perceptive summary of the literature on illness narratives, see Fairchild, "Polio Narratives" (n. 17), pp. 491–97.

21. John Gunther, *A Fragment of Autobiography: The Fun of Writing the Inside Books* (New York: Harper and Row, 1962), p. 9.

22. Ibid, p. 6.

23. Ibid., p. 60.

24. Ibid.

25. Ibid., p. 45.

26. John Hayward and Geoffrey Keynes, eds., *The Complete Poetry and Selected Prose of John Donne and The Complete Poetry of William Blake* (New York: Random House, 1941), p. 239.

27. The book's dust jacket stated that neither the publisher nor the author was profiting from the account, and that the proceeds would be donated to cancer research. John proposed that he and Frances share a portion of the funds; "I thought of dividing the rest," he wrote, "between Deerfield, Memorial, or some other hospital (in the form of a specific endowment in Johnny's name for tumor research if the sum is considerable enough)," and he also considered making a donation to Gerson or using some to pay their medical expenses (John Gunther to Frances Gunther, [1949], box 4, folder 175, Frances Gunther Papers, Schlesinger Library, Radcliffe Institute, Harvard University, Cambridge, Mass. [hereafter, FGP]).

28. After the unexpected loss of her daughter, Frances sought professional advice. One physician replied that the medical community knew little about the cause or nature of thymic death. Another termed it an "unavoidable accident" (L. Emmett Holt, Jr., to Frances Gunther, 7 June 1929, carton 2, folder 46, FGP).

29. Frances Gunther, 8 May 1948, box 1, folder 15, FGP. Elaine Scarry, in *The Body in Pain: The Making and Unmaking of the World* (New York: Oxford University Press, 1985), drew from varied sources such as Amnesty International publications, transcripts of personal injury trials, poems, and disease narratives to uncover and examine a language of pain. Scarry argued that through records written by patients themselves, friends, and relatives, or captured in institutional case histories, "the most radically private of experiences begins to enter the realm of public discourse" (p. 6). The Gunthers repeatedly addressed the physical pain that Johnny experienced during his prolonged illness and emphasized how little their child suffered; however, *Death Be Not Proud* and the personal writings of John and Frances exposed their intense distress over the failure of their marital relationship, the repeated exacerbations of Johnny's illness, the incurability of his disease, and the loss of their son. Although I do not attempt to analyze or measure their grief,

I use readers' responses to these four implicit themes to show
the power of the Gunthers' voices in this regard. For a more
complete account, see Scarry, *Body in Pain*.

30. In private notes, John Gunther called Frances's section
"beautifully, movingly, exquisitely written," but he also criticized
its contents (marginal notes, draft of "A Word from Frances,"
n.d., box 44, folder 18, John Gunther Collection, Special
Collections Research Center, University of Chicago Library,
Chicago, Ill. [hereafter, JGC]). He summarized the two sections
as, "I tell a story and she tells of a relationship and how you
stand it when a relationship is broken by something external";
he opined: "It's so much by a *woman*. Women *are* different
from men. It's so *warm*. But mine is *strong, solid*" (notes labeled
"Diary," n.d., box 44, folder 18, JGC [emphasis in original]).

A Farewell to Arms
(Ernest Hemingway)

"Hemingway's Uncanny Beginnings"
by David M. Wyatt,
in *The Georgia Review* (1977)

Introduction

For David M. Wyatt, Hemingway's beginnings announce his novels' endings: the dark, barren spaces where those who have known pain await their death while pondering dying. In this excerpt from his article on Hemingway's five main novels, Wyatt calls *A Farewell to Arms* "Hemingway's most fatal book." Focusing on loss and nothingness, Wyatt explores the "fascination with death that recurs throughout Hemingway's work," noting how Frederic Henry, the protagonist of *A Farewell to Arms*, is "caught in the middle." Wyatt sees that "Frederic's inability to go forward or backward proceeds from one anxiety," the fear of death, the one thing in this world "one learns how to do."

Hemingway has a hard time imagining beginnings but an easy time inventing ends. Middles challenge him most of all. His novels

---

Wyatt, David M. "Hemingway's Uncanny Beginnings." *The Georgia Review* (Summer 1977): 476–501.

constantly anticipate, when they do not prematurely achieve, the sense of an ending. Our surprise at heating Anselmo say "I am an old man who will live until I die" turns upon the prolonging *until* and measures our disbelief that Hemingway will actually let such a life happen. Living from birth to death through a long life proves difficult of depiction for a writer trying to stave off death by continually adumbrating it. Hemingway's beginnings have the uncanny effect of raising the very specter of the end against which they are so concerned to defend. In the attempt to forestall annihilation by preempting it, Hemingway loses hold on the present. His moments of immediate experience unshadowed by future loss are rare indeed. His present tense, abundant as it is, registers itself as the tension of a consciousness caught between the trauma of the "before" and the fear of the "after." Hemingway's pleasure in the "now" is a largely apocryphal experience. Short stories, consumed in the limit of a single sitting, can protect us from the gathering sense of doom which becomes, in all but one of Hemingway's five major novels, his central effect. For writing novels of any length excites as much tension as it releases. The sense of option felt while beginning to write (or read) proves to be an oppressive irony when all that can be foreseen is the outstretched interval of time that must be filled. Why bother filling, Hemingway everywhere suggests, what will only be certainly lost?

[...]

A Farewell to Arms is Hemingway's most fatal book. While it promises the most life, it delivers nothing but loss. The imagination of disaster intrudes even into the strenuously pacific opening:

> In the late summer of that year we lived in a house in a village that looked across the river and the plain to the mountains. In the bed of the river there were pebbles and boulders, dry and white in the sun, and the water was clear and swiftly moving and blue in the channels. Troops went by the house and down the road and the dust they raised powdered the leaves of the trees. The trunks of the trees too were dusty and the leaves fell early that year and we saw the troops marching along the road and the dust rising and leaves, stirred by the breeze, falling and the soldiers marching and afterwards the road bare and white except for the leaves.

> The plain was rich with crops; there were many orchards of fruit trees and beyond the plain the mountains were brown and bare. There was fighting in the mountains and at night we could see the flashes from the artillery. In the dark it was like summer lightning, but the nights were cool and there was not the feeling of a storm coming.

At first this voice appears simply to report what it sees. It sounds in touch with seasons and elements. We stand aside here and conserve ourselves. The water flows, the troops pass, the leaves fall. Everything else spends itself. Yet high summer—a time of ripeness—somehow becomes late fall. We are manipulated into the season of loss. Parallel syntax presents an army of falling leaves. Men are "marching" and leaves are "falling," and through this parataxis they become all too easily confused. The leaves last; the men disappear. What remains is the emptiness of landscape—"a road bare and white"—which the human presence interrupts but cannot master.

The narrator subtly repeats this involvement of the reader in a fall that is at once natural and human. To say that "the nights were cool and there was not the feeling of a storm coming" is to protest too much. Yes, the storm is denied—but why is it ever envisaged? In *A Farewell to Arms* potential turbulence has more presence than actual peace. What Frederic Henry anticipates, Hemingway actually precipitates. A storm is exactly what Catherine fears: "I'm afraid of the rain because sometimes I see me dead in it." The storm looms over the entire novel, and inevitably breaks.

Yet this is not the only disaster the beginning obliquely foreshadows. More striking is Frederic's projection of pregnancy. As he watches the troops march by he notices "under their capes the two leather cartridge-boxes on the front of the belts, gray leather boxes heavy with the packs of clips of thin, long 6.5 mm. cartridges, bulged forward under the capes so that the men, passing on the road, marched as though they were six months gone with child." Through abundant detail Frederic attempts to establish the probability of what he sees. But the metaphoric leap from carefully measured cartridges to carefully measured pregnancy is so idiosyncratic as to reveal more about the mind of the beholder than what he beholds. Even before Frederic conceives a child, he seems to "feel trapped biologically." Projection allows him to assign to others what he feels as threatening to himself. Yet he no more negates this possibility than he does the chance of a storm. Frederic is trapped within *superstitious* narrative. While seeming to open into possibility, it really *stands still over* the very fear that it starts out to exorcize. As if to prove this, a storm quickly develops. The sudden reversals of *In Our Time* are condensed into single sentences: "One day at the end of the fall when I was out where the oak forest had been I saw a cloud coming over the mountain. It came very fast and the sun went a dull yellow and then everything was gray and the sky was covered and the cloud came on down the mountain and suddenly we were in it and it was snow." The storm is upon us before we have time to feel it coming. Yet we will learn to get ready. The novel educates us in anticipating the worst.

Such presentiments are uncanny. They make us uneasy because they so often come true. They express a fascination with death that recurs throughout Hemingway's work. Such recurrence suggests that every encounter with death aggravates rather than allays the fear of it. It is a repression which continually fails and so must repeat itself—a repetition compulsion. Freud argues that an anxiety which "can be shown to come from something repressed which *recurs* . . . would then be no other than what is uncanny." Repetition is a home away from home. What we repeat must be familiar, yet why would we repeat it if that were so? "The uncanny is in reality nothing new or foreign, but something familiar and old-established in the mind that has been estranged only by the process of repression." Freud speculates that "many people experience the feeling of the uncanny in the highest degree in relation to death." But the feeling can proceed as well from another source:

> An uncanny experience occurs either when repressed infantile complexes have been revived by some impression, or when the primitive beliefs [e.g., fear of the dead] we have surmounted seem once more to be confirmed. Finally, we must not let our predilection for smooth solution and lucid exposition blind us to the fact that these two cases of uncanny experience are not always sharply distinguishable. When we consider that primitive beliefs are most intimately connected with infantile complexes, and are, in fact, based upon them, we shall not be greatly astonished to find the distinction often a rather hazy one.

Hemingway's version of the uncanny certainly blurs this distinction. As we have seen, his career formally begins with a story that fuses and confuses birth trauma, castration anxiety, suicide, fear of dying, and fortune telling. Frederic Henry is the legitimate heir of Nick Adams. His primitive fascination with ends rehearses a universal anxiety over origins.

Caught in the middle, Frederic is a man with no belief in middles. His one memory of childhood defines this sense of limbo:

> The hay smelled good and lying in a barn in the hay took away all the years in between. We had lain in hay and talked and shot sparrows with an air-rifle when they perched in the triangle cut high up in the wall of the barn. The barn was gone now and one year they had cut the hemlock woods and there were only stumps, dried tree-tops, branches and fireweed where the woods had been. You could not go back. If you did not go forward what happened? You never got back to Milan. And if you got back to Milan what happened?

Here Frederic's inability to go either forward or backward proceeds from one anxiety. Later, his thoughts about his dead child show how a fear of dying derives from an ambivalence over the conditions of birth:

> He had never been alive. Except in Catherine. I'd felt him kick there often enough. But I hadn't for a week. Maybe he was choked all the time. Poor little kid. I wished the hell I'd been choked like that. No I didn't. Still there would not be all this dying to go through. Now Catherine would die. That was what you did. You died. You did not know what it was about. You never had time to learn. They threw you in and told you the rules and the first time they caught you off base they killed you.

Frederic renounces Jake's hope that learning to live in the world might help one to know what it was all about. In this world, dying is what one learns how to do.

In one of the endings he ultimately rejected, Hemingway admits through Frederic that life is open-ended in a way his stories refuse to acknowledge:

> I could tell about the boy. He did not seem of any importance then except as trouble and god knows I was bitter about him.

Anyway he does not belong in this story. He starts a new one. It is not fair to start a new story at the end of an old one but that is the way it happens. There is no end except death and birth is the only beginning.

Once the belief that death is the only plausible ending has been raised to the level of an aesthetic principle, the end of a novel cannot coincide with the birth of a son. Something has to give, and in the final version starting gives way to stopping. Hemingway had to reject this ending if he was not to openly dramatize the conflict between the rules laid down by his technique and the "way" things really happen. He chooses to kill the boy and so avoids having to expose his art as a defense against the facts of life.

So the book is stillborn. Like the child, "it had never been alive." It never knows an interval of time free from intimations of mortality. We do not experience its middle as a discovery of its end. Nothing is allowed to seem lasting. Our insecurity is founded on untimeliness. Wounds inevitably come, but, what is worse, at wholly improbable moments. "I was blown up while we were eating cheese." The rule governing the future is that what cannot be predicted cannot be imagined.

Yet Hemingway finally does get love into a book. "I do what you want" announces a kind of consummation never before represented by him. But it will not be represented here; with these words Chapter XVII ends. Our disappointment with *A Farewell to Arms* comes less from fastidious omission, however, than from Hemingway's refusal of this "splendid chance to be a messiah." Love is always something had on leave, stolen from fate. Throughout, Frederic treats his love for Catherine as something already over—as recollection. His "mistake was this," Kierkegaard argues in *Repetition*, "that he stood at the end instead of the beginning." Yet he goes on to admit that

the man who in his experience of love has not experienced it thus precisely at the beginning, has never loved. Only he must have another mood alongside of this. This potentiated act of recollection is the eternal expression of love at the beginning, it is the token of real love. But on the other hand an ironic elasticity is requisite in order to be able to make use of it … It must be true that one's life is over at the first instant, but there must be vitality enough to kill this death and transform it into life.

Frederic has the requisite irony but not the elasticity and so begins and proceeds by "seeing it all ahead like the moves in a chess game." Would we begrudge Hemingway his oft-criticized romance were it not betrayed from the start to so bitter an irony? If books can be defined by how they end—tragedy with the death of the hero, comedy with the birth of a new society—then romance never ends and irony ends before it begins. The two modes are simply incompatible. *A Farewell to Arms* might have been Hemingway's best novel had he opened himself more to the awkward and sometimes silly lovemaking many readers find so embarrassing. Embarrassment is precisely what Hemingway dreads and what he must overcome. But he cannot imagine a future that is not foreclosed in advance because he cannot trust in the basic facts of human continuity: procreation and married love. While Hemingway remains capable of depicting a series of carefree sexual encounters, he fails to invent a hero who truly domesticates the uncanny place.

HEART OF DARKNESS
(JOSEPH CONRAD)

"Lying as Dying in *Heart of Darkness*"
by Garrett Stewart, in *PMLA* (1980)

INTRODUCTION

While Joseph Conrad's *Heart of Darkness* is often read as an allegory of self-exploration, one in which the movement to the inner Congo is seen as an introspective turn, the novel's ending complicates such a mystical reading. For as the novel ends, Marlow, the soothsayer, poised as a Buddha at the novel's onset, lies to Kurtz's fiancée, the "Intended." What do we make of this lie? What is its significance? Why does Conrad foreground the lie in the text? These are the questions to which Garrett Stewart responds, hypothesizing that Marlow's lie is emblematic of a greater lie: Western civilization's many idealistic lies masqueraded as truths, truths used to justify evil ends, most notably the extermination of "the brutes," as Kurtz's scrawled message on his monograph identifies Africans, those who stand in the way of Western "progress." For Garrett, such unbridled idealism leads to the kind of horror Kurtz has enacted, not only the murder of countless "Others," but also the death of the spiritual in modern culture.

Stewart, Garrett. "Lying as Dying in *Heart of Darkness*." *PMLA* Vol. 95, No. 3 (May 1980) 319–331.

> It is indeed impossible to imagine our own death; and whenever
> we attempt to do so we can perceive that we are in fact still
> present as spectators.
>
> —Freud, "Our Attitude towards Death"

Lying is dying. So says Marlow, and so Conrad is out to demonstrate,
even at the expense of his own narrator. "There is a taint of death, a
flavour of mortality in lies" (p. 27),[1] Marlow announces early in *Heart
of Darkness*, but the final words he quotes from himself in the novel—
his consoling statement to Kurtz's devoted fiancée that her lover
expired uttering her name—constitute his own lie about a dying man's
last words. Thus lie's fatal taint makes rot even of a man's deathbed
integrity. It infects and cancels that unflinching power of speech at
mortality's point of no return which Conrad calls in *Lord Jim* the
"triumph" of expression "in articulo mortis" (p. 233; Ch. xli), his own
expression evoking the English word "articulation" as well as the Latin
idiom for "turning point." The full import of Marlow's self-indicting
charity is bound to elude us if the imagery of death has not been carefully logged. *Heart of Darkness* is the deviously mapped quest for a
sequestered space beyond geographical coordinates, a recessed sector
of the soul to which only death, firsthand or secondhand, can guar-
antee passage. Negotiating the further transit from Kurtz's renowned
deathbed utterance to Marlow's appended lie (itself, as I try to show, an
indirect death scene), detecting the continuity between main plot and
coda, is one of the most troublesome maneuvers in Conrad studies. Yet
taking the scent of lie's taint, as it emanates from the symbolic corpses
and metaphoric decay that litter the course of the story, is the best way
of tracing Conrad's equation of death and deceit. Whether political,
moral, or psychological, mendacity is the most mortal of sins, against
ourselves and others. Although Marlow equivocates, Conrad is there
behind him to warn us that the lies of Western idealism mislead us
to death. The plot of *Heart of Darkness* is in part a political autopsy of
imperialist myths. A level-headed seaman named Marlow, teller of his
own tale, journeys to the Congo as steamer captain for a European
trading company; hears rumors about another agent of the company,
an eloquent mastermind named Kurtz; later discovers that the man
has submitted to, rather than suppressed, the natives' savagery, with its
hints of cannibalism and sexual license; finally meets up with Kurtz,
remaining by his side to hear the man's deathbed judgment on his

own degeneracy and diabolism; and then returns to Europe to lie about Kurtz's "worthy" end in order to give the man's fiancée something to live for and with. Marlow's trek toward Kurtz, first by water, then by land, is made now in the wake of a generalized epidemic of death, now in the footsteps of walking specters: a dead march to the heart of a defunct and festering ideal of European superiority. Though the novel's "adjectival insistence,"[2] which so famously annoyed F.R. Leavis, centers nowhere more relentlessly than on permutations of "dark" and "deadly," "tenebrous" and "moribund," the effect is one not so much of morbid atmospherics as of moral asperity, an attack on death-dealing imperialist motives and the truths they obscure.

Heart of Darkness harkens back to origins. It suggests that a naked exposure of the human ego, unshielded by civilization and its self-contents, to a world of savagery presumed to be far beneath it is, in the long evolutionary run, only a baring of the soul to the most primally rooted human impulses. To plumb the native is to come up against the innate, apart from all cultural or racial demarcations. Even before Marlow begins his African narrative proper, he ruminates that the Thames, on which he and his fellow seamen are traveling, has also been, as far back as the Roman colonization, "one of the dark places of the earth" (p. 5). Apropos of the story to come, this initial sense of a primordial blackness triggers an association, more than gratuitous, with "death skulking in the air, in the water, in the bush. They must have been dying like flies here." In Roman England under the pall of colonization, yes, just as in Africa, where Marlow found everywhere "the merry dance of death and trade ... in a still and earthly atmosphere as of an overheated catacomb" (p. 14), where trade rivers were "streams of death in life" (p. 79).

Beyond the sinister topography of the African landscape, which lays bare the inevitable brutality of imperialism as itself a mode of death, Marlow has also faced his own private demise in an embodied omen. On leaving the company offices in Europe, he must pass by those black-garbed, knitting women, the sibylline harpies and harbingers of death, to whom departing agents seem to sense as the appropriate valediction "Morituri te salutant" (p. 11). As one about to die, or narrowly to skirt his own death, Marlow shortly after encounters two European predecessors, predeceased, on his way to what he calls (recalling a metaphor from its grave) the "dead center" of Africa. First he hears reports of the anonymous Swedish captain who "hanged himself on the road" (p. 79)—no one knows exactly why, but no one is surprised—and later he learns certain details about an earlier Nordic fatality, the Dane Fresleven, who was Marlow's immediate predecessor in the post of company agent and who was conveniently murdered by a representative of the jungle so that Marlow could step "into his shoes" (p. 9). Marlow, sensing the mortal stakes in his adventure and unwilling to content himself with the mere report of Fresleven's death, searches out the corpse in the jungle, become by now a skeletal memento mori with grass growing through its ribs.

Marlow therefore achieves in life what the rest of us receive from such stories as the one he spins: he procures an intuition of his own end in the doom of a surrogate. Yielding us the "warmth which we never draw from our own fate,"[3] or in Conrad the chill of recognition, the death scene is art's perpetual bequest to life, though its insights may too easily be forfeited. One of the chief motives for a death scene in literature is thus in *Heart of Darkness*, and never more so than with the final death of Kurtz, devolved on a character within the fiction, indeed the narrator, who gravitates to the death of the Other, first with the nameless Swede and much more urgently with the murdered Fresleven and then twice later, as we will see, to savor the extremity otherwise unavailable to consciousness. The reader, through character—as Marlow, through rumored dooms, skeletons, finally dying men—comes within the safe proximity of his or her own end, a death by imaginative proxy. To vary Shakespeare, in art we ruminate our ruin at one remove, as Marlow's mortuary agenda so complexly exemplifies up to, and even after, his own feverish brush with death following immediately on the death of Kurtz.

Kurtz himself is introduced as the barely living fulfillment of the mortal fate of Marlow as contemplated through his double, Fresleven—though such thoughts hover at the level of mere foreboding, without as yet any explicit parallel between Marlow and Kurtz, except that they are both European agents in Africa. When Kurtz makes his long-delayed appearance Marlow describes him too, like Fresleven, as a skeleton, "the cage of his ribs all astir, the bones of his arms waving" (p. 60). In a scene that looks forward to the remarkable epiphany in *The Magic Mountain* where Hans Castorp sees latent within him, by way of an X ray, his own corpse, Kurtz as breathing skeleton keeps company with the remains of Fresleven as a death's-head memento mori. As Kurtz emerges from his blankets "as if from a winding-sheet" (p. 60), his moribund condition is also personally retributive, an oblique revenge on himself, as arch imperialist, for those untended dying natives in that "grove of death" (pp. 17–18) Marlow had earlier come on, all of whom were reduced to skeletal "bundles of acute angles." In tandem with this ironic reprisal for Kurtz—the witherer withered—is another symbolic pattern of poetic justice, for Kurtz has also been shriveled to an image of the precious corrupted element, the cold ivory, in which he has traded and debased his humanistic ideals. The mania for this dead bone strikes Marlow from the first as having a "taint of imbecile rapacity" like (as with lying for that matter) "a whiff from some corpse" (p. 23), and when Kurtz appears on the scene to personify that greed, his all-but-fossilized being seems like "an animated image of death carved out of old ivory" (p. 60).

Even before Kurtz's first onstage appearance a premature and precipitous description of him as a breathing corpse broke into Marlow's chronological narrative, providing a glimpse of the story's haunted destination. Marlow cannot keep down the need to tell his auditors in advance that the visionary encounter with genius he had gone in search of would never be more than spectral—the eviscerated Kurtz reduced, by the time Marlow first sees him, to a disembodied voice in a "disinterred body" (p. 49). Exploring Marlow's preoccupation with Kurtz *as voice* leads us to recognize the logic of such a premature intrusion, for it argues the deepest logic of the novel's first full-dress death, which frames this premonition, the wordless end of a subtly partial doppelgänger for Marlow and Kurtz together in the former's native helmsman. Marlow can share in Kurtz's slaying self-knowledge because "it"—what was left of the man, his neutered "shade" or "wraith" (p. 49)—"it could speak English to me. The original Kurtz had been educated partly in England." Thus Conrad quietly implicates England, and Marlow as Englishman, in Kurtz's European hubris and diseased idealism—and of course implicates himself, too, as British-educated master of nonnative English eloquence. I introduce Conrad's famed English, not just Marlow's expert story-telling, because the local stress on the risks and responsibilities of rhetorical power seems to broaden outward into a comment on the dark expressiveness that brings us the story in the first place.

Marlow admits that his grandiose expectations of Kurtz center on the man's vocal eloquence, for "I had never imagined him as doing, you know, but as discoursing.... The man presented himself as a voice," possessing as his only "real presence" the "gift of expression, the bewildering, the illuminating, the most exalted and the most contemptible, the pulsating stream of light or the deceitful flow from the heart of an impenetrable darkness" (p. 48). Marlow realizes the double nature of language, its power to illuminate and ennoble but also to corrupt, and he imagines Kurtz as a disembodied annunciation of this very duality. Kurtz's wasted person when finally encountered bears out this sense of him as language incarnate, for his flesh has withered to the bone, leaving only a speaking soul, a direct effluence from the heart of darkness. And it is a death scene, as so often in literature, that will finally put to the ironic test this power of eloquence. It is important to note, also, that we have a piece of transcribed as well as merely rumored eloquence that ties Kurtz not only to Marlow as a speaking "presence" but again to Conrad, this time as author. Before returning to the narrative of the trip upriver, Marlow slows to summarize a report Kurtz had written for the International Society for the Suppression of Savage Customs; even here the dangerous underside of rhetorical flourish is apparent: "It was eloquent, vibrating with eloquence, but too high-strung ... a beautiful piece of writing.... It made me tingle with enthusiasm. This was the unbounded power of eloquence—of words—of burning noble words ... the magic current of phrases." Kurtz exposes the danger of the verbal genius that delivers him to us as a prose incarnation, for at the end of his manuscript he had scrawled into view that dark-heartedness which, like his greatness, is charged by the current of his magniloquence, though rendered now in a sudden truncation of all burning and burnished phrase: "Exterminate all the brutes!" Rhetorical sonority in a moral vacuum boils down to a curt, criminal injunction, and the dream of piercing eloquence that Conrad shares with Marlow, especially in this most "high-strung" and overwrought story, and that both share with Kurtz, an eloquence obsessively stressed in this digression, stands confessed in its essential emptiness. Voice must mean what it delivers, and even Marlow as narrator here—though not Conrad, who is an ironic step or two to the side—protests too much in his brooding reiterations.

To follow Conrad more deeply into the relation of voice to death and darkness, we must note the strategic location of this digression on Kurtzian verbal virtuosity. Closing off the intrusive reverie, Marlow writes: "No, I can't forget him, though I am not prepared to affirm the fellow was exactly worth the life we lost in getting him" (p. 51). He is referring to his murdered helmsman, a man of no words at all lanced to death in a native attack meant to keep the rescue party from removing Kurtz. "I missed my late helmsman awfully. I missed him even while his body was still lying in the pilot-house." Despite Marlow's deep-seated racism, death solidifies the sense of human commonality, for stabbed through the side, the otherwise negligible "fool-nigger" suddenly "looked at me over his shoulder in an extraordinary, profound, familiar manner, and fell upon my feet" (p. 46). It is the "familiarity" of a soul that knows its own death in the common body. The nameless savage, civilized only enough to enable him to serve the mechanical function of steering, has no English in which to voice the mysteries of his injury and his death. Yet even untutored mortality has its voiceless eloquence: "I declare it looked as though he would presently put to us some question in an understandable language, but he died without uttering a sound. . . . Only in the very last moment, as though in response to some sign we could not see, to some whisper we could not hear, he frowned heavily." Death speaks to, but not through, him an unspeakable something, the whisper of incommunicable revelation, and the resulting frown "gave to his black death-mask an inconceivably sombre, brooding, and menacing expression"—that last noun used in only one of its senses and awaiting completion in the articulate death of Kurtz. Kurtz too has his facial expressions carved in the death mask seemingly hewn of his coveted ivory, but he dies vocally transmitting, as well as receiving, the "whisper" from beyond. The moment of death for the helmsman is precisely marked by a transition in the prose across one of Conrad's most stunning flourishes of the "gift of expression." In this jungle world where death is so treacherously slurred with life, where the landscape itself evinces a Coleridgean "life-in-death," the syllabic momentum of Conrad's studied euphony smooths and blurs one noun into its stretched sibilant antonym, the stare of life into the blank of death: "The lustre of inquiring *glance* faded swiftly into vacant *glassiness*" (my italics). But one death, so vividly imagined and so final, immediately leans forward to become the preview of another.

Almost at once, by a deviously pertinent non sequitur, Marlow adds to the pilgrim at his side: "And, by the way, I suppose Mr. Kurtz is dead as well by this time." So begins the frenetic early digression on Kurtz and on the fear of a lost opportunity for an audience with him, imagined only as an audition of his voice in the aftermath of the helmsman's voiceless demise. Just as Marlow is changing the subject— or is he?—from one certain death to a probable one, he is tearing off the shoes filled with the blood of the helmsman who fell at his feet, imploring but mute, as if in a last brotherly supplication. Certainly we are to recall the dead Fresleven and Marlow, on that earlier captain's death, stepping "into his shoes." Now it would seem that Marlow's own life's blood has been shed into them in a symbolic blood brotherhood with his pilot that amounts to a sudden doubling at the point of death. If we assume Conrad is preoccupied with such secret sharing as part of a coherent symbolism in this story, we must begin to range and discriminate Marlow's dead or dying doppelgängers. At first almost a matter of statistical survey or impersonal backdrop, then slowly driven home, even internalized, the surrogate deaths gather step by step toward an excruciating revelation.

En route, the death of the helmsman is an important and rarely discussed middle term. Immediately after the conjecture of Kurtz's probable death, Marlow returns to the death of the pilot to suggest a closer tie than expected between himself and his helmsman: " . . . for months I had him at my back—a help—an instrument. It was a kind of partnership. He steered for me—I had to look after him" (p. 52). One is brawn, physical instrumentality, the other percipience and concern; one muscle, the other mind; and death serves to distinguish, but at the same time to bond, them "like a claim of distant kinship affirmed in a supreme moment." When we note later that the same phrase, "supreme moment," is used for Kurtz's death (p. 71), we have the parallel unmistakably confirmed. Providing a cool head to Kurtz's tortured soul, Marlow pilots for Kurtz as the helmsman has done before for Marlow. The psychological crux here is a vexing crisscross of doubles that lingers in the imagination until it sorts itself into shape. Though allegory may seem too bald a term for the nested subtleties of Conrad's elusively apportioned psychology, some appreciation of pattern on our part is essential.

If Kurtz is the heart or soul of darkness repressed beneath the accretions and delusions of civilization, what is Marlow's relation, obsessive as it is, to Kurtz? As organizing and expressive consciousness, passionately desirous of the Kurtzian eloquence so as better to tell the Kurtzian secrets, Marlow is mind—we might say ego or even superego—to an id identified with those dark lusts in the jungle.

When Kurtz tries to return to the jungle, Marlow must prevent him. Mind must detect and control the unconscious atavistic urges, repress the regressive. This is what Marlow indirectly admits when he has caught up with the escaping Kurtz in the underbrush: "Soul! If anybody ever struggled with a soul, I am the man" (p. 67). Of course many have had such conflicts, but usually with their own soul. In the psychic scheme of this novel, however, all things external seem to radiate from Marlow as percipient center, even the jungle incantation in this very scene, for "I confounded the beat of the drum with the beating of my heart, and was pleased at its calm regularity" (p. 66). But only Kurtz knows the true rhythms of that native darkness and embodies them symbolically as the objectified buried interior of Marlow's consciousness. In the introduction to a joint edition of this novel and *The Secret Sharer*, Albert Guérard points out that Conrad's departure from such classics of doppelgänger fiction as Poe's *William Wilson* and Dostoevsky's *The Double* reflects a shift away from the pattern whereby "the second selves of the heroes are embodiments of the accusing conscience."[4] Instead, the Conradian double tends to embody a "more instinctive, more primitive, less rational self," a relation in which the helmsman certainly stands—and falls—to Marlow. So too with Kurtz in relation to Marlow, though at the last moment the unconscious life does seem to spew forth a voiced conscience, accusatory and horrible. Interested also in the doppelgänger, Richard Ellmann has suggested that we might go outside the narrative to see Kurtz as a shearing off of one part of Conrad, whose Polish name Korzeniowski abbreviates by transliteration to Kurtz.[5] When Conrad in *Heart of Darkness* decided to test such delvings and divisions of self against its ultimate cancellation in death, however, he inserted the helmsman as the middle term that would help render such death in its twin definition—physical mortality as well as the closure of consciousness—and thus augmented the allegory of his terminal partnerings.

The helmsman, Kurtz, and Marlow form a triangle of body and soul equidistant from the overseeing mind. A mere "instrument" of the white imperialist, yet a physical tool rather surprisingly missed when his awareness has vacated the body, the helmsman is the animal, or preconscious, side of Marlow, primitive but no more initiated into darkness, perhaps, than Marlow. His going is the death of the body, mortality at its lower common factor, in which the "distant kinship" claimed for the first time is merely the fraternity of those who, born for death, are thus, regardless of color, human. Death democratizes as it levels, the corpse of the Other becoming the body of a brother. First a skeleton in tall grass, now a bodied but speechless demise, soon the death throes of an almost incorporeal eloquence: these are the stages of Marlow's face-to-face confrontation with mortality, one on one, or one on naught.

For this confrontation, the "whisper" that registers as a glint in the helmsman's eye must eventually be given voice, even if it is "The horror! The horror!" that Kurtz "cried in a whisper" (p. 72). Since, in his murderous panic to remain behind, the ailing Kurtz must have seen his desperate unfitness for return both to civilization and to its curative ministrations, must have known that the life he lowered himself to in the wilderness had slain his European illusions and had spelled death all along, the final welling up into utterance of his self-denunciation is not only belated but posthumous. Like spiritual corpses before him in Dickens, George Eliot, and Hardy, Kurtz dies offstage just moments after his last words. (We must wait for the manager's black servant to stick his head in the cabin door and say— with "scathing contempt" but, because of his untrained grammar, without the verb of being that lends paradox to most predications of death—"Mistah Kurtz—he dead.") Direct representation of demise would be redundant for this "disinterred" wraith, whose terminal disease had long before done its worst.

The symptoms of Kurtz's jungle fever are, like the words that punctuate its final stage, a direct tapping of spiritual essence. Though understated in its allegorical causation, his is one of those classic deaths of the literary tradition whose etiology wavers between physiology and symbolism. Not only did he live a spiritual death, but the death he dealt to others returns to him with the gruesome suitedness of his physical end. We have watched allusions accumulate from the start to the traditional effect that as he has slain, so he is laid low; as he lusted, so death covets him. When we first see him he is wasted to the inanimate matter of his obsession, his face an ivory death mask; the maker of skeletons and corpses, he is collapsed now to a heap of bone. Morally as well as bodily the jungle has claimed him, and its endemic death now overmasters him by punitive reversal: Africa "had taken him, loved him, embraced him, got into his veins, consumed his flesh, and sealed his soul to its own by the inconceivable ceremonies of some devilish initiation" (p. 49). His terminal sickness is merely the pathological insignia of his soul's disease. Kurtz dies lingeringly of a fever contracted at the heart of the primordial. Something he encounters there meets no resistance, immunological or spiritual; it first inflames, then gradually emaciates him, eating him up from within. This contact is one of the overdetermined weddings of medicine and morality against which, once they become more than a literary figuration, Susan Sontag rails so passionately in *Illness as Metaphor*.[6] They are, of course, the very lifeblood of classic fictional dying, where dramatic sense must be made from the onset of mortal absence.

With just this purpose in mind, Marlow comes to the death of Kurtz with expectations fashioned by myth or literature or both: "Did he live his life again," Marlow asks in one of the clichés of extinction, "in every detail of desire, temptation, and surrender during that supreme moment of complete knowledge?" (p. 71). Kurtz himself has another mortuary formula haltingly in mind just before the end, not Marlow's "drowning man archetype" but another facile parallel between life and its end: "I withdrew quietly, but I heard him mutter, 'Live rightly, die, die . . .' I listened. There was nothing more." To such swallowed clichés has Kurtz's superb rhetorical gift dwindled. We struggle to recognize a stuttered version, caught in Kurtz's throat, of some balked orthodox formula like "Live rightly, die rightly"—sacred to religion as well as to all those nineteenth-century fictional deaths by aesthetic predestination. Only the converse (if any such formulaic correspondence) could be true for Kurtz, and full fictional honesty demands that, live however you have chosen to live, the fact is simply that you die, not crystallizing your *raison d'être* but canceling it. Kurtz, knowing this no doubt, cannot get beyond the predication of death— "die, die," the broken record of a broken soul. Yet he is still struggling to sum up in his scorching last words, "The horror! The horror!" The whispered repetition raises for us an even more teasing question: Why twice? Is there a thanatological recipe present here too? "He had summed up—he had judged. 'The horror!'" Both summation and judgment are comprehended in that single word, repeated in Kurtz's actual words once for each—the horror that has been perpetrated, the horror that descends as judgment, either in this pitiless and empty death or in whatever damnation there could be to come. Not until the coda of the novel, when the horror is deceitfully expurgated only to grin from the very depths of its denial, will the full doubleness of its reference be implicitly whispered.

Contaminated by the "horror," Marlow himself shortly falls ill and nearly gets himself buried along with Kurtz, but instead of focusing on his own near death, Marlow insists that "It is his [Kurtz's] extremity that I seem to have lived through" (p. 72). The idiomatic preposition "through" reminds us that only another's death can be undergone without finality, lived up to the moment of and worked past to its other side. And this is for Marlow, of course, not displacement or evasion, at least the first time around, for Kurtz's soul is not some phenomenon entirely removed from him. Allegorically, if we may say so, Kurtz *as soul* represents—below the level of the still-repressive consciousness for which Marlow *as mind* has stood—the buried anguish and guilt of Marlow's own soul, as the helmsman had earlier stood for, and in the stead of, Marlow's bodily self in his multistaged encounter with oblivion. In his book on Conrad's relation to autobiographical narrative, Edward W. Said suggests that *Heart of Darkness* exaggerates the entire first-person mode to a crisis point, where the reportorial or ruminative impulse no longer has the benefit of retrospect. Drawing on Schopenhauer, Said writes that the "only possible meeting between thought and action is in death, the annihilation of both. For the mind to accept death as a solution of the difficulty would be to accept the devastating irony that permits the destruction of the consciousness, the only faculty capable of enjoying the solution."[7] Conrad's early tales instead, according to Said, "posit a compromise in which the agent usually dies . . . and the reflecting mind continues still uncertain, still in darkness." The mind, miraculously sustained beyond the symbolic death of body and soul, remains puzzled with the potentially creative questioning of artistic distance. Again we must note the emphasis on voice, on the articulated end of experience that provides the matter of reflection. Kurtz's death before the eyes and especially the ears of Marlow is best read as the death not of a man alongside a man but of a tragic agonist in the presence of a receptive, if finally too timid, interpreter. One student of Conrad has suggested that Kurtz evokes "from the sensitive Marlow feelings akin to the traditional emotions of pity and terror."[8] Death is cathartic; it boasts the revelatory "compression" (Marlow's own term) of literature pitched to its "supreme moment," where the consciousness, of reader or audience or here "partner," can move, instructed but unconsumed, through the death of the Other.

If this weathering of death by a double were advanced as a *modus moriendi* in life, however, rather than in tragic art, a basic premise of existentialism, as phrased in emphatic italics by Heidegger, would be directly violated, for *"No one can take the Other's dying away from him"* (Heidegger's italics).[9] Death is undeflectably one's own, for its "end" has a teleological component that is irreducibly private, the coming from potential into presence, always final, of being's fullness—for Kurtz that complete, and completely recognized, "horror," a corruption damningly one's own even while universalized. Kurtz therefore projects the latent predilection of the human race for darkness, a prepossession that when ripened to completeness becomes the very definition of death, the end (to vary Heidegger's "being-toward-death") of a tragic being-toward-darkness. In a characteristic run of ontological argot, Heidegger sums up the principle of mortal individuality by saying that "coming-to-an-end implies a mode of Being in which the particular *Dasein* [roughly "Being"] simply cannot be represented by someone else" (p. 286). Yet what is true existentially, true to life, cannot be true to art, or art would fail us precisely where we most need the intervention of a shaping consciousness. Art's tragic figures must die for us, and for Marlow in our place.

The notion that Kurtz elicits from Marlow the "traditional emotions of pity and terror" that, say, Kurtz or Faust or any other tragic figure evokes in us as audience is developed at some length in Murray Krieger's valuable chapter on Conrad in *The Tragic Vision*. For Krieger, *"Heart of Darkness* is effective as an ideal archetype of the literature of the tragic vision, giving us an exemplary version of the relations between representatives of the ethical and of the tragic realms." By his "relation to Marlow," that is, Kurtz becomes in his fatally concentrated self-revelation "an allegory of the role that the visionary and the literature in which he figures are to play for those of us who are interested but not ourselves committed totally."[10] Marlow is entirely aware, too, of the role he has assigned to his articulate double as doomed visionary, even as we note how throttled and nihilistic is Kurtz's so-called tragic recognition. Death by proxy, terminal vantage through a ritual scapegoat, may be entirely a literary invention, but it is one Marlow tries hard to validate from his experience, for it alone offers him a model of death with understanding, however

horrible, to contrast with the nonepiphanic pallor of his own approach
to the brink:

> I was within a hair's breadth of the last opportunity for
> pronouncement, and I found with humiliation that probably I
> would have nothing to say. This is the reason why I affirm that
> Kurtz was a remarkable man. He had something to say. He
> said it.... True, he had made that last stride, he had stepped
> over the edge, while I had been permitted to draw back my
> hesitating foot. And perhaps in this is the whole difference;
> perhaps all the wisdom, and all truth, and all sincerity, are just
> compressed into that inappreciable moment of time in which
> we step over the threshold of the invisible. (p. 72)

Marlow, the moral consciousness who dips into the heart of tragic
darkness but returns on guard, thus embodies what Krieger calls "the
ethical resistance to the tragic" in which "moral strength resides" (p.
155). I should like soon to qualify this statement, for the tragedy in
Heart of Darkness and the irony seem more pervasive than Krieger
believes, Marlow's admirable "restraint" more like repression and
delusion. Nevertheless, Krieger's point about the central dichotomy
between moral percipience and tragic vision is well taken. It suggests
that the order of art attempts to soften existential extremity by
molding it to understanding and, further, that death by proxy may be
taken as a test case for the entire narrative and dramatic enterprise,
the knowing voice transmitting visionary experience into the receptive
mind as the essential transaction of all fictional tragedy.

If Marlow is no more than an eavesdropper on tragedy, our medi-
ator between visionary depths and the everyday, then the considerable number of critics who find him receiving Conrad's unqualified
assent, even in his supposedly benign final lie, would be correct.
Marlow, who aligns lies and death in his own mind, knows better. On
any reading of the novel, one understands Marlow's awe at Kurtz's
deathbed pronouncement, but why should the Marlow of majority
opinion be at all dismayed that he too, no more than nearing that
"last opportunity" for statement, could not muster Kurtz's extremity
of self-judgment? Why should a man of complex ethical sensitivity
who has "kept his head" through demonic tribulations feel diminished by comparison with a life so single-mindedly surrendered to

blackness that a reverberating disyllable, like Keats's "forlorn," can toll its retribution? Or we can put the question another way: In this allegory of "homo duplex"—to use the term that Edward Said fitly borrows from Conrad's letters[11]—how lightly can we afford to take a doubling of the climactic denomination, "The horror! The horror!"? Not only a dead echo within the soul but a resonance with the darkness outside, in another dichotomy not only summation but also judgment, this doubleness seems further to indict both parties at the scene, Kurtz as well as Marlow—passing judgment on the former's exaggeratedly depraved soul, but only as it concentrates the potential horror of "all the hearts that beat in the darkness."

And perhaps there is one final doubling of "the horror" to consider, when Marlow lies to Kurtz's Intended that "The last word he pronounced was—your name." That we never know her name, so awkwardly withheld from the reader, that indeed her title "Intended" seems to incarnate in her all the original Kurtz's best blind intentions, admits her even more readily than otherwise into the sphere of his searing universal revelation: the horror in me (as Kurtz might have said), the horror in all, even in her, the nameless abstract ideal. A lie that would liquidate the tragedy, Marlow's fib exposes the lie of idealism that generates it. Marlow himself, however, has a lesser motive in mind when he falsifies Kurtz's death. Criticism often senses something vaguely contaminating as well as consoling about this lie, but what is *mortal* about it goes undiscussed. As I hope now to show, Marlow's last words about Kurtz's last words are the death knell of his own tragic apprehension, the squandering of Kurtz's delegated revelation on a squeamish deceit. They signal, in fact, some measure of the very death of self Marlow thought he had slipped past, for that "flavour of mortality" in lies leaves its acrid taste throughout the last scene.

Given what we know of Marlow's ultimate attitude toward the Congo experience, the surprise is that criticism can so widely persist in thinking Marlow's whitewashing capitulation merely a white lie, a sacrificial violation of his own spiritual insight out of humanist charity. When he pontificates early on about lie's taint, the point is hammered home as a personal revulsion. Lying "appalls me"; it is "exactly what I hate and detest in the world"; it "makes me miserable and sick, like biting into something rotten would" (p. 27). One must doubt whether it could be simply for the solace of another that he later submits himself to his spiritual death. His strict ethical theorem, the equation of death with lying, is even in the early context no stray remark, for it threads untruth to death in the causal nexus of the European experience in Africa. What dying and lying have in common is that they both induce decay, the psychic moribundity and physical decomposition visible everywhere on that colonized landscape we traverse on our way to the death of Kurtz. The novel's largest lie is the one that premises its experience: the ultimately self-revenging hubris of imperial impulse. The question is what degree of collusion in this untruth Marlow, long its implicit critic, ultimately allows himself to take comfort in.

Against the muddied tide of critical opinion, Eloise Knapp Hay, writing about the political novels of Joseph Conrad, has helped us to see how the political self-deception of Marlow serves to discredit him as a morally reliable narrator.[12] For though we read the novel as a progressive disclosure of European delusions in Africa, we must recall that Marlow's words of introduction are uttered from the vantage of retrospect, uttered and thus undercut. Having seen the darkness at the heart of Europe's colonizing onslaughts, he can still say, with a combination of political acuity and idealistic confusion: "'The conquest of the earth, which mostly means the taking it away from those who have a different complexion or slightly flatter noses than ourselves, is not a pretty thing when you look into it too much. What redeems it is the idea only. An idea at the back of it; not a sentimental pretence but an idea; and an unselfish belief in the idea—something you can set up, and bow down before, and offer a sacrifice to. . . .' He broke off" (p. 7). Despite his witnessing to the inevitable corruption that comes from white imperialism, Marlow would seem to be saying that without "selfishness" Kurtz could have succeeded, and yet the very claim is demolished by the religious imagery of bowing and sacrificing. Idealism degrades itself to idol worship, as we know from the perverse exaltation and adoration of Kurtz in the jungle, his ascent to godhead.

The inbred spoilage of an ennobling ideal was also sketched out with the first jungle victim we heard about in any detail, the Danish captain Fresleven, who began as "the gentlest, quietest creature that ever walked on two legs" (p. 9). Yet he was murdered by a native while "mercilessly" beating an African chief over some misunderstanding about two black hens. After all, Marlow says without surprise, "He had been a couple of years already out there engaged in the noble cause, you know, and he probably felt the need at last of asserting his self-respect in some way." Thus is the nobility of the white man's grand burden sapped and trivialized. Marlow's parenthetical "you know" (such things taken for granted by us far-thinking Europeans) teeters uneasily between sarcasm and apologetics; Marlow himself is unsure how to feel about his beloved idealism, however fine and selfless, when it can be so readily undermined, here and of course with Kurtz, by eruptions of the ego in sadistic self-assertion. Indeed Kurtz seemed at first the very embodiment of this "noble cause," but too much its incarnation in the long run, too little its acolyte. If Kurtz somewhere held to any glimmer of his original "idea," he must have lost sight of it entirely amid the blackness of his end. Does Marlow mean to imply, however, that Kurtz is the kind of "sacrifice" the idea deserves? Surely Kurtz died in the name of his idea's death, not its perpetuation, died at the hands of his own traitorous neglect of the ideal. There are, Marlow is so far right, purposes in themselves sublime, but when they are implemented by persons in power the danger is always that others will be sacrificed to the ghost of idealism's grandeur, cannibalized by its rhetoric and its personal magnetism. Bowing down, we tend to give up our vigilance. In line with the imagery of adoration, Marlow himself is twice described in the prologue as an inscrutable effigy, first with a posture and complexion that "resembled an idol" (p. 3) and later, just before his defense of imperialism, with "the pose of a Buddha preaching in European clothes and without a lotus-flower" (p. 6). His own person partially incarnates that idolatry masquerading as an almost religious truth—in another key, Kurtz's idealism turned demonic—which is the monitory center of his tale. Though Marlow knows the evils of white suppression at first hand, he represses them far enough from consciousness to leave continued space for the European idealism he still shares with "the original Kurtz."

Recognizing this, we are a far cry from the sympathetic treatment given Marlow's lie about Kurtz's sustained greatness in the most recent, and on this point not untypical, book about Conrad: "Marlow's lie to her, strain as we may, obstinately remains an ordinary white lie, a humane expression of compassion without devious moral implications and by no stretch of the imagination can we regard it as evincing a form of corruption of his part."[13] H.M. Daleski is thus taking direct issue, and he means to, with Conrad's own statement that in "the last pages of *Heart of Darkness* ... the interview of the man and the girl locks in—as it were—the whole 30,000 words of narrative description into one suggestive view of a whole phase of life, and makes of that story something quite on another plane than an anecdote of a man who went mad in the Centre of Africa."[14] To side with Conrad against many of his critics in this is to note, for one thing, Marlow's often discussed view of women as cocooned dreamers whom a touch of reality would wilt. Though on the one hand this helps explain his eagerness to protect the Intended from the truth, on the other hand Marlow should have learned better—given another woman he has met—by the time he sees Kurtz's fiancée. When the Intended wails her disbelief in Kurtz's absolute absence, Marlow joins her silently in this faith in the man's perpetuity: "I saw him clearly enough then. I shall see this eloquent phantom as long as I live." But his specter is, to use Conrad's suggestive language, "locked in" also to Marlow's haunted vision of the Intended and of another dark woman superimposed on her image, Kurtz's black liaison from the jungle: "... and I shall see her, too, a tragic and familiar Shade, resembling in this gesture another one, tragic also, and bedecked with powerless charms, stretching bare brown arms over the glitter of the infernal stream, the stream of darkness" (p. 78). When this sentence is followed immediately by the Intended's ambiguous intuition about Kurtz's death, the feminine pronoun itself is rendered ambiguous by the narrative's overlapping of two spectral images, as if the black (or brown) soul mate is whispering a cryptic truth through the tremulous voice of the white woman's delusion. We have just heard about the tragic African shade, and then: "She said suddenly very low, 'He died as he lived.'" Two "she"s obtain, one obtruding from the past, to reinforce both the Intended's myth and at the same time the darker reality that Kurtz's "tenebrous" consort in the jungle had no reason to doubt as he was torn from her.

Marlow has seen two colors of the feminine heart and thus of the human heart artificially construed as Other. But the Intended carries her savage sister inside her, just as Marlow envelops Kurtz. Dark truth lurks beneath blanching delusion, and both women, copresent in the narrator's mind's eye, are ill-consorted emanations of Marlow as well as of Kurtz. Marlow's early allusion to Brussels as "a city that always makes me think of a whited sepulchre" (p. 9) comes entirely clear only after we have grown to recognize Kurtz as the personified corpse of the *civis* and its hypocrisy; Marlow, returned to the "sepulchral city" (p. 72) as if for entombment himself, washes it the whiter with the bleach of deceit in the course of his lying interview with the Intended. We now see his previous remark about defending female illusions more clearly too as the self-protective gesture to which he briefly admits even during his much earlier allusion to the Intended: "Did I mention a girl? Oh, she is out of it—completely. They—the women I mean—are out of it—should be out of it. We must help them to stay in that beautiful world of their own, *lest ours gets worse*" (p. 49; my emphasis on Marlow's revealing afterthought). When Marlow reflects at the end, in his own final words to us, that the alternative to his lie "would have been too dark—too dark altogether," he is speaking not only on her behalf but on his own, in rebuttal to the tragic truth vouchsafed to him in Kurtz's death and repressed in Marlow's own approach to that end, as well as being repressed, by timid necessity, in his subsequent return to civilization.

Marlow repeatedly describes his experience in Africa, and especially with Kurtz, as a "nightmare," and this is never more telling a metaphor than in Marlow's drawing back from the ultimate fate of Kurtz. Psychological truism has it that we never dream our own death, even in the worst of nightmares—that we always wake to consciousness within an inch or so of the abyss. So with Marlow's nightmare. We can neither dream nor, according to Freud, even force ourselves to imagine with any cogency our own demise. Marlow, therefore, must wake up from another's fatal nightmare just in the nick of time's tilting over into eternity. Only later is the lie of idealism unconsciously resurrected from its own death scene in order to be traded on as the barter of return, the inevitably exacted price of repatriation to the European community. Kurtz's revelation is a sweeping death sentence, the end point of an asymptotic nightmare that Marlow holds off in order to come back and go on. Kurtz's abject but profound darkness dims to a "grey skepticism" in Marlow that is not only the trivialization but the very ticket of return.

If, back at the sepulchral hub of Europe, the Intended's dark counterspecter, that feminine apparition from our savage source, might only be held to a shadowy depth that does not impinge so remorselessly on consciousness, the woman of Faith might still manage to embody for Marlow an ideal he could "bow down before," offer his own misguided and mortal "sacrifice" to in the form of that deadly lie. As he said earlier of Kurtz: "I laid the ghost of his gifts at last with a lie." These gifts of insight into darkness must be laid to rest, or else Marlow would have nothing left to revere. Kurtz's revelation of "the horror" is fatally incompatible with genuflection. Since we know that Marlow's own idol-like person seems an outward sign of such internalized idealism, internalized at the expense of full truth, we sense the reflexivity: "bowing my head before the faith that was in her, before that great and saving illusion that shone with an unearthly glow in the darkness, in the triumphant darkness from which I could not defend her—from which I could not even defend myself" (p. 77). With devious valor, however, he attempts this self-defense, and by preserving such a feminine dreamworld he hopes to prevent his own from "getting worse," making good the grammatical and psychic parallelism in "defend her ... defend myself." For Marlow (to risk again the boxing off of a more expressive complexity) is ultimately homo quadruplex, a wholeness reified into the mental powers of assimilation (as well as repression) played off against lower and would-be higher functions: mind against body in the helmsman, heart or soul in Kurtz, and finally a supervening and repressive Faith in the Intended. In this fourfold "allegory," eventually unfolded, she represents pure idealist intentionality preserved against the corrosive truth of experience, but preserved by being interred along with the buried truth in a sarcophagal unreality.

Daleski follows his critique of Conrad's coda with this sentence: "Consequently, it is difficult for us to make any meaningful connection between the lie and death" (p. 75). But we are now in a position to make this connection amid the metaphors of spiritual deadliness and posthumous defeatism that litter the coda as much as they do the tale itself. Marlow's untruth is lethal precisely because it kills the meaning of a death. There is a corollary to the proposition that lying is a kind of dying. Truth, even grasped only in death, is a defiance of death, a notion hallowed in British fiction's treatment of demise. Kurtz's self-realization, about the "horror" his life and death would have epitomized, rendered his image deathless in the mind, a perennial admonishing phantom, except that the lie kills it. Partly to abet Marlow in this homicidal denial, two of the most trusted mortuary formulas of fiction, each a version of death by epitome, are invoked with some verbal and thematic deviousness in connection with Kurtz's death, one early, one late. When Marlow realizes that the name Kurtz, meaning "short" in German, is belied by the man's considerable height, he says—as if forgetting (because wanting to, no doubt) the cauterizing truth telling of Kurtz's last utterance—that "the name was as true as everything else in his life—and death" (p. 60). Marlow's own retrospective account seems colored, obscured, by the late meliorating lie eventually summoned to slay Kurtz's black epiphany. Marlow does, however, recognize the "true" consonance of Kurtz's life and death in another sense, for the persistent specter of Kurtz's ghost calls up this postmortem observation: "He lived then before me; he lived as much as he had ever lived ... a shadow darker than the shadow of the night" (p. 75). Ghostliness is at one with his ghastly aura in life. There is further evidence in the coda that Conrad, if not Marlow, has the mortuary tradition in literature specifically in mind, with its often rigorous equations between death and identity. When, hoping for solace, the Intended clutches at the time-tested heroic prescription, "He died as he lived," Marlow's mock iteration, "His end was in every way worthy of his life," not only secretly reverses the moral judgment implicit in her faith, even as he preserves some of that faith for her and for himself, but helps us see the additional irony to which Marlow, in the throes of untruth, is no doubt blinded. The epitomizing apothegm of death is traditionally phrased with a change in tense—"He died as he *had* lived"—with pluperfect brought to perfection (in the existential sense) in the preterit. The Intended, however, has unwittingly summarized the nature of a corrupt life coextensive with death and equivalent to it: the long-pending end of a man who, again, "died as he lived." Living a lie of moral superiority, lies being deadly, Kurtz died *while* he lived ("as" in this sense), his death scene true to life in its very deadliness. What Céline would call "death on the installment plan" is, however, a truth about Kurtz that is itself sabotaged and assassinated.

An equally mordant telescoping of tense arrests us in the most curious passage in this coda, where Marlow seems more than usually aware that his words may fail to capture his only half-glimpsed purpose: "For her he had died only yesterday. And, by Jove! the impression was so powerful that for me, too, he seemed to have died only yesterday—nay this very minute. I saw her and him in the same instant of time—his death and her sorrow—I saw her sorrow in the very moment of his death. Do you understand? I saw them together— heard them together" (p. 76). Her black-draped mourning is Kurtz's darkness visible; her untarnished faith is the lie overlaying his fatal eloquence. For her Kurtz died yesterday, while for Marlow, who somewhere knows the truth, he dies in the instant, every instant, of her deluded mourning, in which Marlow now colludes. The faith Marlow so sustains, in and through its feminine vessel, is a faith that kills, that denies the tragic content of the death scene—as if Kurtz himself had not inched over the edge into revelation. And so in Marlow's mind's-eye vision—a palimpsest of mourning superimposed on simultaneous death—Kurtz's *present* deathbed, symbol of the present murder of his very meaning, and the Intended's immolation on the bier of his memory are, after all, "locked together." They give us death's poisonous aftertaste in the mouth of untruth. If this is an even bleaker reading of the story's denouement than usual, at least it seeks to respect the tragic potential of the previous climax, the legacy of insight willed by a cruel but lucid death.

For in the Intended's dedication to Kurtz's misunderstood and idealized shade there is, we come finally to see, a heart-denying lie that is equivalent to the death it euphemizes, a lie that rests at the heart of the death it originally causes. In short, such faith in moral supermen breeds the death of its own heroic avatars in their all too human incarnations. Marlow cannot separate the black of Kurtz's end from that of his fiancée's mourning, because he uses her suffering as an excuse to deflect the full import of the former tragedy, reducing it to futile pathos. This vicious circle is imaged as an almost hallucinatory superimposition, her continuing grief over and above her idol's recurring death. And it renders sickeningly visible the link between death and delusion just before the sustaining lie is tendered. If we can answer affirmatively Marlow's "Do you understand?" then this appalling double image becomes the symbolic configuration of death as lie incarnate, corpse and killing delusion seen in line with the same vanishing point, spiritual negation zeroing in on a void.

NOTES

1. Conrad, *Heart of Darkness*, ed. Robert Kimbrough (New York: Norton, 1963). Subsequent references are to this edition. The quotation from *Lord Jim* is also from the Norton Critical Edition, ed. Thomas C. Moser (New York: Norton, 1968).

2. Leavis, *The Great Tradition* (London, 1948; rpt. New York: New York Univ. Press, 1964), p. 177.

3. Walter Benjamin, "The Storyteller," *Illuminations*, ed. Hannah Arendt, trans. Harry Zohn (New York: Schocken Books, 1969), p. 101.

4. Guérard, Introd., *Heart of Darkness* and *The Secret Sharer*, Signet Classic ed. (New York: New American Library, 1950), p. 11.

5. Ellmann, *Golden Codgers: Biographical Speculations* (New York: Oxford Univ. Press, 1973), p. 18.

6. Sontag, *Illness as Metaphor* (New York: Farrar, 1978).

7. Said, *Joseph Conrad and the Fiction of Autobiography* (Cambridge: Harvard Univ. Press, 1966), p. 113.

8. Paul L. Wiley, "Conrad's Skein of Ironies," originally published in Kimbrough, ed., p. 226.

9. Martin Heidegger, *Being and Time*, trans. John Macquarrie and Edward Robinson (1927; rpt. New York: Harper, 1962), p. 284.

10. Krieger, *The Tragic Vision: Variations on a Theme in Literary Interpretation* (New York: Holt, 1960), p. 155.

11. Said, *Beginnings: Intention and Method* (New York: Basic Books, 1975), pp. 104, 130.

12. Hay, *The Political Novels of Joseph Conrad: A Critical Study* (Chicago: Univ. of Chicago Press, 1963); see esp. Hay's treatment of Marlow's lie, pp. 150–54.

13. Daleski, *Joseph Conrad: The Way of Dispossession* (London: Faber and Faber, 1977), p. 75.

14. Letter to his publishers, William Blackwood, 31 May 1902; quoted by Daleski, p. 73.

IN COLD BLOOD
(TRUMAN CAPOTE)

"Faith and Tragedy in *In Cold Blood*"
by John McClain,
University of North Carolina at Asheville

Lawrence Grobel: *Although they so cold-bloodedly murdered a family of four, you didn't think they should have been killed, did you?*

Truman Capote: No. I'm very much against capital punishment. (Grobel 118)

In Cold Blood tells the story of two types of death: death by murder and death by legal execution. The view of capital punishment expressed in this essay's epigraph comes from an interview Truman Capote gave in the early 1980s, a view unchanged from that he offered when he published *In Cold Blood* in book form, fifteen years earlier, in January 1966 (Plimpton 41). His opinion about capital punishment and the way *In Cold Blood* implicitly seeks to persuade readers of that opinion created a controversy that has not died. From the notable range of praise and criticism surrounding *In Cold Blood*, perhaps one label for it would satisfy everyone: it is a masterpiece—of controversy.

The book relates the story of six deaths. First to die are Herbert William Clutter, his wife Bonnie, and Nancy and Kenyon, two of their children. The last to die are the two who killed them, Perry Smith and Dick Hickock. *In Cold Blood* also emphasizes the role of

Alvin Dewey, the lead investigator in solving the case, who knew all the principal characters (described as "principals") personally as well. No one disputes that Smith and Hickock indeed killed the Clutters and were in turn killed by the state of Kansas, legally. But Truman Capote unites all six deaths under his title, *In Cold Blood*, provoking a problematic question for the reader: if all of these deaths are premeditated, in fact "in cold blood," what moral, if not legal, status does capital punishment have compared to criminal murder—especially for the predominantly Christian members of the communities affected? Capote purports *In Cold Blood* to be a work of nonfiction; all the principals were real people and the events presented happened. But he also claims for the book the status of a novel, a literary form traditionally understood as fictional. What then is *In Cold Blood*? How can the reader gauge its truth, considering Capote's belief that capital punishment is truly wrong?

In Cold Blood should be read as Capote's indictment of capital punishment in the United States, the moral of the book being that all six deaths are wrong. His aesthetic theory and practice of the nonfiction novel create the truth of that moral, connecting it to the Western tradition of the "tragic." He himself said of *In Cold Blood*: "I came to understand that death is the central factor of life. . . . The experience served to heighten my feeling of the tragic view of life, which I've always held . . ." (Norden 123–124). Capote's remarks are not offhand conceits. He uses the word "tragedy" often in the book. He claims that the book has a "hero," the devout Alvin Dewey (Clarke *Too Brief* 283). *In Cold Blood* presents capital punishment as a "tragedy" for a society rooted in Christian faith, suggesting that the "tragedy" is in part due to Christian support of it.

The epigraph Capote selected for *In Cold Blood*, François Villon's *Ballade des pendus* (*Ballad of the Hanged Men*), sets the tone for the book: "Brother humans who live on after us / Don't let your hearts harden against us / For if you have pity on wretches like us / More likely God will show mercy to you" (Kinnell 209). Villon's verses plead with, but also warn, their readers. How does *In Cold Blood* similarly evoke pity, a key tragic theme?

Capote sticks to the facts of the case. How he organizes those facts and reveals information—especially *when* he reveals information—conditions the reader for a certain emotional reaction. Who is the narrator who does this? Several times Capote uses an unnamed figure referred to as a "journalist" or "reporter" to present information that only this figure could have heard. This figure must be the narrator of the book, Capote himself (Capote *In Cold Blood* 216, 259, 281, 331, 335). But no Capote—by name—appears in the book. He avoids first-person voice entirely, a characteristic Capote prided himself on: "The great accomplishment of *In Cold Blood* is that I never appear once. There's never an *I* in it at all" (Grobel 116).

Why is this important? Capote states, "Ordinarily, the reporter has to use himself as a character, an eyewitness observer, in order to retain credibility. But I felt that it was essential to the seemingly detached tone of that book that the author should be absent" (Capote *Music* xviii). Note that he states "the seemingly detached tone of that book." Capote is not detached from the events of the story. But how does Capote make his case objectively and in the voice of a seemingly neutral writer? With his (near) invisibility. He wants to present, as he states in his subtitle for the book, "A True Account of a Multiple Murder and its Consequences." The "truth" in *In Cold Blood* is a "distillation of reality" (Capote *The Dogs Bark* 397). It is novelistic because Capote arranges the material creatively, though the material itself is not fiction. He states, "Journalism ... moves along on a horizontal plane, telling a story, while fiction—good fiction—moves vertically, taking you deeper and deeper into character and events. By treating a real event with fictional techniques ... it's possible to make this kind of synthesis: thus, the nonfiction novel" (Steinem 240). He does not want to express directly his view of capital punishment. It becomes an implicit persuasion, an argument against capital punishment without an arguer. "'I make my own comment by what I choose to tell and how I choose to tell it. . . . [for] in the nonfiction novel one can also manipulate . . . to step into the story myself to set the reader straight" (Plimpton 32). Capote puts himself into the story via his "selection, by the way he assembles the facts and actual quotes" (Steinem 240).

How does this technique work in *In Cold Blood* specifically? Capote structures his "account" with four major parts, in sequence: "The Last to See Them Alive," "Persons Unknown," "Answer," and "The Corner." In the first part he describes western Kansas as a place where "horses, herds of cattle, a white cluster of grain elevators rising as gracefully as Greek temples are visible long before a traveler reaches them" (Capote *In Cold Blood* 3). This is also Christian country, "within the Bible Belt

borders, and therefore a person's church affiliation is the most important factor influencing his class status" (34). Roman Catholics and a
handful of Protestant denominations comprise the majority: Method-
ists, Baptists, Episcopalians, and Presbyterians. Here Herbert Clutter,
48, and his wife, Bonnie, 45, lived in Holcomb, a suburb of the county
seat of Finney County, Garden City, "in the middle—almost the exact
middle—of the continental United States" (33). Both native Kansans,
they had four children; Nancy, 16, and Kenyon, 15, still lived at home
on the family's River Valley Farm. It consisted of the house, three
barns, more than eight hundred acres and three thousand more rented
acres. Eveanna Jarchow, their eldest, lived in Illinois with her husband
and son. Beverly, the next, was studying to be a nurse in Kansas City.
The family prospered from hard work and skill. They were respected.
The Eisenhower administration appointed Herbert Clutter to the
Federal Farm Credit Board. They were faithfully Methodist. Evidence
of the seriousness of religious association in the area was that Nancy's
boyfriend, Bobby Rupp, was a Roman Catholic, "a fact that should
in itself be sufficient to terminate whatever fancies she and this boy
might have of some day marrying" (8).

Part I also introduces the killers. Dick Hickock, a fellow Kansan,
was from Olathe, a suburb of Kansas City, where his parents and
brother owned a small farm; they were poor, respectable, and unre-
markable. He had a "normal" life with his relatives, his parents and a
brother, with whom he maintained cordial contact for the rest of his
life. He completed high school, where he did well as a student and
athlete. Too poor to go to college, he went to work at various jobs
including as an auto mechanic; he married twice and fathered three
children, lived beyond his means, went into debt and then into crime:
check fraud, burglary, and eventually the murder of the Clutters—all
by the age of 28. In contrast to Hickock, Capote reveals most of Perry
Smith's background in Parts II and III. When we first meet Smith
he has been on parole from prison for several months and is waiting
to meet Hickock in Olathe. They decide on the last details of the
plan already agreed upon, a plan "flawlessly devised" with the "alleged
perfection of his overall-design" (37). The motive: robbery of the cash
in a safe in Herbert Clutter's office, described to Hickock by another
cellmate. They also had agreed to leave "no witnesses" (37).

Capote juxtaposes scenes of the Clutters in their routines with
the oncoming arrival of Hickock and Smith at their home. Capote

foreshadows events ominously: "then touching the brim of his cap, he [Herbert Clutter] headed for home and the day's work, unaware that it would be his last" (13); "Now, on this final day of her life, Mrs. Clutter hung in the closet the calico housedress . . ." (30); in her Bible a bookmark states, "'Take ye heed, watch and pray: for ye know not when the time is'" (30); and Nancy laid out her clothes for church the coming Sunday morning; "It was the dress in which she was to be buried" (56).

A "fate" awaits them. Early Sunday morning, November 15, 1959, the four Clutters are murdered at River Valley Farm. First neighbors find them, then law enforcement officers. Nancy was "shot in the back of the head with a shotgun held maybe two inches away" (62); Bonnie was "shot pointblank in the side of the head" (63); Kenyon was "shot in the face, directly, head-on" (64); and Herbert was "shot, all right, the same as Kenyon—with the gun held right in front of his face . . . his throat had been cut, too" (64-65). Part I ends with Hickock and Smith back in Olathe. Capote omits, at this point in the story, those witnesses who were the very last to see the Clutters alive: the murderers themselves, Hickock and Smith.

Nor does Capote present their perspectives on the night of the murders in Part II, "Persons Unknown." Only at the end of Part III, "Answer," does Capote relate Hickock and Perry's stories of that night, their confessions—160 pages, nearly half the length of the book—after his setup to that fateful evening as described in Part I. Hickock and Smith were arrested December 30, 1959; their confessions followed over the next several days. In between the dates of the murders and confessions Capote presents more than just the sequence of events as they happened in those approximately six weeks.

Capote continues in "Persons Unknown" and "Answer" with the juxtaposition of scenes of different characters, their stories, and perspectives with which he began *In Cold Blood*. Capote counterpoints Hickock and Perry's roaming after the murders—to Mexico, back to Kansas, to Miami, back west through Texas until caught in Las Vegas—with new characters, notably Alvin Adams Dewey. Dewey is also a native Kansan, a friend of the Clutters (a member of the same First Methodist church), and a career man with the Kansas Bureau of Investigation stationed in Garden City. He heads the subsequent investigation.

Capote also juxtaposes time. In Part II, "Persons Unknown," and Part III, "Answer," he alternates the investigation taking place in the present with Perry Smith's life before the murders. As portrayed by Capote, Perry Smith's life was terrible by any standard. He was born in rural Nevada, one of four children. His parents were rodeo professionals; the family moved around—to California, Alaska, back to Nevada. They moved as well into deadly dysfunction. Eventually past their prime for the rodeo circuit and failing as entrepreneurs, his mother, Florence Buckskin, a full Cherokee, left his father, Tex John Smith, with all four children for San Francisco. Perry was six. With little supervision at home, Perry joined gangs and was sent to various detention homes, Christian-affiliated and not. The physical, emotional, and racial abuse he received in such places instilled in him an emphatic atheism he would hold to for the rest of his life. Over the years his mother became a sexually promiscuous alcoholic and died in an alcohol-induced coma. His brother, Jimmy, killed himself with a shotgun, the same shotgun Jimmy discovered that his wife had used on herself in their home. Jimmy was a compulsively jealous husband who feared his wife would become like his mother. One sister, Fern, had followed in their mother's alcoholic path, falling or jumping, while drunk, out of the window of a hotel room and being killed by a passing taxi.

Perry sought escape from his family. He joined the Merchant Marine at 16, then eventually the Army, serving in Korea, where he was awarded the Bronze Medal. After his service he was in a serious motorcycle injury that required six months of hospitalization; he was to suffer continuous pain in his legs. Finding himself on the loose, unable to find work or maintain a relationship with his father, he fell into a "career" of burglary. Caught and sentenced, he would meet Dick Hickock in prison in Kansas. His one remaining sister, Barbara (presented in *In Cold Blood* as Mrs. Frederic Johnson), had not seen and not wanted to see her brother for four years. Finally came the Clutters' murder when Smith was thirty years old.

Throughout Parts II and III Capote sorts the facts of Smith's life with a layering of multiple perspectives: Smith's surviving sister's, his father's, and Smith's own view of his relatives' views of him. Accusation, recrimination, pity, regret, fear, and just plain hatred soil those perspectives as the Smiths relentlessly repeat the pain they have shared and continue to share. Capote describes Smith's sister's general view of them: "She had said she was afraid of Perry, and she was, but was it simply Perry she feared, or was it a configuration of which he was a part—the terrible destiny that seemed promised the four children of Florence Buckskin and Tex John Smith?" (183).

Capote also juxtaposes the miseries of Smith's life with the misery Alvin Dewey's family, a wife and two sons, undergo as he strives to solve the case. The family is devoutly Methodist: "A belief in God and the rituals surrounding that belief—church every Sunday, grace before meals, prayers before bed—were an important part of the Deweys' existence" (105). But the Clutter murders challenge their faith. Alvin is "haunted" by their deaths (148). His physical health suffers: "In fact, during the past three weeks, Dewey had dropped twenty pounds" (149). For "His state of mind was bad; he was emaciated; and he was smoking sixty cigarettes a day" (165). Capote reports a horrific dream of Dewey's in which he sees Herbert Clutter with his murderers—Smith and Hickock. In his dream they end up in Valley View Cemetery where the Clutters are buried, as is Dewey's father. He imagines Smith and Hickock hiding behind his father's headstone. They disappear, laughing, as he shoots at them. In the disappointment he feels at their escape, he experiences "a despair so mournfully intense that it awakened him" (197). He had fallen asleep in the sheriff's office. Now awake, "it was as though he were a feverish, frightened ten-year-old; his hair was wet, his shirt cold-damp and clinging" (197).

Capote increasingly presents Dewey's reactions to Smith as the emotional center of the book, reactions key to *In Cold Blood*'s "tragic" agenda. When Smith offers his first confession to Dewey, on their way to Garden City for trial, Dewey hears Smith's own sense of being someone he does not recognize. Smith: "And yet—How can I explain this? It was like I wasn't part of it. More as though I was reading a story" (240). At one point in the robbery, a robbery that did not find a safe with the promised cash, he thinks to leave Hickock there by himself. Then he assaults Herbert Clutter: "I didn't want to harm the man. I thought he was a very nice gentleman. Soft spoken. I thought so right up to the moment I cut his throat" (244). He describes how he shot him, out of pity, as Clutter struggled to breathe through his bloody, cut windpipe; then he shot Kenyon. Then Dick, he claims in this, his first confession, shoots the two women upstairs. (Smith, later confirms Hickock's claim that he himself killed all the Clutters.) Capote describes Dewey after hearing Smith's initial account as "without anger—with, rather, a measure of sympathy—for Perry Smith's life had been no bed of roses but pitiful, an ugly and lonely progress toward one mirage and then another" (246). Capote is clear, however, that Dewey, at this point, remembering the suffering the Clutters went through, "hoped to see Perry and his partner hanged— hanged back to back"(246). Part III, "Answer," ends with their arrival in Garden City. Because Capote has structured his book so that the murders are understood in the context of Smith's life, will the reader identify with Dewey's initial reaction of sympathy?

In Part IV, "The Corner," Capote provides further context for Dewey's initial sympathetic reaction to Smith. Capote borrows the name for his concluding section from the name inmates at the Kansas State Penitentiary give to the building containing the gallows, hanging being the means of execution in Kansas. Their trial began on March 22, 1960, in Garden City, their lawyers rejecting the idea of having the trial elsewhere because Garden City "is a religious community. . . . And most of the ministers are opposed to capital punishment, say it's immoral, unchristian; even the Reverend Cowan, the Clutters' own minister and a close friend of the family" (266). Indeed, all the jurors turn out to be "family men . . . and were seriously affiliated with one or another of the local churches" (273).

Due to the willful determination of Dewey's investigation and some lucky breaks, the prosecution triumphed. Found guilty and sentenced to death, Hickock and Smith were transferred to the Kansas State Penitentiary for Men in Leavenworth, Kansas. With new lawyers and various appeals, the first execution date for both, May 13, 1960, moved to October 25, 1962, then to August 8, 1963, then to February 18, 1965. Finally, both executions took place on April 14, 1965. Hickcock was thirty-three years old, Smith thirty-six. They had been on death row in side-by-side cells for nearly five years.

"The Corner" concentrates on the justifiability of their death sentence. The only possible defense (to save their lives, not free them) would be pleas of insanity. But such a defense was severely restricted in Kansas, where courts adhered to the M'Naghten Rule. It "recognizes no form of insanity provided the defendant has the capacity to discriminate between right and wrong—legally, not morally" (316). No gray areas. Dr. W. Mitchell Jones, who testified on their behalf, was asked if he had an opinion on their capacity. He answered "yes" regarding Hickock and was allowed to say no more, legally (294). For Perry he said he had no secure opinion. And that, legally, was all he was allowed to say.

In both instances Capote, the narrator, intervenes: "However, had Dr. Jones been allowed to speak further, here is what he would have testified ..."—regarding Dick (294). Regarding Smith, "But had Dr. Jones been permitted to discourse on the cause of his indecision, he would have testified ..." (296). What would Dr. Jones have said? Hickock "shows no sign of mental confusion or disorientation. His thinking is well organized and logical and he seems to be in good contact with reality" (294). But he has "a severe character disorder'" (295) and "signs of emotional abnormality" (294). Smith, on the other hand, "shows definite signs of severe mental illness" (296). He finds that Smith "is oriented, hyperalert to things going on about him, and shows no sign of confusion" (297). But his "present personality structure is very nearly that of a paranoid schizophrenic reaction" (298). Capote provides information that no judge, juror, or spectator can know. But the readers of *In Cold Blood* know.

Capote adds more psychiatric "testimony" for *In Cold Blood*'s readers. A Dr. Joseph Satten examines Smith's case in particular. He believes that when "Smith attacked Mr. Clutter he was under a mental eclipse, deep inside a schizophrenic darkness, for it was not entirely a flesh-and-blood man he 'suddenly discovered' himself destroying, but 'a key figure in some past traumatic configuration'" (302). What was the "traumatic configuration?" Capote's implicit answer: Smith's whole life.

Returning to the trial itself, Capote then includes an exchange after the jury leaves to evaluate the case, between a newspaper man, Richard Parr, and an unnamed reporter:

> Parr: "What's unfair?"
> "The whole trial. These guys don't stand a chance."
> "Fat chance they gave Nancy Clutter."
> "Perry Smith. My God. He's had such a rotten life—"
> "Many a man can match sob stories with that little bastard. Me included ... but I sure as hell never killed four people in cold blood."
> "Yeah, and how about hanging the bastard? That's pretty goddam cold-blooded too." (305–306)

Capote follows these comments immediately with the views of a Reverend Post who heard the exchange. "Capital punishment is no

answer: it doesn't give the sinner time enough to come to God. Sometimes I despair" (306). These comments echo those from a letter to the
Garden City *Telegram* by Bonnie Clutter's own brother, Howard Fox,
whom Capote had mentioned earlier in the book: "'The deed is done
and taking another life cannot change it. Instead, let us forgive as God
would have us do'" (107).

Does *In Cold Blood* end with such forgiveness, pity, mercy? It does
not end with the executions. Dewey, a believer in capital punishment,
its purported deterrent effects, and its justice, witnessed the hangings.
But in Capote's account he could not watch Perry Smith being killed.
"Dewey shut his eyes; he kept them shut until he heard the thud-
snap that announces a rope-broken neck" (340). Capote takes a hard
case, a committed, devout, and decent man of the law, Alvin Dewey,
and suggests doubt. He writes that for Dewey, "Perry possessed a
quality, the aura of an exiled animal, a creature walking wounded,
that the detective could not disregard" (341). Dewey remains unsatis-
fied. He "had imagined that with the deaths of Smith and Hickock,
he would experience a sense of climax, release, of a design justly
completed" (341).

Capote the literary artist provides the release, the catharsis the
detective wanted—while Hickcock and Smith are still alive. He
relates a chance meeting nearly a year earlier, before the hangings,
between Dewey and Susan Kidwell, Nancy Clutter's best friend and
the one who found her body. They meet at Valley View, the Garden
City public cemetery where, earlier in *In Cold Blood*, Dewey had his
ferocious nightmare about the murderers hiding behind his father's
headstone. Now he finds himself there again, but awake and happy, as
he proceeds to weed his father's grave peacefully. He and Susan have
a passing conversation in which they imagine alternative presents and
futures, of those still living, and for those, like the Clutters, who are
dead. Then Dewey heads home. Thus Capote ends his book. Again,
this interlude that Capote selects for his ending for *In Cold Blood*
takes place while Hickock and Smith live. To Dewey this quiet event
"had somehow for him more or less ended the Clutter case" (341). But
Capote presents this episode as a memory. When Dewey finds himself
at the violent executions he *remembers* "a design justly completed." Is
it now?

One can read *In Cold Blood* as Capote's indictment of capital
punishment without, of course, seeing it as a defense of the murderers.

They were murderers. But Capote describes them as "brothers in the breed of Cain" (260), a revealing association for his book. Cain, the first son of Adam and Eve, murdered his brother, Abel. God punished him with banishment, not death. God showed mercy, just as François Villon asserts in *In Cold Blood*'s epigraph. God forbade anyone else from killing him. Cain goes on to marry, father a son, and build a city. Dewey and his community would know well this story from Genesis, just as in true classical tragedy the audience would know the story beforehand. Capote's selection of this reference shows in part how his point of view creates the moral of *In Cold Blood*. Throughout he writes of the "tragedy in Holcomb" (54) and the "Holcomb tragedy" (247); the book's structure guides the reader as it presents many classic tragic themes: suffering, pity, fear. Who is the protagonist who experiences all of these and, Capote suggests, achieves a new and ambivalent awareness? The character still standing at the end—the one who knew the Clutters and Dick Hickock and Perry Smith—is Alvin Dewey, a faithful witness to an America in tragic conflict with itself and an actor within that drama, one whom Capote distills into a work of art.

WORKS CITED

Capote, Truman. *Music for Chameleons*. New York: Random House, 1980.

———. *The Dogs Bark: Public People and Private Places*. New York: Random House, 1973.

———. *In Cold Blood*. New York: Random House, 1965.

Clarke, Gerald. *Capote: A Biography*. New York: Simon and Schuster, 1988.

———. *Too Brief a Treat: The Letters of Truman Capote*. New York: Random House, 2004.

Grobel, Lawrence. *Conversations with Capote*. New York: New American Library, 1985.

Kinnell, Galway. *The Poems of François Villon*. Lebanon, N.H.: University Press of New England, 1982.

Kroll, Jack. "*In Cold Blood* . . . An American Tragedy." *Newsweek* 24 January 1966: 59–63.

Macdonald, Dwight. "Cosa Nostra." *Esquire* 65.4 (April 1966): 44, 46, 48, 58, 60, 62, 64.

Malin, Irving, ed. *Truman Capote's* In Cold Blood: *A Critical Handbook*. Belmont, California: Wadsworth Publishing Company, 1968.

Nance, William L. *The Worlds of Truman Capote.* New York: Stein and Day, 1970.

Norden, Eric. "*Playboy* Interview: Truman Capote." *Truman Capote: Conversations.* Ed. M. Thomas Inge. Jackson, Miss.: University Press of Mississippi, 1987. 110-163.

Plimpton, George. "The Story Behind a Nonfiction Novel." *Truman Capote's In Cold Blood: A Critical Handbook.* Ed. Irving Malin. Belmont, California: Wadsworth Publishing, 1968. 25-43.

Steinem, Gloria. "A Visit with Truman Capote." *Glamour* April 1966: 210.

Waldmeir, Joseph J. and John C. Waldmeir, eds. *The Critical Response to Truman Capote.* Westport, Conn.: Greenwood Press, 1999.

In Memoriam
(Alfred Lord Tennyson)

"The 'Way of the Soul'"
by A. C. Bradley, in *A Commentary on Tennyson's* In Memoriam (1929)

Introduction

Tennyson's *In Memoriam* is one of the finest elegies in English literature. Written during the sixteen-year period following the death of Tennyson's dearest friend, Arthur Henry Hallam, *In Memoriam* records the many changes the author went through after this tragic loss and represents his own coming to terms with death and dying. In "The 'Way of the Soul,'" A.C. Bradley focuses on the "passionate grief and affection" of the poem, calling the poem a "victory over sorrow." Bradley traces the way that "the grief and the struggle are portrayed in all their stages and phases throughout months and years," noting that "each is depicted, not as it may have appeared when the victory was won, but as it was experienced then and there." Thus, for Bradley, the poem deals ultimately with one of the greatest mysteries we contemplate when we think about death and dying: the nature of the immortal soul.

Bradley, A.C. "The 'Way of the Soul.'" *A Commentary on Tennyson's* In Memoriam. Third revised ed. London: MacMillan, 1929 (third edition, first published in 1910). 36–48.

It is a fashion at present to ascribe the great popularity of *In Memoriam* entirely to the 'teaching' contained in it, and to declare that its peculiar position among English elegies has nothing to do with its poetic qualities. This is equivalent to an assertion that, if the so-called substance of the poem had been presented in common prose,[1] the work would have gained the same hold upon the mass of educated readers that is now possessed by the poem itself. Such an assertion no one would make or consciously imply. The ordinary reader does not indeed attempt to separate the poetic qualities of a work from some other quality that appeals to him; much less does he read the work in terror of being affected by the latter; but imagination and diction and even versification can influence him much as they influence the people who talk about them, and he would never have taken *In Memoriam* to his heart if its consoling or uplifting thoughts had not also touched his fancy and sung in his ears. It is true, however, that he dwells upon these thoughts, and that the poem is often valued by him for its bearing upon his own life; and true again that this is one reason why he cares for it far more than for elegies certainly not inferior to it as poems. And perhaps here also many devotees of poetry may resemble him more than they suppose.

This peculiar position of *In Memoriam* seems to be connected with two facts. In the first place, it alone among the most famous English elegies is a poem inspired by deep personal feelings. Arthur Hallam was a youth of extraordinary promise, but he was also 'dear as the mother to the son.' The elegy on his death, therefore, unlike those on Edward King or Keats or Clough, bears the marks of a passionate grief and affection; and the poet's victory over sorrow, like his faith in immortality, is felt to be won in a struggle which has shaken the centre of his being. And then, as has been observed already, the grief and the struggle are portrayed in all their stages and phases throughout months and years; and each is depicted, not as it may have appeared when the victory was won, but as it was experienced then and there. In other elegies for example, scarcely anything is to be found resembling the earlier sections, which describe with such vividness and truth the varied feelings of a new grief; scarcely anything, again, like the night-poems (LXVII. ff.), or the poem of the second anniversary (XCIX.), or those of the third spring-time (CXV., CXVI.). Stanzas like these come home to readers who never cared for a poem before, and were never conscious of feeling poetically till sorrow opened their souls. Thus much of *In Memoriam* is nearer to ordinary life than most elegies can be, and many such readers have found in it an expression of their own feelings, or have looked to the experience which it embodies as a guide to a possible conquest over their own loss. 'This,' they say to themselves as they read, 'is what I dumbly feel. This man, so much greater than I, has suffered like me and has told me how he won his way to peace. Like me, he has been forced by his own disaster to meditate on "the riddle of the painful earth," and to ask whether the world can really be governed by a law of love, and is not rather the work of blind forces, indifferent to the value of all that they produce and destroy.'

A brief review, first of the experience recorded in *In Memoriam*, and then of the leading ideas employed in it, may be of interest to such readers, and even to others, as it may further the understanding of the poem from one point of view, although it has to break up for the time that unity of substance and form which is the essence of poetry.

The early sections portray a soul in the first anguish of loss. Its whole interest is fixed on one thing in the world; and, as this thing is taken away, the whole world is darkened. In the main, the description is one of a common experience, and the poem shows the issue of this experience in a particular case.

Such sorrow is often healed by forgetfulness. The soul, flinching from the pain of loss, or apprehensive of its danger, turns away, at first with difficulty, and afterwards with increasing ease, from the thought of the beloved dead. 'Time,' or the incessant stream of new impressions, helps it to forget. Its sorrow gradually perishes, and with its sorrow its love; and at last 'all it was is overworn,' and it stands whole and sound. It is not cynical to say that this is a frequent history, and that the ideas repelled in section XC. are not seldom true.

Sometimes, again, the wound remains unhealed, although its pain is dulled. Here love neither dies nor changes its form; it remains a painful longing for something gone, nor would anything really satisfy it but the entire restoration of that which is gone. All the deeper life of the soul is absorbed in this love, which from its exclusively personal character is unable to coalesce with other interests and prevents their growth.

In neither of these extreme cases is there that victory of which the poet thinks even in the first shock of loss, when he remembers how it has been said

> That men may rise on stepping-stones
> Of their dead selves to higher things.

In the first case there is victory of a kind, but it is a victory which in the poet's eyes is defeat; the soul may be said to conquer its sorrow, but it does so by losing its love; it is a slave in the triumph of Time. In the second case, the 'self' refuses to die and conquers time, but for that very reason it is bound to the past and unable to rise to higher things. The experience portrayed in *In Memoriam* corresponds with neither case, but it resembles each in one particular. Sorrow is healed, but it is not healed by the loss of love: for the beloved dead is the object of continual thought, and when regret has passed away love is found to be not less but greater than before. On the other hand regret does pass away, and love does not merely look forward to reunion with its object but unites freely with other interests. It is evident that the possibility of this victory depends upon the fact that, while love does not die, there is something in the soul which does die. The self 'rises' only on the basis of a 'dead self.' In other words, love changes though it does not perish or fade; and with the change in it there is a corresponding change in the idea of its object. The poem exhibits this process of two-fold change.

At the beginning love desires simply that which was, the presence and companionship of the lost friend; and this it desires unchanged and in its entirety. It longs for the sight of the face, the sound of the voice, the pressure of the hand. These doubtless are desired as tokens of the soul; but as yet they are tokens essential to love, and that for which it pines is the soul as known and loved through them. If the mourner attempts to think of the dead apart from them, his heart remains cold, or he recoils: he finds that he is thinking of a phantom; 'an awful thought' instead of 'the human-hearted man he loved'; 'a spirit, not a breathing voice.' This he does not and cannot love. It is an object of awe, not of affection; the mere dead body is a thousand-fold dearer than this,—naturally, for this is not really a spirit, a thinking and loving soul, but a ghost. As then he is unable to think of the object of his love except as 'the hand, the lips, the eyes,' and 'the meeting of the morrow,' he feels that what he loves is simply gone and lost, and he finds his one relief in allowing fancy to play about the thought of the tokens that remain (see the poems to the ship).

The process of change consists largely in the conquest of the soul over its bondage to sense. So long as this bondage remains, its desire is fixed on that which really is dead, and it cannot advance. But gradually it resigns this longing, and turns more and more to that which is not dead. The first step in its advance is the perception that love itself is of infinite value and may survive the removal of the sensible presence of its object. But no sooner has this conviction been reached and embraced (XXVII.) than suddenly the mourner is found to have transferred his interest from the sensible presence to the soul itself, while, on the other hand, the soul is no longer thought of as a mere awful phantom, but has become what the living friend had been, something both beloved and loving (XXX.). This conquest is, indeed, achieved first in a moment of exaltation which cannot be maintained; but its result is never lost, and gradually strengthens. The feeling that the soul of the dead is something shadowy and awful departs for ever, and step by step the haunting desire for the bodily presence retires. Thought is concentrated on that which lives, the beauty of the beloved soul, seen in its remembered life on earth, and doubtless shown more fully elsewhere in a life that can be dimly imagined. At last the pining for what is gone dies completely away, but love is found to be but stronger for its death, and to be no longer a source of pain. It has grown to the dimensions of its object, and this object is not only distant and desired, but also present and possessed. And more—the past (which is not wholly past, since it lives and acts in the soul of the mourner) has lost its pang and retained its loveliness and power: 'the days that are no more' become a life in death instead of a 'death in life'; and even the light of the face, the sound of the voice, and the pressure of the hand, now that the absorbing desire for them is still, return in the quiet inward world.

Another aspect of this change is to be noticed. So long as the mourner's sorrow and desire are fixed on that which dies they withdraw his interest from all other things. His world seems to depend for its light on that which has passed away, and he cries, 'All is dark where thou art not.' But as his love and its object change and grow, this exclusiveness lessens and its shadow shrinks. His heart opens itself to other friendships; the sweetness of the spring returns; and the 'mighty hopes' for man's future which the friend had shared, live again as the dead friend ceases to be a silent voice and becomes a living soul. Nor do the reviving activities simply flourish side by side with love for this soul, and still less do they compete with it. Rather they are one with it. The dead man lives in the living, and 'moves him on to nobler ends.' It is at the bidding of the dead that he seeks a friendship for the years to come. His vision of the ideal man that is to be is a memory of the man that trod this planet with him in his youth. He had cried, 'All is dark where thou art not,' and now he cries,

> Thy voice is on the rolling air;
>   I hear thee where the waters run;
>   Thou standest in the rising sun,
> And in the setting thou art fair.

For the sake of clearness little has been so far said of the thoughts of the mourner regarding the life beyond death. These thoughts touch two main subjects, the hope of reunion, and the desire that the dead friend should think of the living and should even communicate with him. The recurrent speculations on the state of the dead spring from this hope and this desire. They recur less frequently as the soul advances in its victory. This does not mean that the hope of reunion diminishes or ceases to be essential to the mourner's peace and faith; but speculation on the nature both of this reunion and of the present life of the dead is renounced, and at last even abruptly dismissed (CVII., CVIII.). The singer is content to be ignorant and to wait in faith.

It is not quite so with the desire that the dead friend should now remember the living, and should even communicate with him. True, this desire is at one moment put aside without unhappiness (LXV.), and it ceases to be an urgent and disturbing force. But long after the pining for the bodily presence has been overcome, it remains and brings with it pain and even resentment. It seems to change from a hope of 'speech' or 'converse' to a wish that the dead should in some way be 'near' to or 'touch' the living; and thus it suggests the important group of sections XC.–XCV. Here the poet even wishes at first for a vision; and although he at once reflects that neither this nor any other appeal to sense could convince him that the dead was really with him,[2] he does not surrender either here or later (CXXII.) the idea of some more immediate contact of souls.[3] On the other hand, he is not sure that the idea is realised, nor does his uncertainty disturb his peace. What he desires while he remains on earth is contact with 'that which is,' the reality which is half revealed and half concealed by nature and man's earthly life, and which, by its contact, convinces him of the reason and love that rule the world; and, as now he thinks of his friend as 'living in God,' he neither knows nor seeks to know whether that which touches him is to be called the soul of his friend or by some higher name.

It appears then that the victory over sorrow portrayed in the poem is dependent upon a change in the love felt by the living for the dead, and upon a corresponding change in the idea of the dead. And some readers may even be inclined to think that the change is so great that at last the dead friend has really ceased to be to the living an individual person. He is, they will say, in some dim fashion 'mixed with God and Nature,' and as completely lost in 'the general soul' as is Adonais in Shelley's pantheistic poem: and so the poet's love for him has not merely changed, it has perished, and its place has been taken by a feeling as vaguely general and as little personal as the object to which it is directed. As my purpose is neither to criticise nor to defend the poet's ideas, but simply to represent them, I will confine myself to pointing out that the poem itself flatly denies the charge thus brought against it, and by implication denies the validity of the antitheses on which the charge rests. It is quite true that, as the poet advances, he abandons all attempts to define the life beyond death, and to form an image of his friend, 'whate'er he be.' It is quite true also that he is conscious that his friend, at once human and divine, known and unknown, far and near, has become something 'strange,' and is 'darklier understood' than in the old days of earthly life. But it is equally clear that to the poet his friend is not a whit less himself because he is 'mixed with God and Nature,' and that he is only 'deeplier loved' as he becomes 'darklier understood.' And if the hope of reunion is less frequently expressed as the sense of present possession gains in strength, there is nothing in the poem to imply that it becomes less firm as the image of reunion becomes less definite. The reader may declare that it ought to do so; he may apply to the experience here portrayed his customary notions of human and divine, personal and impersonal, individual and general; and he may argue that whatever falls under one of these heads cannot fall under the other. But whether his ideas and his argument are true or false, the fact is certain that for the experience portrayed in *In Memoriam* (and, it may be added, in *Adonais* also) they do not hold. For the poets the soul of the dead, in being mingled with nature, does not lose its personality; in living in God it remains human and itself; it is still the object of a love as 'personal' as that which was given to

> the touch of a vanished hand,
> And the sound of a voice that is still.

NOTES

1. This, in strictness, is an impossible supposition.
   Anything that could be so presented would not be really the substance of the poem.
2. His reflections on the difficulty or impossibility of any such proof are expressed in XCII. with a conciseness which is characteristic of Tennyson and conceals from many readers the full force and bearing of his thoughts.
3. This idea is not confined to *In Memoriam*. Tennyson, we are told, thought 'that there might be a more intimate communion than we could dream of between the living and the dead, at all events for a time' (*Memoir*, I. 320).

"THE JILTING OF GRANNY WEATHERALL" (KATHERINE ANNE PORTER)

"A Coming of Death Story: Katherine Anne Porter's 'The Jilting of Granny Weatherall'"
by John McClain, University of North Carolina at Asheville

In my end is my beginning. [The epitaph on Katherine Anne Porter's grave.]

There is at the heart of the universe a riddle no man can solve, and in the end, God may be the answer. (Porter, *Collected Essays* 7)

In "The Jilting of Granny Weatherall" (1930), Katherine Anne Porter creates one of her supreme achievements as a modern writer concerned with death and dying. Death's physical fact only initiates Porter's art and themes. As important as the fact of literal death is for her stories, the psychological plots, the characters' development (or failure to develop) into adults, their interpretation of the meaning of death, individually and personally, and sometimes universally, comprise Porter's true subjects. To narrow the point, one could argue that not death, but the fear of death, pervades much of her work, as an identifiable philosophy and literary approach.

Porter is a distinctive voice sounding on distinctively modern themes, such as the horror of our mortality and the desperation of our religious belief. Like many authors writing near the turbulent beginning of the twentieth century, Porter was a modernist writer, one who used dreams, interior monologue, and stream of consciousness—all experimental forms—to convey her characters' confusions about the meaning of life when death is accepted as a cataclysmic fact. To understand Porter's "coming of death" theme and the way Porter deals with death in "The Jilting of Granny Weatherall," a brief comparison with another of Porter's stories, the classic coming-of-age short story "The Grave," might be helpful.

As "The Grave" begins, the two protagonists, Paul, age twelve, and his sister Miranda, age nine, live in rural Texas, the setting of Porter's own childhood. The year is 1903. They have begun one of their numerous hunting expeditions for small game when they run across their abandoned family cemetery. The land has been sold and the bodies of their relatives moved to a public graveyard. After finding some souvenirs in the former graves, such as a coffin's screw head in the shape of a silver dove and a gold ring, they continue to hunt. A kill is made, one that suddenly and emphatically awakens in Miranda a more mature understanding of the connections between birth, life, and death—all in one image.

Paul shoots a rabbit. He discovers while skinning it—"Miranda always had fur coats for her dolls, for though she never cared much for her dolls she liked seeing them in fur coats" (*Collected Stories* 366)—that the rabbit was pregnant. He opens the bag and he and Miranda see the bunch of little unborn rabbits, "their unbelievably small delicate ears folded close, their little blind faces almost featureless" (366). They both realize that the rabbits were about to be born, Miranda stating, "I know, like babies" (367). After her initial thrill with the scene, the "bloody heap" disgusts her. "'I don't want the skin,' she said, 'I won't have it'" (367). Paul colludes with Miranda to keep the event a secret, which she does. She forgets about it until twenty years later, when an association provokes the memory.

In a market in a foreign country, Miranda sees candies in the shape of baby animals. Porter writes how "the smell in the market, with its piles of raw flesh and wilting flowers, was like the mingled sweetness and corruption she had smelled that other day in the empty cemetery at home ..." (367). Together, these sensations produce the violent memory of the slaughtered mother rabbit and her unborn young: "The episode of that far-off day leaped from its burial place before her mind's eye" (367). What happened?

Clearly "The Grave" is a coming-of-age story with its attention to the awakening in a child of the realities of life, sex, birth, and death.

But what understandings of life and death does Miranda attain from them? Porter describes Miranda as "reasonlessly horrified" (367) by the vision and the memory as "dreadful" (368). Immediately before its eruption Porter presents Miranda's initial coping with the dead rabbits, when still a little girl, as a state of "confused unhappiness," (367) a state that Miranda never addresses or deals with, at least not consciously, for "Miranda never told, she did not even wish to tell anybody" (367). This key event in Miranda's growing up remains primarily an emotional one, of horror and confusion mixed. The importance of its violence and the violence of its importance is indisputable given the shock and force of the vivid memory. But its meaning remains problematic, as does, perhaps, Miranda's maturity itself. Is she a twenty-nine-year-old woman or still a confused nine-year-old girl? Or perhaps, more simply, Miranda had no more to learn. "The Grave" omits a character, even the idea of a certain character, that one might think would belong given the story's time and place: Where is God?

As in much of her fiction, Porter employs an array of potent Christian religious symbols in "The Grave," especially Roman Catholic ones: the dove, the wedding ring, the graves themselves with the ceremonies naturally associated with them. But she avoids any explicit mention of God in "The Grave." This absence betrays Porter's point: Faith is in the grave. The relevance of faith is in the grave for Miranda and indeed her family, a part of their decline in all ways (they had to sell the land of their private cemetery). "It was said the motherless family was running down, with the grandmother no longer there to hold it together" (364-365). Some (nameless) characters mention the Bible, characters "who had treated her grandmother with most sincere respect" (365). But Porter has Miranda view these characters with derision as "bad-tempered old crones" (365) when they stare at her tomboy clothes. "They slanted their gummy old eyes sideways at the granddaughter [Miranda] and said, 'Ain't you ashamed of yoself, Missy? It's aginst the Scriptures to dress like that'" (365). In no way does a positive or even articulated religious faith play an important part for Paul and Miranda in "The Grave." For apparently it has no important place in Porter's telling of this coming-of-age story.

In "The Jilting of Granny Weatherall" Porter creates another type of coming-of-age story, this one set in an individual's old age. The story portrays the death of the title character by narrating her last day of life. Porter explores how Granny Weatherall dies, how she sees herself as she dies, and how she interprets her life from her realization of death's imminence.

As the story begins Granny is in bed and ill. She does not lose consciousness, but her mind drifts haphazardly, uncontrollably for the most part, as she observes the actions and concerns of those around her (Doctor Harry, her daughter Cornelia, and her priest, Father Connolly), remembers incidents from throughout her life, and even plans for the future. She attempts to talk to Doctor Harry, Cornelia, and Father Connolly, but too often her speech sounds vague, distorted, and too soft for them to understand. Her talking to herself and her thinking to herself (interior monologue) remain focused for a while. From what she says, to others and to herself, Ellen "Granny" Weatherall would appear to have led a fearless life. She recovered from a jilting at twenty years of age—her betrothed, George, left her alone at the altar. She married another, John, and had four children with him: Cornelia, Lydia, Jimmy, and Hapsy. With hard work, heroic patience, and determination, she survived John's early death as well as Hapsy's (her youngest, in childbirth), all the while achieving relative material prosperity. Granny Weatherall had to be tough, on others and on herself, to succeed. She judged (and still judges) and bossed (and still bosses) those around her, but she is also self-critical. Her notions of the failings or inadequacies of her relations include stern judgments regarding her relationship with herself.

In what turns out to be her last day alive, her attitude toward her own death lacks contentment, perhaps feeding her dissatisfaction with her life, its efforts, and its apparent successes. Instead, "While she was rummaging around she found death in her mind and it felt clammy and unfamiliar" (82). She reasons that "She had spent so much time preparing for death there was no need for bringing it up again. Let it take care of itself now. . . . Now she couldn't be worried. She hoped she had better sense now" (82). But something interferes with such sense: the still painful memory of her jilting and the concern that she might be jilted again by someone or something else. She states, seemingly unequivocally, that "God, for all my life I thank Thee. Without Thee, my God, I could never have done it. Hail, Mary, full of grace" (84). But one prayer, certainly, remains unanswered: George. "For sixty years she had prayed against remembering him . . .," but his hellish memory remains, dominating her mind (84).

Granny fights to stay alive by fighting to understand her life. Was this a life with a secure faith in a fair God, a faith that would justify all her work and intentions? She goes back and forth between belief and doubt. At one point Porter writes, "Granny felt easy about her soul.... She had her secret comfortable understanding with a few favorite saints who cleared a straight road to God for her" (86). But with death closer at hand, Porter describes how "The rosary fell out of her hands and Lydia put it back. Jimmy tried to help, their hands fumbled together, and Granny closed two fingers around Jimmy's thumb. Beads wouldn't do, it must be something alive" (88). She needs something alive and, apparently, faith will not do. She *rejects* the rosary. She rejects her death. "She was so amazed her thoughts ran round and round. So, my dear Lord, this is my death and I wasn't even thinking about it. My children have come to see me die. But I can't, it's not time. Oh, I always hated surprises" (88). Her thoughts run round and round because she cannot literally run herself. She can hardly move at all. She is dying. She proves her lack of faith energetically with a demand for evidence: "'God, give a sign!'" (89).

No sign appears. Her will grasps the epiphanic moment: "Oh, no, there's nothing more cruel than this—I'll never forgive it. She stretched herself with a deep breath and blew out the light" (89). *She* decides her end, an act that, in itself, is a rejection of faith.

The story presents one day, the last day, of Ellen Weatherall's life. Is it fair to see it, and the last moments of that last day, as representative of a life, one proved by this last day to be a life governed by the fear of death? In her life Ellen did everything right. Indeed, everything looked right. But did she ever have a secure sense of what was right or wrong? She states, "It was good to be strong enough for everything, even if all you made melted and changed and slipped under your hands, so that by the time you finished you almost forgot what you were working for. What was it I set out to do? she asked herself intently, but she could not remember" (83). In delirium, she lists her accomplishments to herself, grounding them in a prideful sense of herself:

> She wasn't too old yet for Lydia to be driving eighty miles for advice when one of the children jumped the track, and Jimmy still dropped in and talked things over: 'Now, Mammy, you've a good business head, I want to know what you think of this?'

... Old. Cornelia couldn't change the furniture around without
asking. (83)

Nevertheless, does this outward show of strength and determination
disguise a lifelong struggle to maintain conviction and find meaning?
All the way back sixty years to her jilting by George: "Oh, no, oh, God,
no, there was something else besides the house and the man and the
children. Oh, surely they were not all? What was it? Something not
given back ..." (86). These questions without answers reveal a sense of
accomplishment, yes, but motivated by what? A fear of failure, a fear
of chaos (her hatred of surprises), and lack of control? For Granny
Weatherall all is order, duty, and clarity. "It was good to have everything clean and folded away with the hair brushes and tonic bottles
sitting straight on the white embroidered line: the day started without
fuss ..." (81). But such ordering does not display true and secure belief
in the ultimate purpose of it all, or of life or God. Again: "Oh, no,
oh, God, no ..." (86). George's jilting surprised her first, informing a
lifetime of apprehension. Now God's surprise completes the pattern,
life to death.

In the end, how is Granny's life, with its regret, insecurity, and fear,
so different from Miranda's in "The Grave," with its hints at what her
life might be? As Miranda is a twenty-nine-year-old woman who in
some ways remains stuck, emotionally, at nine years of age, so Granny
Weatherall is an eighty-year-old woman still emotionally "stuck" at
twenty. Miranda's innocence died the day the rabbit was killed; it
is problematic to see if anything replaced it. Granny Weatherall's
innocence died the day George jilted her. Her efforts to forget that
death with a life full of success appear to have been built on sand. In
"The Jilting of Granny Weatherall," as in the case of much of Porter's
fiction, coming of age depends upon the death of something and,
finally, the awareness of the universality and personal nature of death.
Appreciation of death may be fundamental in all such literature. But
with Porter, the fear of death follows from a problematic religious
faith. This kind of fear informs the entire lives of her characters.

Does this fear inform Porter's life? Might such fears be the key
to understanding not just Porter's characters but the writer herself?
Appreciating something of Porter's "I" on this subject can help us
interpret "The Jilting of Granny Weatherall." We can piece this "I"
together somewhat from two of her other stories.

Only twice in her fiction does Porter resort to a first-person narrator—first with the short novel "Hacienda" (1935), then in her last short story, "Holiday" (1960). Both of these stories reveal hints of Porter's perspective on death. "Hacienda" fictionalizes Porter's interactions with the Russian film director Sergei Eisenstein and his efforts to complete his film *Que Viva Mexico!* during the summer of 1931. The story takes place primarily at a pulque plantation. Pulque is a thick, alcoholic drink, much imbibed by Indians in Mexico. Porter describes the character Andreyev's (Eisenstein's) approach to the Indians and the social atmosphere, the drugged social sensibility that the pulque production creates: "The camera had caught and fixed in moments of violence and senseless excitement, of cruel living and tortured death, the almost ecstatic death-expectancy which is in the air of Mexico" (Porter 143). She also describes the American producer of the film, Kennerly, a self-consciously clean and tidy figure, physically speaking, but sordid in outlook and attitude toward Indians and Mexico in general. But Porter portrays him as a character with some psychological provocation for his finickiness: the "death-expectancy which is in the air of Mexico. ... It was this terror that Kennerly had translated into fear of food, water, and air around him ..." (143). Kennerly becomes in this short novel a figure deservingly caricatured by Porter: the ugly American tourist visiting a place for profit only. But does not Porter also describe herself as sharing his fears in the end? After an involuntary manslaughter on the movie set and after having smelled for several days the rotting organic smell from the pulque vats, the narrator (Porter) leaves. From the last paragraph: "In the morning there began a gradual drift back to town, by train, by automobile. 'Stay here,' each said to me in turn. ... [But] I could not wait for tomorrow in this deathly air" (170). "Porter" flees the pulque plantation as quickly as she can. Thus she flees "Hacienda."

Porter began "Holiday" in 1920, finally finishing and publishing it in December 1960. The story, its history, and her explanation for the time it took her to complete it occupy unique places in Porter's writing. The voice of the story's narrator and Porter's account of that narrator merit comparison. First, from her preface to *The Collected Stories of Katherine Anne Porter*: "'Holiday' represents one of my prolonged struggles, not with questions of form or style, but my own moral and emotional collision with a human situation I was too young to cope with at the time it occurred; yet the story haunted me for years ..." (v). Second, from "Holiday" itself: "At that time I was too young for some of the troubles I was having, and I had not yet learned what to do with them. ... But this story I am about to tell you happened before this great truth impressed itself upon me—that we do not run from the troubles and dangers that are truly ours, and it is better to learn what they are earlier than later, and if we don't run from the others, we are fools" (407). What was Porter's "emotional collision" and what were "Porter's" troubles?

In this story, the narrator visits a family of German-American farmers in east Texas, the Müllers. She becomes closest, emotionally speaking, to the crippled cook, a mute named Ottilie, whom she discovers finally to be one of the family, a daughter herself. All treat her abruptly, as just the cook. Porter observes their family habits, their impressive work ethic, and their material success. But then a tragedy occurs: A rainstorm nearly destroys the farm. In the process of salvaging whatever is possible, Mrs. Müller, wife, mother, and matriarch, exhausts herself to the point of sickness and dies. On the day of her funeral, Porter writes, "I realized, for the first time, not death, but the terror of dying" (433). She and Ottilie are alone in the house, the rest attending the funeral. She decides to take Ottilie for a ride in the wagon, and "suddenly she [Ottilie] laughed out, a kind of yelp but unmistakably laughter" (434). On the day of her own mother's funeral. Porter's response, "Well, we were both equally the fools of life, equally fellow fugitives from death. We had escaped for one day more at least. We would celebrate our good luck, we would have a little stolen holiday, a breath of spring air and freedom on this lovely, festive afternoon" (435).

Porter begins "Holiday" with a decisive statement: that those who don't run from troubles are fools. But it would seem that death turns out to be *the* trouble, and no one runs successfully from that, not for long. Porter herself could run away, for a while, from the smell of death at the "Hacienda" in Mexico. But she could not run from her own fears of death. Her writings, like the thoughts of Granny Weatherall, run around and around death, trying to find a resolution of meaning, for death and life. Porter chose as the epitaph for her tombstone "In my end is my beginning." Did her awareness of the coming of death allow Porter, at last, a collected coming of age? Porter's own problematic religious faith— "God *may* be the answer" (*Collected Essays* 7, my italics)—may aptly lend to her body of work the title "The Jilting of Katherine Anne Porter."

WORKS CITED

Bayley, Isabel. *Letters of Katherine Anne Porter.* New York: The Atlantic Monthly Press, 1990.

Brinkmeyer, Robert H., Jr. *Katherine Anne Porter's Artistic Development.* Baton Rouge, La.: Louisiana State University Press, 1993.

Johnson, James William. "Another Look at Katherine Anne Porter." *Katherine Anne Porter, A Critical Symposium.* Eds. Lodwich Hartley and George Core. Athens, Ga.: University of Georgia Press, 1969. 83–96.

Porter, Katherine Anne. *The Collected Stories of Katherine Anne Porter.* New York: Harcourt, Brace & World, 1979.

————. *The Collected Essays and Occasional Writings of Katherine Anne Porter.* Boston, Mass.: Houghton Mifflin, 1970.

Unrue, Darlene Harbour. "Katherine Anne Porter's Birthdays." *From Texas to the World and Back, Essays on the Journeys of Katherine Anne Porter.* Eds. Mark Busby and Dick Heaberlin. Fort Worth, Texas: Texas Christian University Press, 2001. 38–49.

————. *Katherine Anne Porter: The Life of an Artist.* Jackson, Miss.: University Press of Mississippi, 2005.

Walsh, Thomas F. *Katherine Anne Porter and Mexico: The Illusion of Eden.* Austin, Texas: University of Texas Press, 1992.

Welty, Eudora. "The Eye of the Story." *Katherine Anne Porter: A Critical Symposium.* Eds. Lodwich Hartley and George Core. Athens, Ga.: University of Georgia Press, 1969. 103–112.

Wescott, Glenway. "Katherine Anne Porter Personally." *Katherine Anne Porter: A Critical Symposium.* Eds. Lodwich Hartley and George Core. Athens, Ga.: University of Georgia Press, 1969. 24–48.

KING LEAR
(WILLIAM SHAKESPEARE)

"*King Lear* and the Psychology of Dying"
by Susan Snyder, in *Shakespeare Quarterly* (1982)

INTRODUCTION

Basing her analysis on both Freud's ideas about death in Shakespeare and on Elisabeth Kübler-Ross's highly influential work *On Death and Dying*, Susan Snyder analyzes *King Lear* as an essay on the dying process. Evaluating *Lear* as an exemplar tragedy, one that forces us to look at death, Snyder focuses on the way readers respond to the play. Asking the key question, "Can it be that what we recognize in *Lear* is the process of dying?" Snyder finds that "Lear's career from that reluctant abdication through struggle and pain to his reconciliation with Cordelia parallels the course of many dying patients observed by Elisabeth Kübler-Ross and other students of death and dying, from initial denial to acceptance." Thus, Snyder sees Shakespeare as an early figure who addressed what are now contemporary concerns: "Now that death is at last being discussed openly, we find as so often that Shakespeare has been there before us."

Snyder, Susan. "*King Lear* and the Psychology of Dying." *Shakespeare Quarterly* Vol. 33, No. 4 (Winter 1982): 449–460.

Pondering "The Theme of the Three Caskets," certain choices-among-three in literature and legend, Freud concluded that in *King Lear* Shakespeare had somehow pierced through the myth's defensive disguises to its original unpalatable meaning. The right choice—the third casket, the third woman—is really death. While students of Shakespeare may well object that a straightforward identification of Lear's third daughter with death says at once too much and too little about the loving Cordelia, many of them have nevertheless heard a ring of truth in Freud's formulation of the play's underlying action: "Eternal wisdom, in the garb of primitive myth, bids the old man renounce love, choose death and make friends with the necessity of dying."[1]

In a sense, all tragedy addresses the necessity of dying. That is, regardless of whether or not the tragic hero is dead at the end (Shakespeare's always are), tragedy's peculiar blend of dignity and defeat expresses our deeply paradoxical reaction to our own mortality. What that mortality means is that the highest human potential cannot be infinite, that death will inevitably undo our treasured, all-absorbing construction—the self. From one point of view, dying feels right. Man is a part of nature, governed, as our vulnerable bodies remind us, by nature's laws of growth and decay. Man is also a moral being with convictions of guilt and unworthiness, a far cry from the God he venerates. At the same time, it is impossibly *wrong* that the precious ego must submit like any oblivious beast to death's imper-sonal blotting-out. We cannot really imagine our own non-being, as Freud observed: "at bottom no one believes in his own death, or to put the same thing in another way, in the unconscious every one of us is convinced of his own immortality."[2] Tragedy provides an objective correlative for this basic ambivalence of ours. Its inevitable downward course toward destruction embodies one reaction: death is right, death comes from inside us. Against this arc of tragic action develops that special dimension of the protagonist we call heroic, which by asserting the ever-expanding human capability protests implicitly that death is wrong, a disaster unfairly imposed by some outside enemy on "else immortal us."[3] Tragic events themselves generate heroic expansion. Oedipus becomes wiser in his searching and suffering than was the confident ruler who opened the play. Macbeth in his agony of conscience and his full experience of despair has explored more of the human condition than the admired military man whom we first meet. It may be that our pleasure in tragedy is owing in part to its power of bringing together what in our psyches simply coexist unrelated, these two reactions of recognition and resistance—bringing them together, not in resolution, which is impossible, but in energizing interaction.[4]

Of course, to say that tragedy enacts our ambivalent response to death and to what death makes absolute, the failure of power and the end of hope, is not at all to say that all tragedies are "about" death. If *King Lear* in fact corresponds to the rhythm of dying, as Freud suggests, it is a special sort of tragedy; and its undeniable special potency may derive from this direct appeal to the very springs of tragic power. No tragedy of Shakespeare moves us more deeply, *involves* us, so that like Dr. Johnson we can hardly bear to look at the final catastrophe. Yet on the surface *Lear* seems remote in both matter and manner from our lives. Lear himself is no Everyman but an autocratic king. He begins the play by abdicating, but even in the act of giving up power he clings to "the name, and all th' addition to a king,"[5] retaining a train of one hundred knights and conducting a bizarre inquest of his three heirs to find out which of them pays him most tribute of love. Goneril and Regan soon reveal themselves as totally selfish, destructive to the point of denying Lear even shelter, so that he must endure the fury of the elements unprotected on a desolate heath. The rejected Cordelia, on the other hand, is so good that she "redeems nature from the general curse / Which twain have brought her to" (IV.vi.206–7). Eventually she seeks out this rejecting father, rescues him, forgives him, and in a way dies for him. Amid these all-or-nothing characters and situations, Lear's sufferings are correspondingly hyperbolical. They push him into complete mental breakdown before he returns to sanity, is reconciled with Cordelia, and in response to her death himself expires in exhaustion. These improbable events are made even more improbable by duplication. Gloucester's children are as archetypal in their moral sets as Lear's and behave with parallel exaggeration. Allowing full impact for Shakespeare's extraordinary language, which ranges in this play from the richly complex to the shockingly simple, we may still ask if there is not something special in this highly stylized dramatic pattern to tap such deep springs of recognition and emotional response.

Can it be that what we recognize in *Lear* is the process of dying? Each of us in that sense is a king who must eventually give up his kingdom. The loss of power and autonomy can be bitter, and the takeover generation will naturally look heartless and ungrateful to the loser. Culture's niceties and abstract concerns are stripped away as death draws closer, yielding to the demands of the ailing body. Mind as well as body may go out of control—a humiliation, but also perhaps a release. Or, under the stress of this fearful new experience, the mind may need to wrestle with the meaning of past life, call into question the principles never before examined. We may hope to win through before the end to peace with ourselves, to make friends at last with the necessity of dying. Lear's career from that reluctant abdication through struggle and pain to his reconciliation with Cordelia parallels the course of many dying patients observed by Elisabeth Kübler-Ross and other students of death and dying, from initial denial to acceptance.[6] Indeed, the stages of response Kübler-Ross outlines in her study all have their correspondences, naturalistic and symbolic, in the action of the play.

I

Symbolism is the more consistent mode in this stylized, half-allegorical play, but Shakespeare has also given in Lear and Gloucester a picture of old age full of naturalistic detail. Lear habitually repeats himself.[7] He is querulous, touchy, as prone as any child to self-pitying tears and impotent threats.

> You see me here, you gods, a poor old man,
> As full of grief as age, wretched in both . . . .
> . . . . . .
>   touch me with noble anger,
> And let not women's weapons, water-drops,
> Stain my man's cheeks! No, you unnatural hags,
> I will have such revenges on you both
> That all the world shall—I will do such things—
> What they are yet I know not, but they shall be
> The terrors of the earth! (II.iv.272–82)

Gloucester has an old man's fondness for the past over the degenerate present—"we have seen the best of our time" (I.ii.112). Lear, even before he goes mad, tends to withdraw to an inner reality where others cannot reach him. Like the old people whom Elaine Cumming and William E. Henry characterized in their study as gradually disengaging from the systems around them, Lear responds not so much to outer as to inner stimuli, and these are likely to come from the past.[8] His "dialogue" speeches are often, as Wolfgang Clemen observed, really monologues. We see him, as in the following passage, tuning fitfully in and out of the life around him.[9]

> *Fool.* Thou canst tell why one's nose stands i' th' middle on 's face?
> *Lear.* No.
> *Fool.* Why, to keep one's eyes of either side's nose, that what a man cannot smell out, he may spy into.
> *Lear.* I did her wrong.
> *Fool.* Canst tell how an oyster makes his shell?
> *Lear.* No.
> *Fool.* Nor I neither, but I can tell why a snail has a house.
> *Lear.* Why?
> *Fool.* Why, to put's head in, not to give it away to his daughters, and leave his horns without a case.
> *Lear.* I will forget my nature. So kind a father! Be my horses ready? (I.v.19–33)

Once, perhaps twice, the old man's mind slips out of the conversation, back to his hasty banishing of Cordelia and then to his more recent affront at Goneril's hands. Later in the play the line between past and present, inner reality and outer, crumbles further as Lear relives sporadically his kingly roles of judge and military leader (III.vi, IV.vi). The dark side of Gloucester's lament for the good old days comes out in Lear's rage against the all-powerful young. He complains of Goneril's neglect, her lack of respect—"to grudge my pleasures, to cut off my train, / To bandy hasty words"—and shows all the bitterness of unwonted dependence on his former dependents when he rehearses for Regan his ironic plea:

> Dear daughter, I confess that I am old;
> Age is unnecessary. On my knees I beg
> That you'll vouchsafe me raiment, bed, and food.

Because he feels so acutely his own loss of function ("age is unnecessary"), his curses on Goneril are directed specifically at her functions of youth, her strength and fertility: "Into her womb convey sterility, / Dry up in her the organs of increase ...."; "Strike her *young* bones, / You taking airs, with lameness!"[10]

II

The intense *physicality* of this play also links it with the process of dying. Action and metaphor both are preoccupied with the body, its demands and vulnerabilities. The plot of *King Lear* has its share of physical violence, perhaps more than its share. There is nothing in the other plays so savage as the scene in which Cornwall and Regan, partners in sadism as well as marriage, put out Gloucester's eyes. Cornwall's servant stabs him and is immediately run through by Regan's sword. Oswald takes a beating from Kent and later a fatal one from Edgar, who also kills his brother in a duel. Goneril stabs herself after poisoning Regan. Cordelia is hanged. Lear is quick in his choler to threaten violence. Others, like Albany, helplessly anticipate it: "It will come, / Humanity must perforce prey upon itself, / Like monsters of the deep" (IV.ii.48–50). Unlike most of Shakespeare's tragic heroes, Lear and Gloucester are made to suffer physically as well as mentally. The audience must register, along with Gloucester's despair, his grotesque mutilated face with wounds where the eyes should be. And in Lear's spiritual ordeal on the heath we are not allowed to forget his physical exposure. "The tyranny of the open night's too rough / For nature to endure.... this contentious storm / Invades us to the skin.... In such a night / To shut me out? Pour on, I will endure.... the pelting of this pitiless storm.... this cold night.... this extremity of skies.... this tyrannous night."[11] All through the storm-scene runs the insistent leitmotiv—cold, cold, COLD, eight times in the space of 184 lines.

These evocations of physical suffering cluster in the middle of the play, although retrospective references continue to remind us of the body's pains and frailties.[12] But the blows, stabs, and buffetings of *Lear* are not confined to dramatic action and situation. They are woven all through the language, so that physical violence dominates the metaphoric world of the play. Caroline Spurgeon found that the imagery of *Lear* keeps in our consciousness "a human body in anguished movement, tugged, wrenched, beaten, pierced, stung, scourged, dislocated, flayed, gashed, scalded, tortured and finally broken on the rack." What is more, evils of the mind or emotions are typically expressed as physical ones.[13] So Lear feels Goneril's contempt as a kick, necessity as a pinch. Britain after the war is a "gor'd state." The sight of the mad Lear is "side-piercing." Oswald in undermining family loyalties is a rat which bites holy cords in twain. Slandered Edgar feels his good name "by treason's tooth bare-gnawn and canker-bit."[14] Most of all, his daughters' ingratitude affects Lear as a gnawing and tearing of his flesh, piercing him like the serpent's fang. "Unkindness" is a sharp-toothed vulture savaging his heart. Goneril's impatient insults also attack Lear's heart physically, "most serpent-like."[15] Goneril and Regan are not only vultures and serpents but pelicans, feeding on their parent's flesh. And behind this image is one even more frightening, of Lear's own body turning against itself. "'Twas this *flesh* begot / Those pelican daughters." Betrayed by his own, he asks in bewildered anguish, "is it not as this mouth should tear this hand / For lifting food to 't?"[16] In the process of dying, the body calls attention to itself. It becomes unreliable, falters before the habitual simple tasks ("Pray you, undo this button"), shames its owner with incontinence or weeping ("these hot tears, which break from me perforce"). Above all, it hurts. As in the language and action of *Lear*, it cannot be ignored.

Nor does Shakespeare spare us the grosser details of infirmity—chilblains, cataracts, corns, plagues, boils, sores, carbuncles, colic, giddiness.[17] The play is haunted by bad smells. Lies, flattery, lust, all are known by their stench.[18] These indeed, as Robert B. Heilman suggests, build up a sense of the world's moral corruption.[19] But it is important that this corruption comes through to us in crudely physical terms that call attention to the process of organic decay, terms appropriate for the drama of aging, decline, and death. We could say of the play as a whole what Lear says of his own hand: "it smells of mortality" (IV.vi.133).

III

The directness of Lear's words is all the more telling for modern audiences in that until recent years mortality has been the great taboo of our society. As many have observed, death became for us what sex was for the Victorians, something from which to avert the eyes. We still do our best to pretend, through a whole system of institutions and conventions, that it doesn't exist. But in the last two decades more and more professionals have addressed their research and analytic efforts to an understanding of dying. Thanatology, newly respectable, draws sociologists, psychiatrists, medical practitioners. Of their many publications, one of the earliest and most influential was Dr. Kübler-Ross's *On Death and Dying*. Her work with dying patients led her to formulate a kind of rhythm of responses through which patients pass as they cope with their imminent mortality. It begins with denial, the dying one refusing to admit his condition. When that defense begins to crumble, confidence gives way to anger: "it can't be me" to "why does it have to be me?" From this perception of the unfairness of personal mortality, one moves naturally to a bargaining posture, offering good behavior in exchange for a release from the sentence of death. But the decline goes on nevertheless, and the resulting sense of loss brings on depression, the grief that anticipates final separation from this life. At last the struggle ends in acceptance. The patient's grip on the world loosens; he is weary, withdrawn, at peace with himself.

In pointing out a similar rhythm in *King Lear*, I do not mean to suggest that Kübler-Ross's five stages represent some universal truth that Shakespeare intuited hundreds of years before the thanatologists. Rather, it seems to me that following out in *Lear* the pattern she postulates—taking dying as a kind of subtext for the play—illuminates the psychological movement of Shakespeare's drama, which in turn can contribute to the thanatologists' study, compelling poetic insight into this last human journey.

IV

The play's "story" is not, of course, of two old men coping with terminal cancer. Lear and Gloucester do not face death overtly until the action is far advanced, and Shakespeare does not dwell on their reactions when the time comes. What the two do face from the beginning is the loss of power—which is, after all, what dying is about: increasing helplessness, dependence on others with the accompanying indignities, autonomy waning until the self has no more function. Gloucester's power is wrested from him. By the middle of the play he has lost his title and lands, and he never regains them. The plot requires that Lear as king initiate his own transfer of power, but two aspects of the abdication are striking. First, the decision seems to have been imposed on him by age and weariness:

> 'tis our fast intent
> To shake all cares and business from our age,
> Conferring them on younger strengths, while we
> Unburthen'd crawl toward death. (I.i.38–41)

For all the King's vigor and authority, he is clearly entering a terminal phase.[20] Second, Lear is by no means psychologically ready to yield up power, whatever he says. Denial, the first stage in Kübler-Ross's rhythm, begins immediately. When he banishes Kent for defending Cordelia, he is exercising automatically, unconsciously, the royal authority he has just supposedly handed over to others. There is a stagy quality to this scene—Lear formally dividing his lands among his daughters in response to their ritual protestations of love—that underlines its unreality for Lear himself. What rings true is his rage at being crossed, both here by Cordelia and Kent and later when Goneril and Regan try to get rid of his retinue of knights. Those hundred knights, as director Grigori Kozintsev realized when he was filming *Lear*, are not separate individuals but a collective representation of Lear's royal way of life.[21] In defending his knights—"My train are men of choice and rarest parts / ... And in the most exact regard support / The worships of their name"[22]—he asserts his own worth as a person. When his daughters chip away at that worth, the worship of his name, by reducing his retinue, Lear reacts with the curses and commands of angry majesty. He ignores the new realities of power, just as he often fails to hear the Fool's jibing reminders that a king with no kingdom is nothing.[23] Another denial sequence occurs when Lear refuses to believe what he sees—that Regan and Cornwall have exercised their new power to put *his* servant in the stocks.

Lear. No.
Kent. Yes.

> *Lear.* No, I say.
> *Kent.* I say yea.
> *Lear.* No, no, they would not.
> *Kent.* Yes, they have.
> *Lear.* By Jupiter, I swear no. (II.iv.15–21)

The self, convinced at the deepest level of its own immortality, rejects even the most direct evidence to the contrary.

V

In *Deaths of Man*, Edwin S. Shneidman observes that, in general, pessimistic diagnoses hit the dying patient less forcefully than those around him. "What is real for the patient is pain, weakness, vertigo, disfigurement. . . ."[24] So, as his daughters' cruelty and his own exposure force on Lear some recognition of his true state, and as the physical element begins to permeate the play's language, Lear responds like the Kübler-Ross patients, with anger. On the heath, his tirade against the elements that batter him challenges the unfairness of fate. *Why me?*

> But yet I call you servile ministers,
> That will with two pernicious daughters join
> Your high-engender'd battles 'gainst a head
> So old and white as this, O ho! 'tis foul.
> . . . . . .
>   I am a man
> More sinn'd against than sinning. (III.ii.21–24, 59–60)

Since in *King Lear* the force that seeks to destroy is most directly embodied in Goneril and Regan, Lear's anger at the storm is a displacement of sorts—one familiar in the dying, who often direct their hostility beyond its true object.[25] Full of his own grievances, Lear also projects his situation onto others. Any obvious misery, like that of Poor Tom, must have been caused by vicious daughters (II.iv). All judgment is arbitrary and unfair (IV.vi). Seeking to answer that outraged "why?" Lear calls his destroyer-daughters to trial. "Let them anatomize Regan; see what breeds about her heart. Is there any cause in nature that makes these hard hearts?" (III.vi.76–78). But Goneril "escapes" from the fantasy-trial, and no judge or doctor can explain Regan's hard heart. The abortive trial, like Lear's rages at the uncaring storm and the absent daughters, underlines how futile anger is in this situation. It can alter nothing.

The trial of Goneril and Regan is also a kind of bargaining process, with Lear pleading against his daughters for his rights. The bargaining instinct observed by Kübler-Ross and others runs all through this phase of the play. Lear promises to be good. "I'll forbear" (II.iv.109); "I will be the pattern of all patience" (III.ii.37). The promises, like those of Kübler-Ross's patients, are not kept. More typically, as in the trial scene, he presents himself to the powers of heaven and earth as unfairly used, a poor old man cheated in his bargain.[26] The giving away of his kingdom is important here. Has he not received a poor exchange for all that he gave his daughters? He reiterates that "all" to his chosen mirror-image, Poor Tom: "Didst thou give all to thy daughters? . . . Wouldst thou give 'em all?" (III.iv.49, 64).

Bargains of the dying which attempt to put off the inevitable do not work, and Lear's pleas get him no reprieve from his daughters or the gods. Like the dying patients observed by Avery D. Weisman and Thomas P. Hackett, he fears insanity: "O let me not be mad, sweet heaven! Keep me in temper, I would not be mad!" (I.v.46–47). But this plea against the extreme loss of control goes as unheard as the others. The dying experience of dislocation and disintegration has seldom found fuller dramatic expression than in Lear's madness. As Weisman and Hackett point out about the process of dying,

> for the patient who experiences it in the vivid, private, intrapersonal world into which no one else can enter, the fear of dying is the sense of impending dissolution or disintegration of all familiar ways of thought or action. The world normally at one with our perceptions suddenly becomes alien, disjointed, and runs along without us.[27]

VI

But if the world of the mad Lear is alien, disjointed, and painful, it also stimulates growth. The king with no kingdom discovers his kinship

with unaccommodated man, recognizes how superficial was his kingly
authority uninformed by human and humane understanding.

> They flatter'd me like a dog, and told me I had the white hairs in
> my beard ere the black ones were there. . . . When the rain came
> to wet me once, and the wind to make me chatter, when the
> thunder would not peace at my bidding, there I found 'em. . . .
> they told me I was every thing. 'Tis a lie, I am not ague–proof.
> (IV.vi.96–105)

Only his unaccustomed exposure on the heath makes him feel for the
houseless heads and unfed sides of the poor who should have been his
concern as king (III.iv.26–36). Only the offhand cruelty of the storm
and his daughters shows him how little justice he dispensed as justicer.
"Change places, and handy-dandy, which is the justice, which is the
thief? . . . a dog's obey'd in office" (IV.vi.153–59). In *The Psychiatrist
and the Dying Patient*, Kurt Eissler speculates from his case histories
that for some persons dying may indeed be a process of growth. Facing
the end enables them to step back from their total involvement in life
and look at themselves from a longer perspective:

> a person may discover the futility of his past . . . he may be
> seized by greatest regret. But . . . this recognition may lead
> to a triumph of individualization, and the final processes of
> structurization during the terminal pathway may provide the
> past life with a meaning which it could never have acquired
> without them.[28]

Given the awesome energy that drives Lear on to his insights,
there is little room in his dramatic career for the fourth stage of reaction described by Kübler-Ross, depression. Certainly he is exhausted
by the end of Act IV, when he is finally reunited with Cordelia, and
the reunion scene hints at "preparatory grief" when the weary King
projects his own death:

> You do me wrong to take me out o' th' grave:
> Thou art a soul in bliss, but I am bound

Upon a wheel of fire, that mine own tears
Do scald like molten lead. (IV.vii.44–47)

Indeed, the vigor of his anger and madness is spent, but the anguish here soon gives way to peaceful acceptance. It is the more passive Gloucester who carries the burden of despair at this stage in the play. Pained in body and mind, he rejects all comfort, sees the gods as careless children who kill men as casually as flies, seeks the end of all consciousness in suicide. Having been brought to grief by trusting his bastard son Edmund, he is guided through this stage by Edgar, who prepares him for final acceptance: "Men must endure/ Their going hence even as their coming hither, / Ripeness is all" (V.ii.9–11).

Lear's progress to acceptance is also marked, perhaps even symbolized, by his shift of dependence from bad children to good, from Regan and Goneril to Cordelia. The play's schematic character groupings—old men of mixed natures surrounded by good and bad offspring—invites us to see the children not only on the naturalistic level, as the nurturing or rejecting takeover generation, but also as aspects of Lear and Gloucester themselves. Lear's orientation to Goneril and Regan makes manifest his resentment at the loss of power, the tortured sense of impending death as both part of him ("'Twas *this flesh* begot ...") and something preying on him from without ("... those pelican daughters"). For all their protested devotion, Goneril and Regan end up offering him only their own ugly version of what Cordelia in her honesty offered at the beginning— that is, "nothing." In this choice-among-three, then, it seems that all three choices are death. The difference is that what was perceived as a hostile force while Lear struggled is a loving presence when the struggle is over. Before acceptance his daughters are assassins. "His daughters seek his death," says Gloucester (III.iv.163); "I have o'erheard a plot of death upon him" (III.vi.89). But in the reconciliation with Cordelia, Lear offers himself freely to death: "If you have poison for me, I will drink it" (IV.vii.71). Cordelia had once thrust upon him an unexpected, unwanted "nothing," which he rejected in a rage of denial. Now he has come to terms with nothingness, the self soon to end. The truth she represented is absorbed. In Act V, after the forces on Lear's side have been defeated, he accepts with equanimity the loss of freedom. So removed is he from outside concerns that he does not care even to see his captors Goneril and Regan. In his lyric invitation to Cordelia, "Come let's away to prison," he envisions himself and her, secure in their apartness, looking on at the world's affairs without caring (V.iii.8–19).

VII

By now many readers are probably objecting that I have fallen into an old trap for *Lear* critics, that of ignoring or refusing to face fully the play's agonizing last scene. Lear's last trauma is not his own death but Cordelia's; and he does *not* go gentle into his good night. True, and in both cases it could not be otherwise, because Shakespeare was writing a tragedy. Whatever psychiatrists may see as desirable adjustment, tragedy's business has always been to assert the self in the face of annihilation, to protest even while bowing to the inevitable. Ending *King Lear* with not one but two deaths— splitting death, so to speak, between Lear and Cordelia—allows the fullest expression of tragedy's ambivalent address to personal mortality. Cordelia dies first. Like the other two daughters, she is in some sense a part of Lear as well as a separate person. Her death is thus an aspect of his own, but its separateness allows Lear to do the impossible, to experience his own death[29] and cry out against the terrible wrongness of it.

> Howl, howl, howl! O, you are men of stones!
> Had I your tongue and ears, I'ld use them so
> That heaven's vault should crack....
>   No, no, no life!
> Why should a dog, a horse, a rat, have life,
> And thou no breath at all? (V.iii.258–60, 306–8)

Lear's *why* brings back, intensified, his earlier angry question. *Why me?* Unable to sustain the awful reality of "no breath at all," he slips at times into denial. "This feather stirs, she lives.... Look on her! Look, her lips, / Look there, look there!" (V.iii.266, 311–12). We seem, in the very face of death, to have gone back to the earliest stages of the Kübler-Ross rhythm. Indeed, Lear's reversion to anger and denial would make sense to many thanatologists who find these stages too neat and see the process of coping with death more in terms of fluctuations between states.[30] Kübler-Ross herself says that the states may exist side by side, and that hope persists through them all.[31] One cannot give up entirely on the breath of life. The feather is never quite still.

Together Cordelia's death and Lear's act out the paradox of mortality as both unnatural and inevitable. Hers is senseless and violent. Edmund has ordered the nameless captain to do away with her, but he repents and sends a countermand. He is, for no good dramatic or moral reason, too late. "I might have sav'd her," says Lear (V.iii.271), and we do in fact feel that *someone* easily might have. Cut off young against all expectation and justice, Cordelia embodies our sense of death as wrong, outrageous. The hanging, the attack from without, expresses our unconscious conviction that, since death cannot be natural to us, it must come as "a malicious intervention from the outside by someone else."[32] Lear, on the other hand, is old and exhausted. As he collapses over Cordelia's body, those looking on see nothing unnatural, only the inevitable end of aging and decay. "The wonder is he hath endur'd so long" (V.iii.317). No outside assassin here, but an internal process of wearing out, experience taking its toll. The enemy is he who would try to interfere with that process:

> he hates him
> That would upon the rack of this tough world
> Stretch him out longer. (V.iii.314–16)

"Ein alter Mann ist stets ein König Lear." Goethe's epigram is about the loneliness of the old, missing their contemporaries and cut off from the next generation. But in the light of recent work in the psychology of dying, it may be true in a deeper way that every old man is a King Lear. Now that death is at last being discussed openly, we find as so often that Shakespeare has been there before us.

Notes

1. "The Theme of the Three Caskets," *Collected Papers*, 4 (London: Hogarth Press, 1925), p. 256.

2. "Thoughts for the Time on War and Death," *Collected Papers*, 4, p. 305.

3. I have borrowed the phrase from Donne's holy sonnet beginning "If poisonous minerals," in which he questions the justice of God's punishment of mankind for Adam's sin. The Jahwist account of the Fall of Man in Genesis, the archtragedy which in Judeo-Christian tradition "explains" death, sets forth the same ambivalence about mortality. Adam belongs to created nature, and when he disobeys God by eating the forbidden fruit he is justly condemned to return to the dust from which he came. But Adam sinned at the prompting of Eve, and Eve at the prompting of the serpent—and the serpent's motives for his act are left a mystery. Thus a contradictory sense grows up that death, rather than proceeding from human imperfection, has been laid upon naturally immortal man by a mysteriously malevolent outside force.

4. I have explored this view of tragedy at more length in the Introduction to *The Comic Matrix of Shakespeare's Tragedies* (Princeton: Princeton Univ. Press, 1979).

5. I.i.136. All Shakespeare quotations are from *The Riverside Shakespeare*, ed. G. Blakemore Evans (Boston: Houghton Mifflin, 1974).

6. Elisabeth Kübler-Ross, *On Death and Dying* (New York: Macmillan, 1969), chapters 3–7; cf., for example, Robert Kastenbaum and Avery D. Weisman, *The Psychological Autopsy* (New York: Community Mental Health Journal, 1968), p. 24, and C. Knight Aldrich, "The Dying Patient's Grief," *JAMA*, 184, no. 5 (4 May 1963), 329.

7. I.i.94; II.iv.15–23; IV.vi.88–92, 187, 203; V.iii.8, 258, 306–12.

8. *Growing Old: The Process of Disengagement* (New York: Basic Books, 1961), p. 127.

9. Wolfgang Clemen, *The Development of Shakespeare's Imagery* (London: Methuen, 1951), p. 134; E.A.J. Honigmann discusses Lear's retreats from present reality in *Shakespeare: Seven Tragedies, The Dramatist's Manipulation of Response* (New York: Barnes and Noble, 1976), p. 109 and pp. 114–15.

10. II.iv.174–75, 154–56; I.iv.278–79; II.iv.163–64; my italics.

11. III.iv.2–3, 6–7, 17–18, 29, 78, 102, 151.

12. Cordelia broods on Lear's ordeal in IV.iii and vii. Lear himself recalls it in IV.vi. Any time the eyeless Gloucester is onstage, of course, such verbal reminders are unnecessary.

13. Caroline Spurgeon, *Shakespeare's Imagery and What it Tells Us* (New York: Macmillan, 1936), pp. 339 and 342–43.

14. III.vi.47–48; II.iv.211; V.iii.321; IV.vi.85; II.ii.73–75; V.iii.122.

15. I.iv.288–89; II.iv.134–35 and 160–61.

16. III.iv.72–75 and 15–16.

17. I.v.9; III.iv.17; III.ii.33; III.iv.67 and IV.i.46 and 64; II.iv.56–57. On the "mother" in the last passage, Kenneth Muir cites one of Shakespeare's sources for Lear, Samuel Harsnett's *A Declaration of Egregious Popishe Impostures* (1603), p. 65. "It riseth ... of a wind in the bottom of the belly, and proceeding with a great swelling, causeth a vary painfull collicke in the stomacke, and an extraordinary giddines in the head": "Samuel Harsnett and *King Lear*," *Review of English Studies*, NS, 2 (1951), 14.

18. I.iv.111–13; IV.vi.96–103 and 127–31. Heilman, cited in the next note, lists several more smell references.

19. *This Great Stage: Image and Structure in "King Lear"* (Baton Rouge: Louisiana State Univ. Press, 1948), pp. 14–17.

20. Freud observed in "The Theme of the Three Caskets" (p. 255) that when one considers Lear as not only old but soon to die, "the extraordinary project of dividing the inheritance ... loses its strangeness."

21. Kozintsev, "*Hamlet* and *King Lear*: Stage and Film," *Shakespeare 1971*, ed. Clifford Leech and J.M.R. Margeson (Toronto: Univ. of Toronto Press, 1972), p. 197.

22. I.iv.263–66.

23. On the communication blocks that dying patients may erect as aids to denial, see Edwin S. Shneidman, *Deaths of Man* (New York: Quadrangle, 1973), pp. 30–31, and Barney G. Glaser and Anselm L. Strauss, *Awareness of Dying* (Chicago: Aldine, 1965), p. 134.

24. Shneidman, pp. 12–13.

25. Kübler-Ross, *On Death and Dying*, pp. 50–52.

26. "You see me here, you gods, a poor old man. . . . Your old kind father, whose frank heart gave all" (II.iv.272; III.iv.20); cf. his complaints quoted above against the heavens as servile ministers, and the *quid pro quo* implication of "more sinn'd against than sinning."

27. Weisman and Hackett, "Predilection to Death," *Death and Identity*, ed. Robert Fulton, rev. ed. (Bowie, Maryland: Charles Press, 1976), p. 304.

28. Eissler, *The Psychiatrist and the Dying Patient* (New York: International Universities Press, 1955), pp. 53–55. Robert Jay Lifton emphasizes that the "ideal death . . . is associated with a realized life," and adds in a note, "Kübler-Ross has been criticized by some for creating overly-schematized stages [see below, n. 30] and for a tendency to idealize dying. . . . More importantly, however, Kübler-Ross has been restating an ancient theme of self-completion from within her compassionate contemporary experience": *The Broken Connection: On Death and the Continuity of Life* (New York: Simon and Schuster, 1979), p. 105.

29. Shneidman points out how paradoxical it is that this great universal human event can be experienced only indirectly, through empathy with others. If one could experience death directly, one wouldn't be dead (*Deaths of Man*, p. 55).

30. Shneidman comments (pp. 6–7), "My own limited work has not led me to conclusions identical with those of Kübler-Ross. Indeed, while I have seen in dying persons isolation, envy, bargaining, depression, and acceptance, I do not believe that these are necessarily 'stages' of the dying process, and I am not at all convinced that they are lived through in that order, or, for that matter, in any universal order. . . . One does not find a unidirectional movement through progressive stages so much as an alternation between acceptance and denial." Cf. John Hinton, *Dying*, 2nd ed. (Harmondsworth: Penguin, 1972), p. 12, Richard Lamerton, *Care of the Dying* (London: Priory Press, 1973), pp. 118–22, and Robert J. Kastenbaum, "Evaluating the Stage Theory," *Death, Society, and Human Experience*, 2nd ed. (St. Louis: C.V. Mosby Co., 1981), pp. 188–91. Glaser and

Strauss stress response as a process rather than a single impact, but they add that "a particular patient's response may stop at any stage, take any direction, or change directions" (*Awareness of Dying*, pp. 121–22).

31. *On Death and Dying*, p. 138.
32. *On Death and Dying*, p. 2.

LORD OF THE FLIES
(WILLIAM GOLDING)

"*Lord of the Flies*: Fable, Myth, and Fiction"
by Arnold Johnston, in *Of Earth and Darkness: The Novels of William Golding* (1980)

INTRODUCTION

As mortals, we must all face dying. Because this is our condition, we can wonder why, if we are all subject to decay, that human beings kill one another. Many works of literature, such as Robert Louis Stevenson's *Dr. Jekyll and Mr. Hyde* and Joseph Conrad's *Heart of Darkness*, depict murderous deeds and explore this inescapable aspect of our lives. Sigmund Freud, founder of psychoanalysis, contended that our unconscious minds are ruled by two drives: one oriented toward pleasure and life (often referred to as *Eros*) and another contrary drive toward destruction and death (*Thanatos*). Regardless of its cause, humanity's capacity for evil is hard to deny or ignore. Arnold Johnston, in his study of William Golding's novels, claims that *Lord of the Flies* is a mythic and symbolic commentary on civilization's inability to "... contend with man's apparently natural and voracious propensity for savagery." While not afraid to point out some of Golding's

Johnston, Arnold. "*Lord of the Flies*: Fable, Myth, and Fiction." *Of Earth and Darkness: The Novels of William Golding.* St. Louis: University of Missouri Press, 1980.

overly didactic passages in the novel, Johnston argues that
Lord of the Flies is a poignant statement on the darker side of
human nature and our compulsion to commit savage acts in
spite of our rationality. Thus, Johnston explores the inhumanity
of human beings and our obsession with dying.

∽ᢁᢍ∼

Lord of the Flies deals, ostensibly, with a group of English schoolboys
who, in the process of being evacuated by airplane from the dangers
of a nuclear war, find themselves alone on a tropical island after their
plane crashes. The boys, ranging in age from about six to thirteen, are
faced with the problem of survival on the uninhabited island while
attempting to attract the attention of passing ships and planes.

The problem of physical existence solves itself—the island is rich
in fruit and game and the climate is favorable. The real problem that
arises among the boys involves their own inner nature, and emerges
most directly from a clash between those who wish to keep a fire
burning on the island's mountain to attract rescuers and those who
wish to hunt and indulge in what at first seems to be the natural
inclination of children toward unrestrained play. The conflict begins in
apparent childish innocence, and reaches its climax in acts of shocking
brutality that carry far-reaching implications of guilt.

Golding has summed up the theme of Lord of the Flies as follows:

> The theme is an attempt to trace the defects of society back
> to the defects of human nature. The moral is that the shape
> of society must depend on the ethical nature of the individual
> and not on any political system however apparently logical or
> respectable. The whole book is symbolic in nature.[1]

As I have mentioned, Golding feels that evil arises from man's
essential being, and he attempts to demonstrate his thesis in this self-
consciously symbolic work which shows civilization totally unable to
contend with man's apparently natural and voracious propensity for
savagery. A systematic probing into the question of man's inherent
good or evil is, without doubt, one of Golding's major concerns; and
in the course of this study I shall attempt to show that his apparent
preoccupation with the problems of survival (Lord of the Flies, The

Inheritors, Pincher Martin) is an important key to understanding both his philosophy and his techniques.

Lord of the Flies falls into that hardy genre of accounts of ship-wreck and survival on tropical islands: *Robinson Crusoe, The Swiss Family Robinson, The Coral Island,* and so forth. Golding particularly wishes the reader to associate his novel with Ballantyne's *The Coral Island.* The two main characters in both books are named Ralph and Jack, and the relationship between the names of Ballantyne's Peterkin and Golding's Simon needs little elaboration. Then, too, there are two direct references to *The Coral Island* in Golding's book, one near the beginning—

> "It's like in a book."
> At once there was a clamour.
> "Treasure Island—"
> "Swallows and Amazons—"
> "Coral Island—"

and one near the end—

> The officer nodded helpfully.
> "I know. Jolly good show. Like the Coral Island."[2]

Frank Kermode and Carl Niemeyer, in separate essays, discuss at some length Golding's use of *The Coral Island* as an ironic parallel to his own novel, pointing out the difference between Golding's vision of human nature and what Niemeyer calls the "cheerful unrealities" of Ballantyne.[3] And Golding himself, in the interview with Kermode, had this to say of his book's connection with *The Coral Island*:

> What I'm saying to myself is, "Don't be such a fool, you remember when you were a boy, a small boy, how you lived on that island with Ralph and Jack and Peterkin.... Now you are grown up, ... you can see people are not like that; they would not behave like that if they were God-fearing English gentlemen, and they went to an island like that." Their savagery would not be found in natives on an island. As like as not they would find savages who were kindly and uncomplicated and

that the devil would rise out of the intellectual complications
of the three white men on the island itself.[4]

Golding's remark about kindly, uncomplicated savages stacks the
anthropological cards a bit heavily against civilized man, and ignores
a number of basic facts about primitive cultures. Of course, *Lord of
the Flies* doesn't allow the reader any "real" savages with whom to
compare the boys, as Golding's artistic sense evidently told him to
avoid confusing the central human issue with such anthropological
quibbles. However, the aforementioned remark does underline Golding's moralistic bias, and points toward a more serious charge that
might be leveled against the novel: that his authorial presence is often
overly obtrusive, either in didactic interpositions or, more seriously, in
unconvincing manipulation of his characters.

In this connection Lionel Trilling says that Golding succeeds
in persuading the reader that the boys' actions result from the fact
that they "are not finally under the control of previous social habit or
convention," but adds that he "should not have credited this quite so
readily of American boys who would not ... have been so quick to
forget their social and moral pasts."[5] For my part, I am unable to see
why Mr. Trilling is unwilling to carry his pertinent critical comment to
its logical conclusion, without involving himself in speculations about
the relative acculturation processes in Britain and the United States.
Had he pursued his doubts to an expression of dissatisfaction with the
credibility of the boys, he would have been on firmer ground, since
there are several points at which Golding's manipulations of narrative
and dialogue do ring false.

Two interrelated but discernibly distinct threads are evident in
Lord of the Flies. One is the actual narrative, detailing meticulously
the boys' descent into savagery; the other is the gradually developed
symbol of the "Beast" that is first suggested by the wholly natural
night fears of the "littluns" and that eventually becomes the object of
worship by the boys-turned-savages. The Beast is an externalization of
the inner darkness in the children's (man's) nature, and its ascendancy
is steady, inexorable, as is the path to savagery, increasing in intensity
with each new regression on the part of the boys. But despite his often
brilliant handling of this apposite motivating symbol of the book, it

is especially during scenes involving the Beast that Golding becomes particularly intrusive.

At one point, for instance, when the assembled boys are discussing the problem of the Beast, Piggy (the pragmatic rationalist) explains: "'Course there isn't a beast in the forest. How could there be? What would a beast eat?'" (p. 77). And the answer, supplied by the chorus of boys, is "'Pig!'"—to which the unmistakable voice of Golding (by way of reminding the reader just what his symbol represents) can be heard to add, "'We eat pig'" (p. 77). And a few pages later Simon, the convulsion-afflicted mystic, says of the Beast: "'What I mean is ... maybe it's only us'" (p. 82). This rather subtle interpretation of human nature from a small boy demonstrates further that Golding is so intent on his moral message that he will not hesitate to make the youngsters dance to his tune.

This assembly scene is central to the novel's development in that it marks the last point at which "civilized" rules and procedures can be said to dominate the boys' words and actions. Grounds for the breakdown of the rules are furnished by dissent among the representatives of order (Ralph, Piggy, and Simon), as Piggy, with his unimaginative rationalist's intelligence, answers Simon's observation with a resounding "'Nuts!'" Even among the "civilized," communication is lacking, and when Jack—leader of the forces of disorder—shouts "'Bollocks to the rules!'" chaos and darkness are ushered in (p. 84).

However, Golding cannot let the matter of the Beast rest here, and after the assembly has dispersed, Ralph, shaken, turns to Piggy and asks, "'Are there ghosts, Piggy? Or Beasts?'" And here the ventriloquist's lips can be seen to move, as Piggy answers: "'Course there aren't. . . . 'Cos things wouldn't make sense. Houses an' streets, an'—TV—they wouldn't work'" (p. 85). Although beautifully camouflaged in boyish diction, the implication that a boy of about ten can reason that the existence of supernatural phenomena challenges the validity of natural law is simply too much to swallow.

A major objectification of man's inner Beast appears in the shape of a pig's head on a stick that Jack and his "hunters" leave as an offering for the Beast. Unknown to the hunters, Simon has been nearby during the killing of the pig, having hidden himself in some bushes at the onset of one of his fits. He is then left alone with the head, thus setting the scene for the most self-consciously symbolic incident in the book. At this point the significance of the book's title becomes evident, as the head, swarming with flies, enters into an imaginary conversation with Simon, a conversation in which Golding, speaking through this grotesque agent, removes any doubts that might still have lingered in the reader's mind with respect to the novel's theme or the source of the evil described therein:

> The Lord of the Flies spoke in the voice of a schoolmaster.
> "This has gone quite far enough. My poor, misguided child, do you think you know better than I do?"
> There was a pause.
> "I'm warning you. I'm going to get angry. D'you see. You're not wanted. Understand? We are going to have fun on this island! So don't try it on, my poor misguided boy, or else—"
> Simon found he was looking into a vast mouth. There was blackness within, a blackness that spread.
> "—Or else," said the Lord of the Flies, "we shall do you. See? Jack and Roger and Maurice and Robert and Bill and Piggy and Ralph. Do you. See?" (p. 133)

The above scene, which places perhaps the greatest strain on the reader's credulity, may be defended as the book's clearest indication that human guilt is pervasive, including even the "good" characters, Ralph and Piggy. However, by comparing this strained encounter between Simon and the head with the scenes immediately preceding and following it, one may see that Golding makes his point there just as clearly and much more effectively.[6]

The killing of the pig by Jack's hunters is a case in point. The pig-hunting of former days has been relatively innocent, but to fully dramatize the deep inner evil that takes possession of the boys after they accept the Beast as their god, Golding depicts more than a mere killing. Conjuring up the most shocking imagery he could use to show the degeneration of these preadolescents, he describes the slaughter of a mother sow in terms of a sexual assault.[7] How better to portray the children's loss of innocence (since children are no strangers to killing) than by picturing them as perpetrators of an Oedipal violation?

... the sow staggered her way ahead of them, bleeding and mad, and the hunters followed, wedded to her in lust, excited by the long chase and the dropped blood. ...

Here, struck down by the heat, the sow fell and the hunters hurled themselves at her. This dreadful eruption from an unknown world made her frantic; she squealed and bucked and the air was full of sweat and noise and blood and terror. Roger ran round the heap, prodding with his spear wherever pigflesh appeared. Jack was on top of the sow, stabbing downward with his knife. Roger found a lodgment for his spear and began to push till he was leaning with his whole weight. The spear moved forward inch by inch and the terrified squealing became a high-pitched scream. Then Jack found the throat and the hot blood spouted over his hands. The sow collapsed under them and they were heavy and fulfilled upon her. (p. 125)

The vividness of this scene makes it both a powerfully realistic component of the essential story and a major contribution to the novel's symbolic scheme. The episode involving Simon and the head, however—especially the "conversation"—is difficult to view in other than symbolic terms, marking it as another nagging flaw in a book that—whatever its thematic concerns—seems committed from the outset to creating believable boys on a believable island. Actually, the mere physical presence of the pig's head, the Lord of the Flies, would have served well without the didactic pronouncements, since "lord of the flies" is a translation of the Hebrew *Ba'al zevuv* (Beelzebub in Greek), implying quite effectively that the head is representative of man's "inner devil."

In any event, the most successful symbolic portrayal of the Beast as man appears earlier in the novel in the form of a dead airman whose parachute carries him in the night to the top of the mountain, where, tangled in the complication of strings, he becomes lodged in a sitting position, the upper half of his body alternately rising and falling as the breeze tightens and slackens the lines. Sam and Eric, the twins, are horrified by this grisly figure when they come to tend the fire, and when a subsequent expedition (headed by Ralph and Jack, but notably excluding Simon and Piggy) climbs the mountain to confirm the twins' garbled report, the following powerful passage shows the Beast impressed forever on the minds and hearts of the boys:

> Behind them the sliver of moon had drawn clear of the horizon. Before them, something like a great ape was sitting asleep with its head between its knees. Then the wind roared in the forest, there was confusion in the darkness and the creature lifted its head, holding toward them the ruin of a face. (p. 114)

This is the experience that accelerates the deterioration of civilized procedures, bringing confusion to the final assembly and committing Jack fully—in a parody of his initial appearance as leader of the choir, or perhaps an oblique commentary on the ritualistic mind—to high priesthood in the dark new religion. And it is to determine the truth of this experience and the nature of the so-called Beast from Air that Simon, after his ghastly interview with the head, courageously ascends the mountain, where he frees the wasted body "from the wind's indignity" (p. 135).

Simon, whom Golding has called quite explicitly a "Christ-figure," comes down from the mountain to carry the truth to the others, but—still weak from his recent attack—he stumbles instead into a ritual reenactment of the pig-killing and is killed by the frenzied and fear-maddened boys, who ironically mistake him for the Beast.[8] And here Golding's sweeping indictment of humanity becomes most nearly complete, for Ralph and Piggy, lured by the prospect of food, have temporarily joined with the hunters and take part, albeit unwittingly, in the murder of Simon. And here, too, at the moment of Simon's death, in the midst of a storm that thunders within as well as around them, the boys are visited by the spectre of human history, embodied in the form of the dead airman. Dislodged from atop the mountain and carried again into the air by the winds, the grotesque figure of the decaying parachutist plummets to the sands, scattering the terror-stricken boys, and sweeps far out to sea. The beach is left desolate save for the small broken body of Simon, which follows the parachutist into the sea:

> Along the shoreward edge of the shallows the advancing clearness was full of strange, moonbeam-bodied creatures with fiery eyes. Here and there a larger pebble clung to its own air

and was covered with a coat of pearls. The tide swelled in and over the rain-pitted sand and smoothed everything with a layer of silver. Now it touched the first of the stains that seeped from the broken body and the creatures made a moving patch of light as they gathered at the edge. The water rose farther and dressed Simon's coarse hair with brightness. The line of his cheek silvered and the turn of his shoulder became sculptured marble. The strange attendant creatures, with their fiery eyes and trailing vapors, busied themselves round his head. The body lifted a fraction of an inch from the sand and a bubble of air escaped from the mouth with a wet plop. Then it turned gently in the water.

Somewhere over the darkened curve of the world the sun and moon were pulling, and the film of water on the earth planet was held, bulging slightly on one side while the solid core turned. The great wave of the tide moved farther along the island and the water lifted. Softly, surrounded by a fringe of inquisitive bright creatures, itself a silver shape beneath the steadfast constellations, Simon's dead body moved out toward the open sea. (p. 142)

The amount and kind of description devoted to Simon's death is ample indication of his saintly role even without Golding's identification of him as a Christ-figure.

All of the obvious parallels to Christ are there—from Gethsemane to Golgotha—and one may easily identify Simon's story with that of many a martyred mystic.[9] But why are they there? Why is Simon there? Is Golding merely speaking with the voice of moral and religious orthodoxy? As his subsequent novels have shown, Golding is not to be labeled so easily. But in those novels one sees a consistent preoccupation with the artist or artist-figure, someone actively engaged in interpreting the human condition: Tuami, the tribal artist in *The Inheritors*; Christopher "Pincher" Martin, the penultimate actor in *Pincher Martin*; Sammy Mountjoy, the guilt-torn painter in *Free Fall*; Dean Jocelin and Roger Mason, creative force behind, and architect of, *The Spire*; Oliver, the confused would-be musician in *The Pyramid*; and Matty Windrove, the naive prophet of *Darkness Visible*.

Viewed in this light, Simon's habitual isolation from the other boys, his obvious inability to communicate to them the "truths" that he grasps intuitively, and finally his death at their hands, reflect the all-too-frequent fate of the artist in society. Of course, all that can be said of the artist's role may be applied to that of the religious or mystic; but again and again in his later works, Golding demonstrates that the nature of his unorthodoxy is its basis in that highly eclectic form of mysticism called art. Like many artists before him, he sees the artist as priest, as interpreter of life's mysteries and possible savior of mankind. Unlike many of his predecessors, though, Golding faces squarely the historical fact that the artist—like other saviors—has met with little success. And in this first novel, Simon should be recognized as the first of Golding's "portraits of the artist," embodying both his pride in the high calling and his frustration at the artist's inability to defend himself against the weaknesses of others, or to transcend his own human frailties. Even more important to a reading of his works as a whole is the realization that, for Golding, the artist is representative of humanity at large, and that Golding finds in creativity the source of man's strength and weakness, his good and evil.

In any case, the aftermath of Simon's death is the last point at which *Lord of the Flies* can be said to picture the existence of a calm and ordering vision. Total disintegration of the civilized forces follows swiftly, beginning with the theft of Piggy's glasses—the source of fire and symbol of intellectual power—by Jack and his hunters, and proceeding through Piggy's murder by the brutal Roger to the final hunt for Ralph, who is to be decapitated and sacrificed like a pig to the Beast.

The description of Piggy's death provides an informing contrast to that of Simon's, showing quite clearly, though subtly, Golding's antirationalist bias:

> The rock struck Piggy a glancing blow from chin to knee; the conch exploded into a thousand white fragments and ceased to exist. Piggy, saying nothing, with no time for even a grunt, traveled through the air sideways from the rock, turning over as he went. The rock bounded twice and was lost in the forest. Piggy fell forty feet and landed on his back across that square red rock in the sea. His head opened and stuff came out and turned red. Piggy's arms and legs twitched a bit, like a pig's after it has been killed. Then the sea breathed again in a long, slow sigh, the water boiled white and pink over the rock; and

when it went, sucking back again, the body of Piggy was gone.
(p. 167)

One notes here the same studious reportage of physical fact as in the passage quoted earlier. But this time Golding concentrates on matter-of-fact particulars, eschewing the angle of vision that might place Piggy's death in universal perspective: whereas Simon is described in language befitting a dead saint, Piggy is pictured as a dead animal. Of course, Piggy's actions immediately before his murder are brave in conventional terms; but his rationalist's faith in order and human perfectibility, ironically undercut throughout the book, seems nowhere more misguided than in this scene (p. 166). The mystic's intuitive recognition that good and evil coexist within man is the spark of his divinity; but the rationalist's denial of such intangible forces chains him forever to the material world of earth and organism.

After Piggy's death, Ralph finds himself being hunted by the other boys. But at the book's climactic moment, just as the "savages" are about to descend on Ralph, a "rescuer" appears in the person of a British naval officer. And at once, in a passage laden with irony, the shrieking painted savages become "a semicircle of little boys, their bodies streaked with colored clay, sharp sticks in their hands ... standing on the beach making no noise at all" (p. 185). The officer, confronted with this scene of filth and disorder, rebukes the boys lamely (as Lionel Trilling might have noted): "'I should have thought that a pack of British boys—you're all British, aren't you?—would have been able to put up a better show than that—'" (p. 186). And Ralph, the book's Everyman, representative of the world of "longing and baffled common-sense" (p. 65), is left to weep "for the end of innocence, the darkness of man's heart, and the fall through the air of the true, wise friend called Piggy" (pp. 186–87).

Several early critics and reviewers of *Lord of the Flies* assailed the book's ending as too neat, if not actually as a question-begging compromise with lovers of happy endings.[10] However, a reflective reading shows that the "rescue" is no rescue at all: throughout the novel Golding is at pains to point out that the major human predicament is internal; the officer solves Ralph's immediate problem, but "the darkness of man's heart" persists. Practically, of course, as Golding says, in a book "originally conceived ... as the change from innocence—which is the ignorance of self—to a tragic knowledge ... If I'd gone on to the death of Ralph, Ralph would never have had time to understand what had happened to him."[11] And on a more sophisticated thematic level he observes, "The officer, having interrupted a manhunt, prepares to take the children off the island in a cruiser which will presently be hunting its enemy in the same implacable way. And who will rescue the adult and his cruiser?"[12]

Returning to the Simon–Piggy contrast discussed earlier, one might also note that it is Piggy, the misguided rationalist, for whom Ralph sorrows, not Simon, the "saint." Besides subtly underscoring Golding's concern for the fate of the artist-mystic, this fact seems to indicate that Ralph's tragic experience has not finally brought him to the sort of self-knowledge that can save him as a man. The implications for humanity at large are clear and unencouraging. Thus, although the officer seems to suggest a deus ex machina, one will be hard pressed to find a happy ending here.

On a broader front, the plot of *Lord of the Flies* has been attacked as both eccentric and specious, either too far removed from the real world or too neatly microcosmic to be true.[14] The first of these charges, that of eccentricity, may be put aside for the time being. After all, removing one's setting and characters from the larger sphere of civilization has long been an acceptable, if not honorable, practice in almost every literary genre and tradition, as witness the success of Melville and Conrad, whose isolated fictional worlds remain real in both their concrete details and their human significance. The source of the objection seems to be predisposed literary tastes, rather than more rigorous aesthetic standards—preference for the novel as typical history, rather than symbolic vision. However, the related charge— that Golding oversimplifies complex truth through manipulation of his microcosmic world—is on firmer ground. And in speaking to this point, one must necessarily return to John Peter's identification of Golding as a fabulist, as well as to Golding's own wish to be seen as a "myth-maker."

The main concern, then, of both opponents and supporters of *Lord of the Flies* is whether or not it functions adequately on its primary, or "fictional," level; or more simply, is the story told convincingly? Peter, in "The Fables of William Golding," assails the novel for its "incomplete translation of its thesis into its story so that much remains external and extrinsic, the teller's assertion rather than the tale's enact- ment before our eyes." And indeed, I have detailed several instances of such didactic obtrusions, including some aspects of character and action that seem more concerned with theme than credibility. However, I would qualify Peter's observation rather strongly, noting that such instances seem more vulnerable to the charge of being extraneous than of betraying Golding's "incomplete translation" of his thesis, which is more than adequately communicated by the rest of the novel.

And what of the rest of the novel? Is it merely a skeleton of thesis incompletely fleshed by concrete detail? Kinkead-Weekes and Gregor are highly emphatic in answering this question: "Physical realities come first for Golding and should stay first for his readers."[15] They devote a long first chapter in their study to a demonstration of the "complex physical truth" of Lord of the Flies, concentrating heavily on the naturalistic clarity and inclusiveness of Golding's description, and arguing that his symbolic representations are often so reflective of life's complexities as to be actually ambiguous, perhaps even too ambiguous to be seen symbolically at all. This latter point is a bit extreme: Golding's main symbolic intentions are clear enough in the novel, even without the many explicit comments he has made since its publication. However, Kinkead-Weekes and Gregor may be excused their overstatement, since so much attention has been paid to the novel's symbolism that its objective vehicles have been too often deemphasized, if not forgotten.

And here, Golding's style becomes a major concern. As Kinkead-Weekes and Gregor demonstrate, Golding's descriptive prose carries the burden of his meaning and—coupled with the inexorable narrative of the boys' descent into chaos—provides the reader with a naturalistically concrete and complex surface world against which to view the symbolic drama. One need only note passages already quoted—the killing of the sow, the deaths of Simon and Piggy—to be convinced that the realities of Lord of the Flies live in the flesh, as well as in the abstract, comprising a universe not oversimplified, but paradoxically diverse, in which beauty and ugliness, good and evil, precariously coexist. The main features of Golding's best description are scientific accuracy and objectivity, combined with a felicitous use of simple adjectives and verbs that can transform his tersely pictured scenes into powerful evocations of transcendent beauty or obsessive ugliness. One thinks here of the extremes of such effects before the sow-killing, when "she staggered into an open space where bright flowers grew and butterflies danced round each other and the air was hot and still" (p. 125), and after, when "the pile of guts was a black blob of flies that buzzed like a saw" (p. 128). Without doubt, Golding's world exists compellingly on its primary level: its strained moments seem more like surface blemishes than structural defects, blemishes that catch the eye because of their dissimilarity to the skillfully woven fabric of the whole.

As for Golding's stature as a maker of myth, one must grant him a considerable measure of success. Certainly, if myth "comes out from the roots of things" and evokes age-old and recurrent human patterns, *Lord of the Flies* is much closer to myth than to simple fable. One may trace its literary roots alone back through the more immediate past (*The Coral Island*), to the ancient past (*The Bacchae*), and on a broader plane one may easily see in the story echoes and parallels from both the political and social dynamics of contemporary civilization (the rise of Fascism, anti-intellectualism) and the religious and philosophical foundations of Western culture (the Old Testament, the Fall, the New Testament, the Crucifixion, as well as nineteenth-century rationalism). Indeed, the very profusion of suggestive patterns in the novel should demonstrate that here is no simple allegorical reworking of the materials of *The Coral Island*, and that irrespective of Golding's initial plans, Frank Kermode properly observes: "In writing of this kind all depends upon the author's mythopoeic power to transcend the 'programme.'"[16] And in this first novel, William Golding displays "mythopoeic power" of an impressively high order. The flaws, the didactic interjections and manipulations remain. But, all in all, one may compare Golding to a puppet master who has wrought his marionettes meticulously and beautifully and led them skillfully through a captivating and frightening drama, while only occasionally distracting the audience by the movement of his strings.

NOTES

1. Golding as quoted in E.L. Epstein, "Notes on William Golding and Pincher Martin," Capricorn Edition of *Lord of the Flies*, p. 250. See also "The War as Awakening" in Jack I. Biles, *Talk: Conversations with William Golding*, pp. 30–52.

2. Golding, *Lord of the Flies* (New York: Coward-McCann, 1955), pp. 30, 186; further parenthetical references in the text are taken from this edition.

3. Frank Kermode, "Coral Islands," *The Spectator*, p. 257; also in William Nelson, *William Golding's* Lord of the Flies: *A Source Book*, pp. 39–42. Carl Niemeyer, "The Coral Island Revisited," *College English*, pp. 241–5; also in Nelson, pp. 88–94, and Baker and Ziegler, Casebook Edition, pp. 217–23.

4. Frank Kermode and William Golding, "The Meaning of It All," *Books and Bookmen*, p. 10.

5. Lionel Trilling, "*Lord of the Flies*," *The Midcentury*, p. 10.

6. Howard Babb, in *The Novels of William Golding*, pp. 26–28, takes a contrary view of this passage, stressing its "visual richness" and "precise diction," and praising Golding's care in creating what Babb terms "the plausible experience of a terrified boy." I would agree with Babb's reading of all the imaginary (or hallucinatory) dialogue.

7. See Golding's brusque reaction to such a sexual reading of the scene in James Keating, "Interview with William Golding," in Baker and Ziegler, Casebook Edition, p. 195; see also Bernard F. Dick, "The Novelist Is a Displaced Person: An Interview with William Golding," *College English*, pp. 480–82.

8. See James R. Baker, *William Golding: A Critical Study*, p. 8, for comparison with *The Bacchae*, and William Golding, *The Hot Gates*, pp. 161–2, for a possible autobiographical source.

9. See Donald R. Spangler, "Simon," in Baker and Ziegler, Casebook Edition, pp. 211–5.

10. See Louis J. Halle, "Small Savages," *Saturday Review*, p. 16, and James Gindin, *Postwar British Fiction*, pp. 196–206, both of which appear in Nelson, *A Sourcebook*, Halle, pp. 5–6, and Gindin, pp. 132–40.

11. Keating, "Interview with Golding," p. 194.

12. E.L. Epstein, "Notes on Golding," p. 250.

13. See Mark Kinkead-Weekes and Ian Gregor, *William Golding: A Critical Study*, p. 64. See also "Piggy" in *Talk*, pp. 11–14, where Golding points out that the description of Piggy as "true" and "wise" is not the author's, but Ralph's.

14. See Frederick R. Karl, *A Reader's Guide to the Contemporary English Novel*, p. 259.
15. Kinkead-Weekes and Gregor, *A Critical Study*, p. 19. See also Babb, *Novels of Golding*, pp. 7–34, for a similar defense of Golding's narrative power.
16. Frank Kermode, "The Novels of William Golding," *International Literary Annual*, p. 18; this article also appears in its entirety in Nelson, *A Source Book*, pp. 107–20, and in part in Baker and Ziegler, Casebook Edition, pp. 203–6.

NIGHT
(ELIE WIESEL)

"Elie Wiesel's *Night* and Dying in the Present Tense"
by Kitty Millet, San Francisco State University

Elie Wiesel's *Night* chronicles the Wiesel family's deportation from Sighet, Hungary, to the camps of Auschwitz and Buchenwald. By the time of his liberation from Buchenwald at the age of sixteen, the narrator Elie will lose his mother, sister, father, his entire community, and his faith to the Nazis. He will understand himself as already dead, characterizing his losses at the camps as an unending night in which he and the other Jewish inmates experience a slow, continuous dying. For most people, death is a finite experience, an end in itself, with obvious boundaries. However, Wiesel tells us of those for whom death is infinite: They are always dying in the present tense. Death and dying are fluid and constant experiences for the Jews of Sighet, for the inmates at Auschwitz and Buchenwald, for those eternally marching, being forced to drag themselves further and further into that night. This gets to the heart of Wiesel's narrative, because this dying suggests a duration impossible to map in hours and minutes.

The Jewish inmates experience a dying that extends far beyond time and space, making it an unbounded experience. Yet even as this unbounded death sweeps up the Jews, it proceeds in stages, stripping them immediately of their civil entitlements, changing them from subjects to "a pack of beaten animals," from bodies to body parts, from mechanistic drives to shadows, and from shadows to corpses. These stages will underwrite the unboundedness as it shifts death from what is knowable to a dying experience that exceeds human perception. In *The Holocaust and Literary Imagination,* Lawrence Langer argues that this shift is a consequence of Auschwitz: Temporality itself is altered by the camps.

But Elie, the Jewish narrator, the student of Kabbalah and Talmud, marks his temporality with the signifiers of Judaism: Its terms, rituals, expectations, and calendar punctuate the life of the observant boy. The year's discreet divisions between Yom Kippur and Passover bracket his childhood, ritually reminding him that God has chosen the Jews and that time itself has been enlisted to bear witness to that fact. Thus Elie's experiences of the unboundedness of death and dying in the camps produce a horrifying conclusion: There is an experience of death that can't be integrated into the fabric of Jewish observance. This will remain with Wiesel, staring at him in the mirror, "never leaving him."

Wiesel alludes to a change in the duration and status of death and dying—its temporality and its effect on Jewish observance—when Moishe the Beadle, "the poorest of the poor of Sighet" and a foreign Jew, returns from an earlier deportation. The native Jews of Sighet have "quickly" forgotten the deportees, but Moishe's unexpected reappearance pushes Elie to ask him about his disappearance:

> One day, as I was about to enter the synagogue, I saw Moishe the Beadle sitting on a bench near the entrance.
>
> He told me what had happened to him and his companions. The train with the deportees had crossed the Hungarian border and, once in Polish territory, had been taken over by the Gestapo. The train had stopped. The Jews were ordered to get off and onto waiting trucks. The trucks headed toward a forest. There everybody was ordered to get out. They were forced to dig huge trenches. When they had finished their work, the men from the Gestapo began theirs. Without passion or haste, they shot their prisoners, who were forced to approach the trench one by one and offer their necks. Infants were tossed into the air and used as targets for the machine guns. This took place in the Galician forest, near Kolomay. How had he, Moishe the Beadle, been able to escape? By a miracle. He was wounded in the leg and left for dead . . . (6)

Recounting his story, Moishe tells Elie of the border crossing and the sudden emergence of the Gestapo. Once the trains have crossed this boundary, the Jews become the property of the Germans and they are consigned to death—the crossing itself suggests a new jurisdiction with its own law. The Gestapo's murder of the Jews takes place "without passion or haste."

Elie discovers that Moishe has changed irrevocably because he has witnessed this massacre. He "no longer mentioned either God or Kabbalah. He spoke only of what he had seen" (7). Thus Moishe's experience of "seeing" his own death recasts him as "a living dead, unfit for life as defined by his community" (Avni 1995). Moishe's changed perception translates into his changed status within Sighet. It also draws attention to how "quickly" the deportees are forgotten, how Moishe has been forced to witness his own death, and how the Jews were "already consigned to death, a final verdict" (Wiesel 10) even before the Nazis arrived in Sighet. Although Moishe has returned to Sighet's Jews, he perceives himself as being on the other side of death. He exists only because of his will to tell, to warn, other Jews of the Nazis' plans. The events of this emblematic scene will circumscribe Elie's experience of death and dying throughout the rest of his narrative.

When the Nazis occupy Sighet, they round up more Jews for deportations. At the same time, the Nazis relocate the remaining families into a smaller ghetto within Sighet. After each subsequent deportation, the remaining Jews quickly forget the deportees and comfort themselves with the rationalization that "the yellow star . . . it's not lethal" (11). As Wiesel points out, the "ghetto was ruled by neither German nor Jews; it was ruled by delusion" (12). Delusion and forgetfulness work in tandem to create an atmosphere in which the Jews fail to grasp the import of these deportations.

On the last night in the ghetto, in his capacity as the leader's son, Elie must awaken sleeping Jews to their own pending deportation. But just repeating the message of their deportation "chokes him" (15). The Nazis' plans for the Jews have already begun to kill him; he tastes his community's death with the repetition of the message. The effect of Elie's message furthers the dying process in his community as "weariness . . . settled in our veins, our limbs, our brains, like molten lead" (16). Their bodies are beginning to register the burden of the final verdict, in that the Jews perceive its burden as an outcome against which they have no energy to fight. That weariness erodes their individual wills, transforming them into a pack of "beaten dogs" (17). In resignation, Elie's community of Jews leaves the ghetto for the last time:

> The procession disappeared around the corner. A few steps more and they were beyond the ghetto walls. . . . There was a little of everything: suitcases, briefcases, bags, knives, dishes, banknotes, papers, faded portraits. All the things one planned to take along and finally left behind. They had ceased to matter.
>
> Open rooms everywhere. Gaping doors and windows looked out into the void. It all belonged to everyone since it no longer belonged to anyone. It was there for the taking. An open tomb. (17)

As the Jews leave, Wiesel notes not only that the objects left behind ceased to matter, but also that the houses themselves are gaping. The buildings themselves resemble tombs. But where are the corpses? Presumably, the Jews who lived in these houses are the corpses forced to march from the ghetto into the void. The Jews have already begun the dying process. They are being forced to march into the void themselves.

When Wiesel describes Elie's first night at Auschwitz, he characterizes it as "one long night seven times sealed" (34). Wiesel sutures night, and the death camp of Auschwitz, together with the notion of the Jewish mystic's seal, and the severity of his depiction can only be understood through the lens of orthodox Judaism and Jewish mystical thought.

In Kabbalistic tradition, there is the belief that the soul has been sealed because of sin so that in our conscious states, we cannot reopen the soul. As the Jewish mystic endeavors to draw closer to God, he must inevitably unseal the soul, "untie the knots which bind it" (Scholem 131) by concentrating on the Divine Name (HaShem). This unsealing releases the mystic into a realm of liberation and transcendence, "the cosmic stream" (Ibid). As Gershom Scholem describes it in *The Major Trends of Jewish Mysticism*, "[T]he seals, which keep it locked up in its normal state and shut off the divine light, are relaxed, and the mystic finally dispenses with them altogether" (137). However, if the mystic, upon entering the cosmic stream, is incapable of resealing his soul, he can become lost in the cosmic stream, damned to and within it. Wiesel's language shifts the cosmic stream to the darkness of the first night at Auschwitz.

In the death camp, when Wiesel declares "the first night ... turned my life into one long night seven times sealed," he marks that there will never be a possibility of unbinding his soul. The death camp has sealed it. Auschwitz's sealing has cut him off permanently from the divine light, casting him and the other Jews with him into an unending night.

> Never shall I forget that night, the first night in camp, that
> turned my life into one long night seven times sealed.
> Never shall I forget that smoke.
> Never shall I forget the small faces of the children whose
> bodies I saw transformed into smoke under a silent sky.
> Never shall I forget those flames that consumed my faith
> forever. . . .
> Never shall I forget those moments that murdered my God and
> my soul and turned my dreams to ashes (Wiesel 34).

At that moment, the effect on Elie of the night's murder of "my God and my soul," suggests that the Divine Name itself has been destroyed, the divine light permanently blotted out. The most vulnerable of the Jewish victims, their children, are now "the small faces ... transformed into smoke." In a role never imagined by the observant, Jewish children will now take the place of those offspring formerly cursed by God. It is as if the sacred narratives underwriting the Jewish experience have been permanently destroyed. The signifiers on which he has relied have been conscripted to serve as the terms of his extermination:

> In one terrifying moment of lucidity, I thought of us as damned
> souls wandering through the void, souls condemned to wander
> through space until the end of time, seeking redemption,
> seeking oblivion, without any hope of finding either. (36)

The specter of the void reemerges here. Instead of Sighet's buildings and houses—those signifiers of home and community—looking out onto the void, Elie realizes that the Jews wander in it already—this exile taking up all others. The void merges then with the darkness; it is the repository for the demonic and the damned who opposed God, for failed creation. Wandering, the signifier of diasporic Jewry, becomes instead an aimless compulsion, "without any hope."

The outlines of the Hebrew Bible, Talmud, and Kabbalah come together in Elie's realization that what has happened to the Jews produces an experience of death and dying that cannot be sanctified (33). As Elie and his father march together toward the crematoria, the Jews around them begin reciting Kaddish, the Jewish prayer of the dead. As they recite, "Yisgadal, veyisgadash, shmey raba ... May His name be celebrated and sanctified ..." (33), Elie questions why he should sanctify the name. Since they are saying Kaddish for their own deaths, Elie's question proposes a death outside the boundaries of sanctification: This death cannot be sanctified. It cannot be brought within the parameters of sanctifying HaShem.

Elie understands, then, the hopelessness of the Jews around him. By the next morning "we had ceased to be men. . . . I too had become a different person. The student of Talmud, the child I was, had been consumed by the flames. All that was left was a shape that resembled me. My soul had been invaded—and devoured—by a black flame" (37). Elie perceives himself as "a shape that resembles" rather than Elie who studies Talmud. His pronouns shift from personal to impersonal, underscoring that his body, like the night itself, has lost specific traits. It has become indistinguishable from the other bodies around him.

This lack of distinctive traits sets up the Jewish body to be reduced to its componentry and its functionality in the camps. The inmates no longer distinguish the boundaries between the stones they touch and their hands (78). Eventually, Elie feels himself reduced to only a stomach:

> At that moment in time, all that mattered to me was my daily bowl of soup, my crust of stale bread. The bread, the soup— those were my entire life. I was nothing but a body. Perhaps less: a famished stomach. The stomach alone was measuring time. (52)

As the boy internalizes this interminable dying, his body colludes with the death around him. The only part of his body that still registers the impulse to live is his stomach.

In this way, Wiesel freights the experience with the image of the stomach "measuring time." The consequences of this act are not lost on Wiesel the inmate. The existential reality of the unending night—its duration—collapses into the Jews' wandering of the void—an unsanctifiable journey—transforming Elie's hunger into the void itself. When Yom Kippur occurs in the camp, Elie realizes that this journey, this duration, was never intended for humans.

> YOM KIPPUR. The Day of Atonement. Should we fast? The question was hotly debated. To fast could mean a more certain, more rapid death. In this place, we were always fasting. It was Yom Kippur year-round. But there were those who said we should fast, precisely because it was dangerous to do so. We needed to show God that even here, locked in hell, we were capable of singing his praises.
>
> I did not fast. First of all, to please my father who had forbidden me to do so. And then, there was no longer any reason for me to fast. I no longer accepted God's silence. As I swallowed my ration of soup, I turned that act into a symbol of rebellion, of protest against Him.
>
> And I nibbled my crust of bread.
>
> Deep inside me, I felt a great void opening. (69)

Elie's choice to eat is a form of rebellion against the God who was silent. In the absence of Judaism's sacred narratives, Elie must look to his father for another narrative the absence of Judaism's sacred narratives that have historically underpinned Jewish existence opens Elie up to a "great void" within him. Although Elie conflates his stomach's measuring time with the "great void," reducing himself to a mechanistic drive, it's still a drive to continue dying rather than the resignation of sliding into death.

In contrast, Zalman, "a young boy from Poland" who runs beside Elie on a long march, has stomach cramps, can go no farther, and drops to the ground with his pants down. Recalling this last image, Elie concludes that Zalman "must have died, trampled under the feet of the thousands of men who followed us" (86). The inmates don't distinguish the inert parts of Zalman's body from their own limbs sinking into the snow and mud. They just continue to run. They are driven to run.

Thus, even though Elie marks the obscenity of his last image of Zalman, lying with his pants down in the dirty snow, Elie cannot stop running. His body works like a machine, making Elie aware only of his own discrete body parts.

> I soon forgot him. I began to think of myself again. My foot was aching, I shivered with every step. Just a few more meters and it will be over. I'll fall. A small red flame ... A shot ... Death enveloped me. It suffocated me. It stuck to me like glue. I felt I could touch it. The idea of dying, of ceasing to be, began to fascinate me. To no longer exist. To no longer feel the excruciating pain of my foot. To no longer feel anything, neither fatigue nor cold, nothing. To break rank, to let myself slide to the side of the road ... (85–86)

Elie's overwhelming desire to let himself "slide to the side of the road," to let himself recede into the earth itself, to finally be free of the marching and running, like Zalman before him, offers him a moment when he can imagine a final end to the machine divvying up his body into its componentry. His discrete parts will cease to exist. For that one moment, Elie thinks of himself as more than a body, an "I" who could find relief from dying by quickly ceding himself to death. Elie maps this tension between the fantasy of an "I" who could forfeit the body and be dead versus an object that is collected, pressed into service as the instrument of another's will.

This tension between a "who" and a "what" crystallizes for Elie in his identification with the dead. Elie recognizes that part of his experience of dying or existing as "a living dead" requires him to see himself in the corpses around him. He identifies with them rather than with the other inmates running next to him. Perhaps one of the most devastating scenes in *Night*, this recognition scene concentrates Elie's attention on his father, the key figure in his identification from the ghetto to the camps. Initially, Elie identified with his father and bore a message that "choked" him; now Elie identifies with his father and he begins to see himself among the bodies of the dead, among the inanimate corpses.

> Beneath our feet there lay men, crushed, trampled underfoot, dying. Nobody paid attention to them. ... I saw myself in every

stiffened corpse. Soon I wouldn't even be seeing them anymore;
I would be one of them. A matter of hours. (89)

Throughout Western literature, recognition scenes serve to establish a protagonist's claim to sovereignty, a narrator's membership
in community, or a character's entitlements. However, Elie is no
king; he is a member of a community of corpses. His entitlements
emerge in death, written on the dead bodies scattered around him.
Elie's displacement of recognition from the inmates to the corpses
suggests a dramatic realignment of community: He constructs it
where he finds claim, from among those who are like him, from
among the dead.

This percepton is startlingly different than that of a non-Jewish
survivor of Buchenwald, Jorge Semprun. Like Wiesel, Semprun states
that he died at Buchenwald; however, he recognizes himself as a ghost
or "a living dead" in the eyes of the other inmates and his liberators.
For Wiesel to see himself then in the bodies of the corpses themselves
implies the crossing of a fundamental boundary on the continuum of
dying. Yet Wiesel refuses to cross the last border in this journey.

Although Wiesel can still recognize himself "in every stiffened
corpse," his father no longer possesses this capacity. As Elie pleads
with his father to "go back to the shed," to seek shelter and not to sink
into the snow as the corpses surrounding them have done, Elie realizes that his father doesn't answer. He's not even "looking at the dead"
(89). His father has become "one of them." This scene echoes several
aspects of Elie's earlier experiences. He fights to keep his father from
becoming silent, a murder similar to the one that claimed his God
on his first night at Auschwitz, a night that began in an unsanctified
darkness and has yet to end.

Elie and his father return to the shed; Elie's father sags into the
earth. He tells his son to sleep—he will watch over him. But Elie
"rebelled against that death," noting that "Death . . . would seize upon
a sleeping person, steal into him and devour him bit by bit" (Ibid.).
Bit by bit, piece by piece, Elie has felt discrete parts of his body being
claimed by the process of extermination. Yet he rebels against being
dead in favor of continuing in the unbounded experience of dying.

A sense of obligation to his father fuels his rebellion. Essentially,
he rejects death, but he accepts the twilight existence of dying.
He construes this acceptance as a mitzvah, a performed duty or

obligation that he bears to his father and not to his God. The force of his mitzvah has been to remain connected to his father, to remember him, to displace the fulfillment or execution of the Nazis' final verdict, through his ability to remember his father. The mitzvah has been his only tether to his survival in dying.

Consequently, when his father finally shows signs of succumbing to death, Elie describes his final moments with him in two ways: first, he realizes that his father who runs past him "like a shadow" (107) neither sees nor recognizes him. In his father's lack of recognition, Elie knows that the son has ceased to be a member of the father's community because the father has chosen death (108). He is already "one of them." Second, Elie still feels the burden of being obligated to his father, the internalized mitzvah of a son honoring his father. The tension between fulfilling the mitzvah versus continuing in the void, to survive in dying, becomes magnified by Elie's realization that his father is close to the end.

> If only I were relieved of this responsibility, I could use all my strength to fight for my own survival, to take care only of myself . . . Instantly, I felt ashamed, ashamed of myself forever. (106)

Elie recognizes that the obligation chafes against his own survival. Just as his father insisted that Elie eat on Yom Kippur, Elie begins to see the caretaking of his father as akin to fasting on Yom Kippur; both acts take away from his ability to keep "running."

But Elie's performance of the mitzvah is not enough to save his father. As Elie wakes up the next morning, his father's cot now belongs to another person. Elie didn't hear them take his father to the crematoria. He doesn't know if his father had died before they burned his body. At this point, Wiesel weaves Jewish tradition poignantly into the reality of the death camp. The night before he had climbed into the top bunk, struggling with his obligations as a Jewish son. Now he considers his father's death from the perspective of a Jewish son.

> I woke up at dawn on January 29. On my father's cot, there lay another sick person. They must have taken him away before daybreak and taken him to the crematorium. Perhaps he was still breathing. . .

No prayers were said over his tomb. No candle lit in his
memory. His last word had been my name. He had called out
to me and I had not answered. (112)

Elie had remained in the state of dying out of an obligation to his
father; he had internalized a mitzvah that required him to remember
his father. Likewise, his father remembers Elie's name at his death. At
that moment, he remembers his son in a gesture recalling the God of
the Hebrew Bible, HaShem, calling to Adam, to any number of his
prophets, to his people, except Elie isn't there. He is not there to say,
"Here am I." The severity of his absence burdens Elie with the understanding that his mitzvah for his father has been irrevocably changed.
He must remember that he wasn't there when his father died. This
partial memory suggests itself as the only way that Elie the son can
sanctify his father's death. Elie must mark his memory with the reality
that at the last minute he was not there. His survival in dying requires
him to remember that he was not there.

After his liberation from Buchenwald, as he contemplates
himself in a mirror, Elie realizes that "[F]rom the depths of the
mirror, a corpse was contemplating me. The look in his eyes as he
gazed at me has never left me" (115). As *Night* ends, Wiesel ponders
the entity in the mirror against who he is after liberation. He will
never be free of the corpse staring at him. He is aware now of an
"I" who can see himself. No longer a stomach, Elie has internalized
the corpses around him. He was one of them. Death and dying
become fluid and constant experiences for the inmates at Auschwitz
and Buchenwald, for those eternally marching, being forced to drag
themselves into that night. This dying suggests a duration impossible to map in hours and minutes because it exceeds common
modes of measurement; however, it does have stages. The inmates
move from subjects to objects, from bodies to body parts, from
shadows to corpses. For the Jewish inmates, dying extends beyond
time and space. This extension makes dying an unbounded experience because it shifts death from what is knowable to an experience
that exceeds any category of perception. Beyond time and space, it
produces dying as an unending present tense. This space had always
been a place for Jewish faith, but after Auschwitz, this place remains
an unsanctified void.

Even more troubling, Wiesel leaves us with the image of the corpse "contemplating him." The corpse never leaves him. Indelibly marked by the camps, Elie Wiesel will drag this corpse with him wherever he goes.

Lawrence Langer argues that temporality itself has been altered because of the camps. Temporality—the category underwriting all human experience—has been altered and, with it, space, obligation, remembrance, faith, and history. The effects of death and dying in the camps are not measured in terms of hours and minutes but rather in terms of a never-ending duration that takes up all the fundamental narratives underwriting Jewish existence and human history, violating them and those who would bear their marks. Thus it remains unsanctifiable.

WORKS CITED

Avni, Ora. "Beyond psychoanalysis : Elie Wiesel's *Night* in historical perspective." In *Auschwitz and After: Race, Culture, and "the Jewish Question" in France*. Ed. Lawrence D. Kritzman. New York: Routledge, 1995.

Langer, Lawrence. *The Holocaust and Literary Imagination*. New Haven: Yale University Press, 1975.

Scholem, Gershom. *Major Trends in Jewish Mysticism*. Ed. Robert Alter. New York: Schocken, 1954.

Semprun, Jorge. *Literature or Life*. New York: Viking Press, 1997.

Wiesel, Elie. *Night*. Tr. Marion Wiesel. New York: Hill and Wang, 2006.

ORESTEIA
(AESCHYLUS)

"Tragedy's Bloody Borders: *The Oresteia*"
by Louise Cowan,
in *The Tragic Abyss* (2003)

INTRODUCTION

In this analysis, Louise Cowan follows the curse of the House of Atrius as it is acted out in the *Oresteia*. Exploring the nether region that we associate with death, dying, and mortality, Cowan sees the *Oresteia* as the ultimate expression of the "tragic abyss." At the center of Aeschylus's work, according to Cowan, lies our tendency to see ourselves and not others, a kind of inherited curse that leads both to death and also to the founding of a human society based on law and not vengeance. Here the will to make a meaningful order and the will to meaningless, rebellion destruction both emanate from the experience of death and dying, an experience that is at once horrific and transformative.

"Who can redeem the blood that wets the soil?"
—Choephoroe, ll. 66–67

Cowan, Louise. "Tragedy's Bloody Borders: *The Oresteia*." *The Tragic Abyss*. Ed. Glenn Arbery. Dallas: Dallas Institute Publications, Dallas Institute of Humanities and Culture, 2003.

According to Robert Fagles, the classical scholar who has rendered what many consider the finest translation of Aeschylus, the Parthenon and the Orestes trilogy are the two noblest achievements of the Greeks' high period, following upon their triumph over the Persians at Salamis and Plataea.[1] Both of these masterworks were created in honor of the gray-eyed goddess Athena, patron of Athens and sponsor of wisdom and excellence. Both bring about a union of the terrestrial and the heavenly in an order of *sophrosyne*, a harmony encompassing an entire cosmos. Further, the crumbling marble edifice and the still intact dramatic trilogy include in this cosmos not only earth and sky, but the chthonic realm under the earth, so that Hades' region of fertility and death is part of the transfigured order. But here the resemblance ends: language can evoke what sculpture cannot even suggest, something that must remain essentially imageless. Aeschylus' drama intuits a place more deeply hidden than the Underworld, a negative region where, as the Furies say, "the terrible is good." Aeschylus is able to make his audience envision a realm of recrimination and chagrin, a black hole in the universe, more deeply hidden even than Chaos and Old Night. Out of this pit, into the murky ground surrounding it, erupt things ordinarily regarded as obscene, as not to be viewed onstage. During the first performance of the *Oresteia*, we are told, the audience fled the theater in horror at the onslaught of these female figures in black with snakes for hair, blood dripping from their eyes. And their visceral impact has little diminished over the centuries. For through these obscenities the creator of Greek tragedy introduced into drama a gargoylian asymmetry that, far from marring the classical balance so marked in the Parthenon and in most of Aeschylus' own lines, enlarged the sphere of imagined space and enhanced its clarity with the deep gloom of the abyss.

The Erinyes, the grim and avenging Furies whom Aeschylus first brought onstage in 458 B.C. and who thereafter form the ground of Greek tragedy, have permanently affected the Western poetic mind. Their origin is obscure. Andre Lardinois informs us that they are mentioned on three Linear B tablets from Cnossos and suggests the possibility in Mycenean times of "a real cult of demons who bore the name of Erinyes" (330–31). According to R.P. Winnington-Ingram, they were once thought of as the "vengeful dead themselves, intent on retaliation" (156). Homer mentions the Furies several times, referring to them as upholders of divine justice. Hesiod declares that they were originally ancient earth goddesses, born from the blood of the castrated Uranus and appointed the task of guarding reproduction and family bonds. By the time Aeschylus encountered them in the arena of his mythopoeic imagination, however, they had long forsaken the positive duties of their role. As he saw them, they inhabited the dark regions of outrage, emerging only from time to time in the bloody territory surrounding the abyss to track down and torment those guilty of crimes against blood kin. In the *Eumenides*, the last play of the Oresteian trilogy, they speak of themselves as the "great fulfillers," who, working with "memories of grief," drive men who have been "banished far from god to a sunless, torch-lit dusk" (392–95). Apollo characterizes them in the same drama as cosmic outcasts. "Born for destruction only, the dark pit," he says scornfully, "they range the bowels of Earth, the world of death, / loathed by men and the gods who hold Olympus" (74–76). And in driving them away from his shrine, he exhorts them:

> Go where heads are severed, eyes gouged out,
> where justice and bloody slaughter are the same,
> castrations, wasted seed, young men's glories butchered
> extremities maimed, and huge stones at the chest.... (183–86)

As Winnington-Ingram writes, "An audience which made its first acquaintance with these infernal powers in the opening scenes of Eumenides—hideous in aspect, cruel in method, truculent in speech, narrowly intent upon avenging a wicked woman, might incline to share the simple detestation of a civilized Apollo for these barbarous creatures and, later, might wonder by what sleight of hand the dramatist transforms them into worshipful and benevolent divinities" (Winnington-Ingram 154). The ambiguity of the Furies thus is central to Aeschylus' vision of tragedy; in them he confronts the chief tragic enigma: the transformation of the painful individual parts into what Gerald Else has called the "redemption-centered whole" (100).

Behind the terrifying eruption onstage of these "gorgons shrouded in black, their heads wreathed, swarming serpents" (*Eum* 1948–50) are implied the depths from which they emerge. They come from "the dark pit," an abyss that indicates a rift in being, a void in the ordered universe, and, if we are to trust Apollo's aversion, a place not of origins but of cast-offs. This repellent region hardly seems the same as

Homer's or Virgil's underworlds of shades; rather, as Apollo testifies, it is a realm of mutilation, of mixed parts, of bitter pain and unappeased *ressentiment*. It was during a time of high aspiration and prosperity, the Greek golden age, that Aeschylus discovered its ominous presence. In a kind of ironic recompense, as it seems, tragedy makes atonement for success by opening up a terrifying gulf until then hidden from consciousness. In both periods of its greatest flowering (fifth-century Athens and sixteenth-century England), the societies out of which it arose were in a heady state of success. We might speculate that the cost of amassing such power and the threat of its misuse prey on the poetic imagination, giving rise to a probing examination of human greatness. According to C.J. Herington, author of the Aeschylus volume in the Yale Hermes series, Aeschylean drama could have come only out of a mind that "at some point had looked on chaos—chaos intellectual, political, and religious" (19). Fifth-century Athens provided such a perspective. But whatever the connection between poet and culture, we have to agree with Gilbert Murray, Gerald Else, and other authorities that Aeschylus "invented" tragedy[2] and that this soldier-hero-poet discovered in the human psyche a region that no inhabitant of the West has been able to forget. Several authorities, however, among them Robert Corrigan, maintain with some persuasiveness that Aeschylus' plays are something other than tragedies—actually, that they are dramas about the gods, divine dramaturgies depicting something more like theomachies than tragic struggles. Aeschylean drama does indeed take place in a different territory from the profoundly human world of Sophocles and Shakespeare. Even so, it seems hardly just to speak of it as pre-tragic, for that label would reduce Aeschylus' grand conceptions to a mere phase in a developmental process. It may be more accurate to think of his dramas spatially, in terms of their location in tragic territory, rather than to view them as part of a temporal sequence, incipient forms of something later to come.

The seven surviving Aeschylean dramas are lyric pageants, apparently all of them parts of trilogies consisting of three related tragic dramas followed by a satyr play. Aeschylus's earliest—*Persians* (472), *Seven against Thebes* (467) and *The Suppliants* (463?)—are quite different in style and focus from the later four, the undated *Prometheus Bound*[3] and the *Oresteia* (458), this latter a trilogy: the *Agamemnon*, the *Choephoroe* (*The Libation Bearers* in Fagles), and the *Eumenides*, or "kindly ones." All Aeschylus's plays, except the *Prometheus*, are about the conflicting drives within the human psyche that trouble both the family and the city. It is not simply that particular families have hidden crimes that, disgracefully, will out. Rather, it is that the mortal condition in itself entails persistent violence. Humanity is made up of borderline creatures, subject to two warring forces and doomed to destroy themselves unless a reconciliation can be effected between such oppositions as male and female, reason and blood loyalty, *polis* and *oikos*. The record of that struggle toward harmony is overtly recorded in two of Aeschylus' trilogies—one, the *Oresteia*, which survives intact; the other, the *Prometheia*, of which only one play remains. In both, Aeschylus uses his powerful lyric sense as a means of exploring the communal source of pain and dread. In probing the roots of myth, he discovers the unlighted caverns of the tragic abyss. Since his time, if tragedy is to be authentic, it must make its way, by whatever means, to this region that he first realized. Some four hundred years earlier Homer had implied Achilles' confrontation with it, and a Homeric hymn had recounted Hera's wrathful flight to this cavernous and forsaken region, but Aeschylus—who wrote some ninety tragedies, introducing a second actor and, in the *Oresteia*, a third—probes the intrusion of this realm into the civic order. His works establish the metaphysical bounds of the tragic in works of art that reveal a fundamental conflict in the nature of being. Some things are so because they cannot be otherwise. And it is by uncovering the hidden horror of the tragic necessity that humanity suffers into wisdom: *pathei mathos*—the terrible insight of the Aeschylean vision.

Once Aeschylus had uncovered the existence of the tragic region, Sophocles and Euripides were not long in looking into its depths. And, two thousand years later, Shakespeare, though he focused more than Aeschylus on the intricacies of character, still based his tragedies not so much on his heroes' individual traits as on their entry into an experience of impenetrable darkness. For tragedy, as Aeschylus first reveals it, is about the invitation of a chosen person into the dimension of the gods, though the way into that dazzling ambience is through the blindness of tragic insight. Those who are marked for such immolation but who refuse the call spend their time, generation by generation, in the bloody ground surrounding the abyss, where they maul and tear each other in acts of retribution. At the heart of the tragic, then, we could say, is the summons to divine inclusion, though it is hardly recognized as such by the victim. The site of entry is made ready by the suffering of a god. There could be no tragedy without the firebringer Prometheus, who crossed over immortal boundaries to bring mortals the gift of comprehension.

Aeschylus thus prepares the tragic ground, and two of his trilogies lay out its parameters. The *Oresteia* describes the horizontal extension of tragedy and the *Prometheia* its vertical heights and depths, though only one part of this latter group of dramas, *Prometheus Bound*, has been preserved. Fragments of a second play, *Prometheus Unbound*, and mention of a third, *Prometheus the Firebringer*, remain to tantalize the scholar. Though most authorities think otherwise, the play that survives seems logically to be the middle play of the trilogy, the one in which the theft of divine fire has already been accomplished, so that the action of the drama consists in the suffering that leads to the final plunge into Tartarus. The setting of the drama is at the world's end, the "jumping off place" in farthest Scythia, where the Titan's servants and fellow gods, at the command of Zeus, nail Prometheus to a rocky cliff. This is the edge of the earth, the cragged region bordering the gulf into which at the end of the drama this heroic, foreknowing Titan will be hurled. Nailed to the ledge, Prometheus thus is the iconic figure of tragedy, becoming the visible sign of a suffering that heretofore unknown to the gods can no longer be viewed as the exclusive and ignominious burden of mortals. It is as though he prepares the way for tragic human suffering, leads the way, so to speak, for mortal being to enter into an immortal ground. Until the final age, the drama makes clear, when a reconciliation will occur, a god is undergoing agony for the human race.

The Prometheus drama seems the absolute paradigm of both the tragic *mythos* and the tragic *ethos*. The protagonist has crossed the line between the human and the divine, has attempted to remake the human project and redefine the ideal concept of justice, and for his hubris is now isolated on a rocky cliff. This "stony place of justice," of which the chorus in *Antigone* later speaks, is, in mythic time, first brought onstage in *Prometheus*; but it recurs perennially in the tragic region of the psyche and in tragic drama as liminal space: the crossroads, the heath, the brazen doorsill, the woods at Dunsinane, the dark halls of the castle at Elsinore. It is the region where the ultimate opposing powers are probed and the necessity of the descent into darkness discovered. The elements of tragic illumination come together in *Prometheus Bound*, not as conscious knowledge but as an icon—an image of suffering divinity that has haunted the Western mind since the play was first performed. *Prometheus Bound*, then, is about the splitting open of the abyss, this rift in being, where those specially called may be brought for their suffering. In it we apprehend the vertical axis of the cosmos, with the protagonist touching (so to say) both the deepest regions of Tartarus and the highest regions of Olympus. The *agon* takes place within this cosmos: Zeus, the principle of intellect and order, struggles with Prometheus, principle of freedom and compassion. As viewers, the audience actually sees neither Tartarus nor Olympus but experiences their location as *transcendent* psychic terrain.

In contrast, the *Oresteia* takes place in the flatlands surrounding the dread chasm, in a murky territory where mortals make their futile attempts to attain justice by evening the score. The chief concern of this sole existent Greek trilogy is the work of art that we call civilization. Depicting the exchange of wrongs in which mortals engage, it goes on to show the possibility of redemption and the way back from the void. It presents the ultimate human dilemma; mortals contend with two laws in their members, two different inheritances: the necessity of living up to the father's code, an urgency primarily of the mind, of ideals, of *nomos*; and the necessity of honoring the mother's heart, a burden primarily of the body, of the vitals, of *physis*. Clytemnestra's baring of her breast to her son is not simply a melodramatic reproach but a reminder of his obligation to the maternal body—all that Apollo disdains. Aeschylus is the first to discern what seems the impossibility of resolution. Mortals being what they are, the gods themselves cannot agree on their proper role. Only stopping and starting over in a renunciation of rights can ensure the continuance of the race.

Steeped in Homer (who preceded him by nearly four hundred years), Aeschylus took the plot of the Orestes trilogy and its main characters from the *Iliad* and the *Odyssey*. But, as Fagles tells us in "The Serpent and the Eagle," the introduction to his translation, Aeschylus "deepened Homer with even older, darker legends and lifted him to a more enlightened stage of culture" (14). Perhaps this is a key to the tragic: the poetic calling up of ancient wrongs and, in a ritualized art piece, spreading their contagion so that they infect the ground around them, bringing about an aesthetic recurrence of their conflicts—which can then, in the simulacrum of an art piece, be resolved. Ultimately, from a new protagonist's making

his way through the tragic territory and daring an encounter with
the void (in which he either calls upon the gods for help or allows
himself to be engulfed by the darkness) emerge the beginnings of
a new order.

In the grim story of the House of Atreus, the turbulence of the
present actions stems from a "spirit" (*daimon*), a curse, that has fallen
on the entire family line. It apparently can have no ending, since it
is passed on from person to person, generation by generation, giving
birth to fresh abhorrences and the renewed necessity of retaliation.
The Chorus of old women declares at the beginning of *The Libation
Bearers*, the second play of the trilogy: "the blood that Mother Earth
consumes / clots hard; it won't seep through / it breeds revenge; and
frenzy goes through the guilty / seething like infection, swarming
through the brain" (LB 66–69). They are describing the dark and
bloody foreground of the abyss, those borders in which people must
continue to live until the curse is lifted. In the driving force of this
seminal drama, we witness the ongoing of the curse until it turns
against itself and is finally exorcised by the practical wisdom, the cour-
tesy, and the persuasion of the goddess Athena.

Herington has written of Aeschylus' plays that they "invoke the
entire environment—human, divine, and ... inanimate." He sees
"ranked side by side, with impartial reverence" the different elements
of the playwright's cosmos: "the political community, the natural
elements, the powers of the bright sky, the powers of the dark earth
who hold the dead in their keeping, and finally the god whom
Aeschylus most often names, Zeus" (1). For, though it is Athena who
accomplishes the specific action of the trilogy, yet it is the mysterious
and powerful Zeus who is over all in Aeschylus' drama, governing the
world, both in its inner and outer aspects, and drawing all to unity. The
chorus chants:

> Zeus, great nameless all in all
> if that name will gain his favor
>   I will call him Zeus. (Agam 161–63)
> . . . .
> Zeus has led us on to know
> that we must suffer, suffer into truth.
>   ... drop by drop at the heart
> the pain of pain remembered comes again,

> From the gods enthroned on the awesome rowing bench
> there comes a violent love. (Agam 177–84)

The "violent love" of the gods is what impels mortals forward, though the buffeting is recognized as love only after suffering has stripped away any purely human aims. For Aeschylus, Zeus is the author of this healing suffering, the enveloping cloud of divinity that gives life value. From human imperfections, from unspeakable deeds, from suffering into truth, even from an encounter with nothingness comes the turbulent divine love intuited by this Greek poet who in his old age, after having fought at Marathon and Salamis, turned to the writing of tragic dramas to be performed before the altar of Dionysus, the god of destruction and renewal.

The trilogy, divided into its three separate plays, enacts the completed drama of the curse on the house of Atreus. The perpetuation of that curse is portrayed in the first play of the trilogy, which depicts the ironically triumphant return of a hero, King Agamemnon, expecting the welcome due a victorious warrior. He is greeted instead by an adulterous wife who has planned her vengeance against him during his ten-year absence. Her chief grievance is the sacrificial death of their daughter Iphigenia, whom Agamemnon slew on the altar at Aulis so that the winds might blow to carry the Achaean ships to the Trojan battlefields. Clytemnestra and her lover Aegisthus—Agamemnon's cousin and bitter enemy—have been living together in the royal palace and contriving the death of King Agamemnon. For it is not only Clytemnestra who holds a grudge against Agamemnon. Aegisthus too has the obligation of revenge, according to the old laws. Atreus—Agamemnon's father—perpetuated the family curse in a feud with his brother Thyestes. The son of Thyestes, Aegisthus, nurses a murderous hatred of Agamemnon and—whether out of natural lust or unnatural desire for vengeance—has become Clytemnestra's lover during the long years of Agamemnon's absence. An evil spirit of revenge indeed lies on the House of Atreus; but Aeschylus is at pains to show that not only this inherited curse but Agamemnon's own actions bring him down. He has heartlessly sacrificed his daughter, has, according to some accounts, slain his wife's first husband and married her by force; stayed away on the battlefields for ten long years; spoiled the altars of the gods at Troy; taken maidens as "meeds of war"; and brought home a royal captive, daughter of King Priam and favorite of Apollo. As the final stroke, in the immediate action onstage, he commits the confirming sin of hubris by stepping on the crimson carpet unfurled before him by his treacherous wife.

In Aeschylean tragedies, the chorus represents the unease of the communal mind, veering alternately from practical, almost platitudinous, advice to haunted conscience, the long-remaining memory of guilt and remorse. In particular, the *Agamemnon* hints of this double mind, this knowing and not knowing, beginning with the watchman's lament about "the hard times come to this house" as he waits for the signal of fire that will announce the fall of Troy and the return of Agamemnon. And the chorus of old men, going through its litany of grief and horror, recalls the death of Iphigenia, sacrificed to propitiate the goddess Artemis that the winds might blow to carry the warships to Troy. Agamemnon had agonized at the thought of staining his hands with his child's blood, but he conceded to it, as the chorus recalls:

> And once he slipped his neck in the strap of Fate,
> > his spirit veering black, impure, unholy
> > once he turned he stopped at nothing,
> > > seized with the frenzy
> > blinding driving to outrage (Agam 217–221)

But Iphigenia is not the only child victim by parental murder in this family. A long sequence of atrocities against its members taints the history of the House of Atreus. Savage retaliation has accompanied savage deeds, all the way back to the earliest ancestor Tantalus, who slew his own children to serve to the bright and appalled Olympian gods. This monstrous crime is repeated in a later generation, when Atreus butchers Thyestes' children as food for their unsuspecting father. Aegisthus fulminates against the atrocity, revealing an imagination sickened by horror:

> He cuts
> The extremities, feet and delicate hands
> > Into small pieces, scatters them over the dish (*Agam* 1624–26)

These lines indicate the savagery that haunts the terrain surrounding the dread abyss, its ominous and horrid foreground, soaked with blood. Within this no-man's-land lies a hint of an even darker curse than murder, one that descends from generation to generation, involving an unthinkable evil—a secret that only tragedy dares recall. Lurking in the shadows at the boundaries of this landscape are ancient memories of familial violations so intimate and dark that cannibalism becomes their symbol. Nothing else could induce the primordial dread that tragedy arouses and then exorcises. Nothing else could so account for the appalled recoil it awakens within us.

This is the terrible root of tragic knowledge that the human race shares in its Great Memory—that we ourselves, not only the gods, are implicated in the horrors that befall the human race. We have it in us to devour each other, but, as Aeschylus knew long before Dante, the human mind immeasurably deepens the abyss, because it can plot a greater horror even than eating another's flesh: not only can intelligence calculate the effect of an unsuspecting kinsmen discovering that he has eaten his own children, but it can also anticipate the satisfaction of revealing through these means a bottomless malice that is absolute and essentially unanswerable.

Some hint of the inevitability of long-hidden things emerging out of that abysmal darkness into light is revealed not only in overt recollections but in the choral chanting of ancient and indefinite wrongs. It is with the ghastliness of this hidden realm that Cassandra is struck as she stands outside the palace, silent and unmoving. Her prophetic insight (a gift of Apollo) enables her to see into the shadows of the invisible. Confronting what she knows will be her own death, penetrating the veil of the underworld with her second sight, she sees the slain children on the housetops, polluting the air with their unavenged injuries:

> ... the babies
>   wailing, skewered on the sword,
> their flesh charred, the father gorging on their parts (Agam
> 1095–97)

Recognizing the pattern of the old wrongs, Cassandra knows them to be perpetuated in the present. She utters a bone-chilling cry. On the housetop are the loathsome Furies, who have crept out of the pit, "a dancing troupe / that never leaves":

> flushed on the blood of men
> their spirit grows and none can turn away
>   their revel breeding in the veins—the Furies!
>   they cling to the house for life ... (Agam 1192–95)

But if these repellent hags are shocking, they have come, as Cassandra knows, on official duty. More familial blood is to be shed. Later, when the dreadful vengeance has been accomplished and Agamemnon lies dead in his bloody robes—Cassandra with him—Clytemnestra speaks of her "masterpiece of justice" and attributes it to a fulfillment of the law: "By the child's Rights I brought to birth / by Ruin, by Fury—the three gods to whom / I sacrificed this man" (Agam 1459–61). She is speaking of Themis, Ate, and the Erinyes, all principles of retributive justice. A few lines later she boasts that "fleshed in the wife of this dead man" lives the "savage ancient spirit of revenge" (Agam 1528–30). But, as the chorus predicts, a further avenger will come—her own son. What Clytemnestra fails to see in this complicated tapestry of justice is that death cannot wipe out death. From the old law of revenge will spring her own death and that of her lover—and the city will be torn with strife until the long chain of repaying wrong with wrong is broken.

If Clytemnestra is deluded about the effects of her own actions, even more deluded is the man she kills. The herald announcing Agamemnon's arrival speaks with an unconscious irony when he recounts Agamemnon's accomplishments:

> He hoisted the pickaxe of Zeus who brings revenge,
> he dug Troy down, he worked her soil down,
> the shrines of her gods, and the high altars, gone!
> and the seed of her wide earth he ground to bits. (Agam 516–19)

In his view, "the man is blest" (521). When Agamemnon comes onstage, he is thus praised as conqueror, as sacker of a city. One recalls that the chorus had earlier proclaimed, out of its prophetic double-edged wisdom, "God takes aim / at the ones who murder many" (Agam 455–56). And now, as though to confirm his hubris, this mighty king treads the crimson carpet Clytemnestra cunningly spreads before him. Yet Agamemnon is neither fool nor villain; he is a man of some nobility who essentially intends the good but who, like most mortals, has inherited ugly secrets, faced ugly choices, and, lacking the courage and discernment to go against the current, has participated in ugly deeds.

The great theme of the trilogy is justice (*dike*), shown to be crowned not in retaliation but in its embrace of all aspects of life in their right order, requiring the help of the gods. The complete tragic cycle, as Aeschylus discovers and as Shakespeare later incorporates into single dramas, moves from destruction to cleansing to building anew. Most tragedies depict only one stage of the completed arc, so that tragic drama seldom enables its viewers to reach the third stage of rehabilitation. But the *Oresteia* devotes its entire last play, the *Eumenides*, to that reconciliation. In it the gods make actual physical appearances and state their arguments, pro and con. This reintegration is the highest reach of the play, the theomachy, the battle of the gods, rendering the trilogy a metaphysical drama—a ritual in which the regal presences of Apollo and Athena themselves are depicted onstage, along with those of the frenzied and cacophonic Furies.

NOTES

1. All citations of *The Oresteia* refer to the Fagles translation.
2. Most authorities agree on this point. Else and Murray have been particularly definite in their statements concerning it.
3. There is no general agreement concerning the dating of the extant Prometheus drama. Some scholars place it at the beginning of Aeschylus's career, some at the end. A few are unwilling to concede that it was written by Aeschylus. For an analysis of current critical opinion on this embattled play, see Herington (*Prometheus Bound*) and Griffith. It seems plausible to follow scholarly tradition and consider the play Aeschylus', written at the end of his career, though it is about beginnings.

   Whatever the date of this play's composition, its mythic time is far prior to Aeschylus' other tragedies, since it traces the opening up of the abyss. Bernard Knox argues for Sophocles' influence on Aeschylus in the portrayal of the Titan's interiority (see his discussion in *Oedipus at Thebes*). His argument is plausible, since Sophocles had probably produced many of his tragedies before Aeschylus wrote his Promethean trilogy and well could have influenced the older dramatist in his portrayal of the suffering Titan. But before Sophocles Aeschylus had divined the presence of the ominous region of the abyss. Writing a bit later, Euripides, with little inkling of the nobility to which characters must aspire if they are to enter into immolation, either destroys his ill-fated protagonists outright or carries them away by means of a *deus ex machina*. Nietzsche may have been right in his dissatisfaction with Euripides, seeing in him the decline of the Greek moment of tragic vision, though the great philosopher may not have entirely understood the reasons for his discomfort.

PARADISE LOST
(JOHN MILTON)

"The Theme of Death in *Paradise Lost*"
by John Erskine,
in *PMLA* (1917)

INTRODUCTION

In "The Theme of Death in *Paradise Lost*," John Erskine argues that mortality is not a punishment from God and the gift of Satan, as readers are often apt to believe, but the gift of God, one designed to end suffering and afford the possibility of spiritual growth. Erskine argues that the theologian in Milton "was persuaded that death was a curse, the result of sin; but the poet in him uttered his true opinion, . . . that death is a heaven-sent release."

The theme of Milton's epic, we are told at the beginning of the poem, is man's disobedience, which brought death into the world. If there is a central doctrine in *Paradise Lost*, it would seem to be that death is the inevitable result of sin. The voice of God declares with severe emphasis that man, once become sinful,

---

Erskine, John. "The Theme of Death in *Paradise Lost*." *PMLA* Vol. 32, No. 4 (1917): 573–582.

> To expiate his treason hath naught left,
> But to destruction sacred and devote,
> He with his whole posterity must die.[1]

Death, then, is peculiarly Satan's gift to man; when the devil entered Paradise, he came, we are told, "devising death to them who lived."[2] Yet in the last two books of the epic Milton apparently contradicts himself; he tells us that death is not a curse but a comforter, not the gift of Satan but the gift of God. That the new account of death should lack none of the authority which the earlier doctrine enjoyed, he puts it also into the mouth of God:

> I, at first, with two fair gifts
> Created him [man] endowed—with Happiness
> And Immortality; that fondly lost,
> This other served but to eternize woe,
> Till I provided Death; so Death becomes
> His final remedy.[3]

To this contradiction between the earlier and the later accounts of death in *Paradise Lost*, this paper would call attention.

A parallel contradiction might be noticed in the earlier and the later accounts of sin. For the greater portion of his epic Milton holds that sin is the essential product of evil, the very child of the devil, and that therefore it can produce nothing but further sin, and death at last. Yet at the end of the poem, after Michael has foretold the blessed age when Earth shall be all Paradise, far happier than the first Eden, it seems to have crossed Milton's thought that perhaps we should have lost something, had our original parents clung to their innocence; perhaps we should have lost some spiritual benefit, which no saint would be without.[4] Adam raises this question—

> Full of doubt I stand,
> Whether I should repent me now of sin
> By me done and occasioned, or rejoice
> Much more that much more good thereof shall spring—
> To God more glory, more good-will to men
> From God—and over wrath grace shall abound.[5]

The idea that sin may serve a good purpose in affording divine mercy something to work on, is unfortunately not unknown to theology, but Milton means more than this ugly paradox. He is expressing a doubt whether what is called sin may not prove to be, here in earthly fortunes, a life-giving benefaction. When Adam confides this doubt to Michael, we expect the archangel to straighten out the remarks into something like orthodoxy; but apparently the heavenly messenger shares Adam's sentiments.

This contradiction in Milton's accounts of death and of sin is here stated somewhat sharply; it is obvious that the illustrations take on a certain exaggeration when isolated from the whole text. It is obvious also that the terms need defining. The death that follows Satan's disobedience, for example, can hardly be identical with the death that follows Adam's sin, for there is no prospect that Satan will cease to exist. Milton has fortunately made clear for us in his treatise on *Christian Doctrine* what he means by Sin and by Death. He there enumerates the four degrees of death recognized by theologians.[6] The first degree "comprehends all those evils which lead to death, and which it is agreed came into the world immediately upon the fall of man"—such evils, he continues, as guiltiness, terrors of conscience, the loss of divine favor, "a diminution of the majesty of the human countenance, and a conscious degradation of the mind." The second degree is spiritual death—that is, loss of innate righteousness, loss of understanding to discern the chief good, and loss of liberty to do good. These two degrees of death are defined in the *Christian Doctrine* as applying to man, but in *Paradise Lost* their effects are traced more relentlessly in Satan, the majesty of whose countenance is gradually diminished, whose mind is consciously degraded, and who at last is without understanding to discern the chief good. But the death with which Adam and Eve are threatened, and which Milton allows to obscure the spiritual decay in their characters, is the third degree of death,[7] the dying of the soul as well as of the body. Milton's opinion is well known, that the soul perishes with the body,[8] and that at the resurrection all men are to be "made alive" again quite literally, the righteous for immortal happiness, and the wicked for the fourth and last degree of death—everlasting torment. Even with these definitions, however, the contradiction remains between the theory that all degrees of death are the result of sin, and God's announcement that the third degree of death, the sleep of the soul between this life and the resurrection, is his merciful gift, man's last remedy.

The definition of sin in the *Christian Doctrine*[9] seems at first less important than the discussion of death, but it suggests certain reflections on *Paradise Lost* which perhaps explain the contradictory accounts of death there given. Sin is defined as disobedience, as transgression of law; and two kinds of sin are noticed—that which is common to all men, and that which is personal to each individual. Personal sin, however, flows from the general guiltiness of the race, and every later form of wrongdoing is traceable to the first disobedience in Eden. We sometimes forget that *Paradise Lost* illustrates "all our woe" as well as the single cause of it, and that Milton was committed by his program to a portrayal not only of the act in which all men with Adam sinned and died, but also of some personal acts in which sinful individuals disclose their ruined disposition. We sometimes fail to observe that whereas Adam and Eve before the fall represent the whole race allegorically, he standing as a symbol for all his sons and she for all her daughters, after the fall they are two individuals, suffering the consequences of a particular sin which they alone committed, and representing the race not allegorically but poetically, as Macbeth or Oedipus represents it. Milton marks the difference by the forms of address which Adam and Eve use toward each other. As Miss Barstow has pointed out,[10] before the fall they address each other in phrases which reflect what Milton conceives to be the universal relation of man and woman—"Daughter of God and Man,"[11] "O thou for whom and from whom I was formed,"[12] "My author and disposer,"[13] but after the fall, when they are become individuals, they call each other simply "Adam" and "Eve." But the change goes deeper than the form of address. The critics of *Paradise Lost* who find Adam and Eve somewhat tiresome and insipid, have probably not read the latter part of the epic; for the moment Milton treats these two characters as individuals rather than as symbolic types, he confesses by implication that to him also the allegorical Adam was a bore, and he spends some effort to give Eve her rights. Her first impulse on eating the apple is to "keep the odds of knowledge in her power,"[14] to be a match at last for that all but omniscient man; but immediately reflecting that when she is extinct, God may create another Eve in her place, she resolves that Adam must share with her in bliss or woe. When Adam, out of magnanimous love, has eaten the apple, determined to die with her, and when he realizes what the sacrifice has cost, he upbraids her in highly individual terms, though still, it must be confessed, with a thought of the superfluousness of woman in general. If his own personality is most revealed in that outburst of wrath and scorn, the character of Eve is discovered in her advice to cheat death;[15] if all their children are to die, she says, they must have no children—perhaps it were best to commit suicide at once. Though Adam hesitates to follow this counsel, giving Hamlet's reason, that beyond the certain sleep of death there may be uncertain adventures, yet his admiration for the advice is sincere and unorthodox.

Milton, then, treats Adam and Eve before the fall as epic characters, who represent the race in a great crisis; but after the fall he treats them as actors in a drama, who reap the results of their past decisions. In the early drafts of his masterpiece, he planned a drama with epic elements; the epic which he finally wrote, however, proved in its best moments to be a drama. What he says of death in the epic part of the story comes with propriety from the mouth of God, whose will, in the beginning of the poem, is illustrated on earth; but what he says of death after the fall might better have been put, not in the speech of God nor of Michael, but in the words of Adam and Eve, since it is the reflection of their dramatic experience. It is natural for Adam, conscious of the loss of happiness, to look on death as a release, but we are shocked when the sentiment proceeds as an epic statement from the deity. When Adam sees that all is not lost, that through the love of God the race may be saved for a second and nobler innocence, it is dramatically fitting that he should be rather proud than otherwise of his sin, which brings about the benefit; but we are surprised that Michael, the epic messenger, permits such demoralizing comfort. How exclusively dramatic the epic becomes when once Adam and Eve are individualized, is clear when we reflect how easily the epic machinery might be spared— the scenes in heaven, the angelic messengers—and how much the important passages would gain if they were converted into a frankly dramatic form. In many of the conversations between Michael and Adam, Adam is really arguing with himself, though one side of the meditation happens to be externalized in the archangel. The scene in which Adam has his first sight of death,[16] is cast in the epic manner; ostensibly Michael is revealing to him the future, the will of heaven. But the effect of the scene is dramatic; we are interested not in the prophecy of Cain and Abel, but in the adjustment of Adam's character to the world before him. The scene, therefore, is essentially a monologue, such as Hamlet might have spoken—the sequence of ideas by which man, starting in horror from his first sight of death, concludes at last that death is a release, a remedy. Michael is not necessary to the episode. Adam's first reaction is of horror at the sight of death; his second reaction is of horror at loathsome forms of life; his third reaction is of resignation, after seeing the penalties of even the gentlest end, old age—the penalties of lost strength, of lost beauty, of blunted senses, of pleasure and cheerfulness foregone. He says at the real end of the monologue—

> Henceforth I fly not death, nor would prolong
> Life much—bent rather how I may be quit,
> Fairest and easiest, of this cumbrous charge.

The famous comment which Michael makes in reply is usually read as an epic speech, a voice from heaven of warning or direction; to ascribe the words to Michael was, however, only Milton's concession to the epic machinery he thought he ought to use. The comment is but a more sententious phrasing of that resignation which Adam had already mastered, after first clinging to life and then loathing it—

> Nor love thy life, nor hate, but what thou livest
> Live well.[17]

That Milton intended to differentiate between Adam and Eve as types and the same characters as individuals, seems evident from the different forms of address they use toward each other; but we wonder if he realized how dramatic his epic became. He may not have been conscious of the extent to which he changed his original scheme, nor of the contradictions he was setting up in the treatment of sin and of death. It was probably with him as with so many other great poets—the theme which he announced proved but a point of departure, what he finally developed was his own nature, and his nature was greater than his theme. The significance of the contradiction in the accounts of death and of sin is that in the later accounts the larger Milton speaks, the poet rather than the theologian. When he was preparing his epic for the press, presumably when he was finishing the last books, he had arrived at an independence in religion which would make the story of Eden distasteful to him."[18] Virtue is obedience, sin is disobedience, says Adam. But obedience to what? The mature Milton was accustomed to obey his own conscience before any ordinance; when he defined sin[19] as transgression of the law, he hastened to say that "by law is here meant in the first place, that rule of conscience which is innate, and engraven in the minds of men." Evidently his epic theme would embarrass him, in so far as it turned upon obedience to a kind of police regulation. But Milton was also, to the end of his days, a renaissance spirit, loving this world as a scene for action, for chivalric virtues; the beautiful paradise which he drew, he may have believed in historically, but he never desired that kind of sequestration for himself. Some passages in the fourth book doubtless represent genuine ideals, yet in the main it is not unfair to say that Milton's true paradise, his ideal world, does not figure in the poem until Adam and Eve are about to be driven from Eden. If he had remained chiefly a theologian, he would have terminated the poem in a decent melancholy, considering what the race, according to the theologian, had lost; but as a matter of fact, when once the sin is fairly committed, the epic becomes appreciably livelier, more liberal, more sympathetic, more hopeful,—and Milton feels free to identify himself with his characters. Though he has diminished the grandeur of Satan's countenance, to show the effect of sin, he cannot bring himself to make the man and the woman less beautiful. God announces that they are not to leave Paradise disconsolate, and they indeed go out in excellent spirits, except for the inconvenience, as Eve laments,[20] of leaving the home one is accustomed to. But for the world before them they had nothing but zest. At last they were to travel and to see life—in short, to have a renaissance career. Here speaks the Milton of the *Areopagitica*: "I cannot praise a fugitive and cloistered virtue, unexercised and unabreathed, that never sallies out and seeks her adversary, but slinks out of the race, where that immortal garland is to be run for, not without dust and heat."

If these contradictory accounts of death and of sin in *Paradise Lost* can be thus reconciled with Milton's character, it is unnecessary to reconcile them with each other. They arise apparently from the double representation of Adam and Eve as allegorical types and as individuals. Imagining them as individuals, Milton allowed his genuine ideals to govern the portrait. The theologian in him was persuaded that death was a curse, the result of sin; but the poet in him uttered his true opinion, after a long and exhausting life, that death is a heaven-sent release. From this conviction he did not again vary; he merely elaborated it in *Samson Agonistes*.

NOTES

1. *Paradise Lost*, III, 207 *sq.*
2. *Ibid.*, IV, 197.
3. *Ibid.*, XI, 59 *sq.*
4. Cf. Kenyon's speech in *The Marble Faun*, ch. L.
5. *Paradise Lost*, XII, 473 *sq.*
6. Chapter XII.
7. Chapter XIII.
8. Milton seems to have made the acquaintance of this idea in Calvin's *Psychopannychia* (Opera, ed. Baum, Cunitz, Reuss, vol. v, p. 168), a tract written in 1534 *against* the idea. The doctrine had been taught by certain of the early Anabaptists, whom Calvin felt it necessary to answer.
9. Chapter XI.
10. Marjorie Barstow, "Milton's Use of the Forms of Epic Address," *Modern Language Notes* (February, 1916), XXXI, p. 120.
11. *Paradise Lost*, IV, 660.
12. *Ibid.*, IV, 440.
13. *Ibid*, IV, 635.
14. *Ibid.*, IX, 820.
15. *Ibid.*, X, 985.
16. *Ibid.*, XI, 461 *sq.*
17. *Ibid.*, XI, 549.
18. Paul Chauvet, *La Religion de Milton*, Paris, 1909. Also Margaret Lewis Bailey, *Milton and Jakob Boehme*, New York, 1914, Chapter IV.
19. *Christian Doctrine*, Chapter XI.
20. *Paradise Lost*, XI, 268 *sq.*

A Separate Peace
(John Knowles)

"The World of War in *A Separate Peace*"
by Jean Hamm,
East Tennessee State University

John Knowles garnered acclaim from all corners with his first novel, *A Separate Peace*. Published in 1959 in Britain and 1960 in the United States, the novel went on to receive both the William Faulkner Award and the Rosenthal Award. *A Separate Peace* explores the relationship between two sixteen-year-olds at a boys preparatory school in New Hampshire. Knowles patterned his fictional Devon school on the prestigious Phillips Exeter Academy he had attended as a teenager. The story's narrator is Gene Forrester, who, after fifteen years, returns to Devon and the site of the most significant experience in his life. As is often true of works with adolescent protagonists, *A Separate Peace* is in some ways a coming-of-age novel. However, this description belies the complexity of a work with an intricate narrative structure and raises enduring questions, including, "What is the source of evil?" and "What is the nature of war?"

The first part of the opening chapter and the final few pages of the novel provide a frame for the core experiences of Gene's youth. The summer of 1942 and the following school year command the major portion of this short novel, just as they have ruled Gene's entire life. Gene tells his own story and seems to be brutally honest about the events. Yet, as is often the case with first-person narratives, the reliability of the book's narrator is questionable. Uncertainty regarding

Gene's reliability is magnified by the passage of fifteen years between the actual events and their narration. Time heightens or diminishes certain aspects of memory, and sometimes individuals remember people and events the way they want to remember them. Yet, time also nurtures perspective and understanding not present in the midst of emotional turmoil. Perhaps readers can accept with confidence only that events of the novel changed Gene, that during the 1942-1943 school year war was being waged both far from campus and within the human hearts on campus and that Gene has returned to Devon to gauge his own growth.

In 1942, against the backdrop of World War II, Devon begins to prepare students for armed service by holding its first summer session, a session filled with contrast. As the oldest boys take part in advanced studies and stringent physical training, the younger boys, including Gene and his roommate Phineas, spend an idyllic summer almost unnoticed by the usually rigid instructors who seem to see them "as a sign of the life the war was being fought to preserve." Devon received news of the war—the bombing of Central Europe, the blitzkrieg, the Tunisian campaign—but remained virtually unaffected. It was a summer spent "in complete selfishness." Even the Devon Woods, which lay beyond the manicured fields and imposing colonial buildings, insulated the boys from the larger society, giving them a separate peace from the rest of the world. Knowles draws a contrast between the Center Common, the heart of the school, consisting of old colonial buildings, balanced and conventional, and the Far Common, which had been a donation from a wealthy woman. The Far Common is too flawless and too opulent to be the real Devon. In contrast to the plain exteriors, the interior of the academic buildings are beautifully ornate, with marble and chandeliers. The narrator says the school exists in a "contentious harmony" with itself and with the world. This descriptive phrase is appropriate not only for the campus, but also for the way individuals live together on campus, for how Gene must live with himself, and for the state in which he sees humanity's existence.

The main characters, Phineas and Gene, were unlikely best friends "at this teen-age period in life." From the beginning, Finny is seen as someone in harmony with himself and nature. Gene, on the other hand, is ill at ease with himself and the world around him. Intellectual, academically successful, and a conformist, Gene is from a wealthy Southern family, but not an aristocratic one. He carefully decorates his room with pictures chosen to cultivate the image of a heritage that he does not possess. Gene's goal is to be the head of his class academically. He sees school, sports, and life as a competition with winners and losers, and he wants to win. In an effort to come out on top, Gene conforms to whatever is asked or expected of him, down to his "West Point stride." Although Gene repeatedly asserts that he and Finny are best friends, he also contends that it is natural to envy one's friends. Gene admits a secret desire to see Finny punished for his misdemeanors and expresses disappointment when Finny gets away with another antic by giving amusing and convoluted explanations to the school authorities. Finny's power of persuasion does not just sway adults: Finny has a hypnotic power that, according to Gene, "traps" him into "acting against every instinct of [his] nature." Although he resents Finny's power, Gene continues to succumb to it and do "stupid things."

In Chapter 4, when Gene fails his first test and puts his academic standing in jeopardy, his animosity toward Finny reaches its zenith. He imagines that Finny hates him and is deliberately sabotaging his studies so that he, Finny, will be the only one on top. Gene and Finny had been even until this point in the narrative: Finny was the top athlete and Gene was the better scholar. After Gene's failure, they have a different evenness; "even in enmity ... both coldly driving ahead for" their own success and hating the other for his achievements. Just at the moment when Gene has fully convinced himself that he and Finny are in a kind of "deadly rivalry," Finny's insistence that Gene study shows him he is wrong. Gene's realization that Finny has never been envious or in competition with him is, ironically, even more maddening for Gene than the imagined rivalry. The thought that they are not alike, that he can never be Finny's equal, is the worst knowledge of all. Still trying to absorb this new understanding, Gene climbs the tree after Finny to take a double jump but shakes the limb and causes Finny to fall.

In contrast to Gene, Finny, a descendant of Boston's gentility, is a gregarious athlete and a poor student. He has little regard for rules and regulations and teases Gene about his conformity. But Finny is a stranger to anger, envy, or hatred. When Finny competes, it is for the joy of the competition. His is a world where "if you really love something, it loves you back," where "nothing bad ever [happens] in sports," and where you "never accuse a friend of a crime if you

only have a feeling he did it." Acknowledged as the best athlete in
the school, Finny has won awards, not for athletic prowess, but for
sportsmanship and gentlemanly conduct on the field of competition.
He would not allow reality—"that when you won they lost"—to
unsettle his conviction that "you always [win] at sports." When
Finny broke the school swimming record with only Gene as his
witness, he did so because he "just wanted to see" if he could. No
longer able to compete after his fall, Finny turns to coaching Gene.
"Listen, pal," he says, "if *I* can't play sports, *you're* going to play them
for me." The young Gene is unable to understand that there is no
room for jealousy or envy in Finny's world.

The relationship between Finny and Gene is one of "contentious
harmony" and the two seem to complete one another. Taken together,
they exemplify the convention of the double in literature. According
to Gordon Slethaug, works that employ the double are generally
those "where the narrator is the main character but where the other
character, his *alter ego*, occupies most of this thoughts" (Slethaug 260),
an apt description of Gene in *A Separate Peace*. Where one boy shines,
the other is lacking. Finny admonishes Gene for not wasting time.
"That's why I have to do it for you," Finny says, and tells Gene that
he is "good for [him] that way." Finny seems unable, or unwilling, to
keep the distinction between his clothes and those belonging to Gene,
often dressing in a mixture of belongings. After Gene causes Finny
to fall, he dresses in Finny's clothes. Looking in the mirror, Gene
sees himself as "Phineas, Phineas to the life. . . . [I]t seemed, standing
there in Finny's triumphant shirt, that I would never stumble through
the confusions of my own character again." Sometimes, Gene says,
he feels his very identity being immersed in Finny's persona. When
Finny remarks that Gene looks as if the fall had happened to him,
Gene replies: "It's almost like it did!"

When Gene returns to school in the fall, he finds that "peace
has deserted Devon" with the gypsy summer. Gene no longer wants
any part of sports because it was "as though when Dr. Stanpole said,
'Sports are finished' he had been speaking of me." Finny's return to
campus is also the return of Gene's peace. The only aid Finny will
accept is from Gene because he sees his friend "as an extension of
himself." Gene absorbs Finny's view of life as much as possible but not
completely, for he has experienced the darker emotions of the human
heart, which Finny has not. Even when he knows with certainty that

Gene caused his fall, Finny forgives him because he believes "it wasn't anything personal." After Finny's death, Gene cannot let go, cannot speak of him in the past tense. "He was . . . present in every moment of every day." Gene attended Finny's funeral but says he did not cry. One does not cry at his own funeral, and Gene "could not escape the feeling that this was" his funeral as well.

That Knowles appropriated the tree as a symbol of man's fall from innocence is clear. The tree, a "tremendous . . . irate, steely black steeple beside the river," already serves as an initiation emblem at Devon. Only the older students jumped from the tree into the Devon River. But for Finny, the tree was "such a cinch" that he was sure they could conquer it as well, and they did. Ironically, the innocent Finny encourages Gene to break the rules and jump from the tree. The tree is later the scene of Finny's literal and Gene's symbolic fall from innocence, a fall from which neither Finny's body nor his spirit can recover. The jump signifies both Gene's and Finny's fall from innocence, but theirs is an intricate fall that does not bring spontaneous knowledge of good and evil; this understanding builds over the summer and winter of 1942-1943. The fall is archetypal, but the story is not a tale in which virtue is rewarded while evil is punished. Nor is the story a reversal of the expected. Neither Finny nor Gene is purely good or evil. Knowles draws no moral for us but leaves us to reflect on the events ourselves.

Yet Finny suffers. From the narrator's vantage, fifteen years removed from the events, Finny is the innocent, and he does nothing to bring about his own fall. He is simply unable to assimilate the reality of human nature into his worldview. Repeatedly, Knowles employs the image of waves washing over the boys, leaving them with greater understanding with each ebb and flow. With each wave, Finny loses vitality. Although Finny breaks rules, they are the Devon rules: skipping meals and classes, going to the beach, wearing his tie as a belt. These infractions have no consequences beyond the campus. The important principles of honor, truth, and fair play are part of his nature. He is unable to conceive of a world in which friends deliberately hurt one another out of jealousy. He escapes the war by pretending it is an illusion, devised by "fat old men who don't want us crowding them out of their jobs." His view of life is based on what should be true rather than what is true (Witherington 798). Because Finny's world is built on naïve falsehoods, he cannot fully assimilate reality. Finny finally believes Gene's report that "Leper's gone crazy" because, he says, "I've got to believe you, at least." With this knowledge, Finny has to admit "that the war was real, this war and all the wars. If a war can drive somebody crazy, then it's real all right."

On the night Finny acknowledges the war is real, his fall from innocence reaches its culmination during Brinker's kangaroo court. Brinker, like the other minor characters, is an exaggeration of human foibles. He is all "Winter efficiency," clubs, organizations, and going after the truth. He does not "want any mysteries or any stray rumors and suspicion left in the air" and believes that "in our free democracy . . . the truth will out." Brinker's reality is just as skewed as Finny's but is much more dangerous to others. When he determines his mission, he goes after it with no regard for consequences. The witch hunt Brinker undertakes with "simple executive directness" in Chapter 11 destroys Finny's illusion of any kind of peace. Finny's initiation is finished with the realization that there is evil in the world, that a friend might act with malice toward another. This knowledge is too much for him to accept. Ultimately, Gene says, "Phineas alone had escaped" the horror of war shattering his "harmonious and natural unity." His escape, however, is into death, and he is forever trapped in the world of Devon, frozen in Gene's memory. Finny is destroyed by his own marrow escaping into his blood. He could not have been saved from his own nature, noble as it was, but in the end, as injurious as his physical falls. Gene's "West Point stride" continues while Finny's grace and free spirit are obliterated, first by his broken leg, then by his broken heart.

Gene's symbolic fall comes when he gives in to "some ignorance inside" and shakes the limb on which he and Finny stand, causing Finny's injury. Rather than being punished because of his action, he seems to prosper. At the beginning of the book, Gene notes that he is now "taller, bigger, . . . [and has] more money and success and 'security' than in the days" he spent at Devon. By putting this space between the events and the telling, Knowles allows Gene to develop a mature understanding, yet it is his nature that enables him to survive. Because Gene is suspicious and untrusting, he is able to tolerate the encroachments of reality and of the world beyond Devon. As an adult, he is able to live in "contentious harmony" with himself and the knowledge of what he did. The lack of immediacy, however, also alters the story itself. Gene, like any other adult narrating his or her childhood memories, sees his sixteenth summer in a different light than when he actually experienced it. Knowles encourages our skepticism by skillfully slipping from the present to the past; readers may not grasp immediately when the mature or adolescent Gene is speaking, and this makes his narration suspect.

A Separate Peace, like Golding's *Lord of the Flies*, depicts adolescents insulated from the adult world of war but unable to escape their own natures. Both books end with the characters confronting war. Both novels present microcosms where boys play war games while the adult world, the supposed rational world, fights and kills. War imagery fills the descriptions of Devon, contrasting with the summer's peace. Finny concocts the Super Suicide Society of Summer Session where boys practice dangerous leaps into the river, making their "contribution to the war effort." Of the game he invented, called Blitzball after the Blitzkrieg, Finny says, "Since we're all enemies, we can and will turn on each other all the time." The sound of trees cracking in the cold is like that of "rifles being fired in the distance," and a snowball fight becomes the "Hitler Youth outing for one day." The tree from which the boys jumped was as "forbidding as an artillery piece." Playful back and forth is described in terms of attack and counterattack. Although Finny can use the war when it fits his purpose, he does not let it become real.

In the second chapter, Finny explains his pink shirt and his belt made of the school tie by saying, "When you come right down to it the school is involved in everything that happens in the war, it's all the same war and the same world, and I think Devon ought to be included." In 1942, however, Devon allows the boys to live in a separate peace, but they are never completely removed from war's effects. They are, after all, human and cannot escape what Peter Wolfe calls "the corrosive ooze of evil" (Wolfe 193). In the midst of winter carnival, another diversion invented by Finny, a telegram arrives from the war, interrupting the innocent fun. Leper, a former classmate, has asked Gene to visit him because he has "escaped" from the army. Gene soon learns that Leper has escaped nothing; his refuge from the war is madness. In the final chapter, the war comes to Devon when the military takes over the buildings in the Far Common. This area, however, is not what the Devon alumnus thought of as the real Devon. Knowles brings a unit of parachute riggers to the school, not with machine guns and artillery, but with sewing machines. Even now, in the midst of war preparation, "peace lay on Devon like a blessing, the summer's peace," the separate peace of that gypsy summer of 1942.

The introduction of an entirely new character in the last chapter, Brinker's father, lends more ambiguity to Knowles' intentions. Mr. Hadley almost substantiated Finny's delusion about the war, except as Gene says, Finny saw it with humor that Mr. Hadley lacks. But Hadley's brand of patriotism is certainly an enthusiastic support of young men going off to fight because "your war memories will be with you forever . . . if you can say you were up front where there was some real shooting going on, then that will mean a whole lot to you . . ." Brinker says that his father "and his crowd are responsible for it! And *we're* going to fight it!" Gene, however, does not blame them because "wars were not made by generations and their special stupidities, but . . . by something ignorant in the human heart."

At the end of the novel, Gene acknowledges that the same darkness that caused him to harm Finny causes humanity to fight against itself. Early in the novel, when the adolescent Gene still views Finny with distrust, the narrator asserts: "It was what you had in your heart that counted." The truth of this statement manifests itself when Finny is able to forgive Gene and when Gene comes to terms with his actions. He has been able to accept that there is an animosity within the human heart without letting the knowledge destroy him. He can do this in part because he had learned from Finny to take in "only a little at a time, only as much as he could assimilate without a sense of chaos and loss." There are indications of Gene's growth within the novel itself. After Finny's return to Devon, Gene says he begins to understand "that sleep suspended all but changed nothing, that you couldn't make yourself over between dawn and dusk." Later Gene feels free to dispose of his "false identity" of Southern aristocracy. "Now I was acquiring, I felt, a sense of my own real authority and worth."

Devon is the place where "Boys Come to Be Made Men." Even in the last pages, however, the extent of Gene's redemption and growth is left deliberately ambiguous. He had returned to Devon to see how far his "convalescence had gone," but questions remain. Is he "changed" by his visit to Devon, can he live in "contentious harmony" with himself, or will the events of fifteen years past continue to prevent him from achieving the private, separate peace he so desires?

WORKS CITED

Knowles, John. *A Separate Peace*. Toronto: Bantam Books, 1982.

Slethaug, Gordon E. "The Play of the Double in *A Separate Peace*." *Canadian Review of American Studies* 15.3 (Fall 1984): 259–270.

Witherington, Paul. "*A Separate Peace*: A Study in Structural Ambiguity." *English Journal* 54.9 (December 1965): 795–800.

Wolfe, Peter. "The Impact of Knowles's *A Separate Peace*." *University of Missouri Review* 36.3 (March 1970): 189–198.

SLAUGHTERHOUSE-FIVE
(KURT VONNEGUT)

"Not Facing Death in Vonnegut's
Slaughterhouse-Five: Escapism and Fatalism
in the Face of War and Trauma"
by Jeff Williams,
Universidad Nacional de La Rioja

The mind resorts to a variety of psychological strategies in order to come to terms with abusive situations, especially traumas such as war, its accompanying near-death experiences and exposure to violence, and the aftermath of mass death. These strategies, or involuntary reactions, can include developing another persona or personality, escaping into a fantasy world, or a combination of the two. Billy Pilgrim, in Vonnegut's *Slaughterhouse-Five, or The Children's Crusade: A Duty-Dance with Death* seems to exhibit some of the classic symptoms of stress-induced schizophrenia—"shell shock"—and he also exhibits a fatalist and nonchalant attitude toward war, mass death, and everyday death. But even though Billy Pilgrim passively sleepwalks through the nonlinear, interchanging moments of his life (a result of his coming unstuck in time), he is not completely devoid of a sense of humanity. When his protective masking slips the reader glimpses Billy Pilgrim's suffering underneath the passiveness, the numbness and "so it goes" attitude. His escapism and fatalistic philosophy do not protect him from the memories of the horrors of mass death and the human suffering that he witnessed and experienced as a POW in Dresden during the infamous U.S. fire-bombing during World War II, and he is not as insensitive or immune to these horrors as the reader is led to believe. Billy Pilgrim is psychologically scarred due to his experiences as an Everyman; the war has robbed him of his innocence and childhood. For Billy Pilgrim, civilization's social costs incurred through war outweigh any social benefits. War equals death and destruction, there are no victors and everyone suffers and loses.

Vonnegut's *Slaughterhouse-Five* was marketed as "a moral statement" (Vonnegut, front cover) and "one of the world's great anti-war books" (back cover). Various literary scholars (e.g., Hinchcliffe, Hume, and Veix) acknowledge that *Slaughterhouse-Five* belongs to the antiwar genre. Also, Vonnegut himself states that it is an antiwar book. The Vonnegut persona in the novel (an unnamed first-person narrator who frames the story in the first and last chapters) responds to a question from a moviemaker who asks if the book project is an antiwar book, "Yes . . . I guess" (3). An acknowledgement that antiwar books are futile and will never end or prevent wars ensues (3-4). Even though wars may be as inevitable as glaciers (3, 4), the Vonnegut persona still agrees not to glorify war or to pretend that wars are fought by men instead of babies (14). He also suggests using "The Children's Crusade" as a title. This crusade refers to the historical propaganda scandal in which children were enlisted to fight for the Crusades but were actually sold into slavery (15-16). Once the Vonnegut character assures Mary that the book will tell the truth about war, senseless killing, and death, he is able to befriend his war buddy's troubled and angry wife.

As an antiwar novel, it is important that Billy Pilgrim's experience represents a general experience and reaction to war and not simply one soldier's point of view. Though a surface reading may tempt the reader into interpreting Billy Pilgrim as a fictionalized Vonnegut or even a fictionalized Bernard O'Hare, a closer reading proves that Billy Pilgrim is an Everyman and that his attitudes toward death act as defense mechanisms, designed to diminish the suffering and traumatization that occurs among the average wartime soldier. Specifically, in a small handful of occurrences, the author and/or O'Hare appears at the same time and in the same location as Billy Pilgrim, thus proving that Billy Pilgrim is not a fictionalized version of the author or his war buddy. When Billy Pilgrim is "packed into a boxcar with many other privates" (67), the reader discovers that "I [Vonnegut] was there. So was my old war buddy, Bernard V. O'Hare" (67). Later, when Billy Pilgrim enters a latrine, again the author is present: "[t]hat was I.

That was me. That was the author of this book" (125). In other places within the story the author or the author and O'Hare are described as standing or marching behind Billy Pilgrim (148, 212) and observing him. These occurrences emphasize that Billy Pilgrim is not a fictionalized version of the author or O'Hare but an Everyman.

The main character's name is further evidence of his Everyman status. Billy's last name, Pilgrim, is an obvious allusion to Bunyan's famous religious allegory of living a spiritual life, *Pilgrim's Progress* (Hinchcliffe). Within the context of Vonnegut's plot line, a woman at a party asks Billy why he is not called William, and Billy explains that his father-in-law encouraged him to have people call him Billy, "because it would stick in their memories. It would also make him seem slightly magical, since there weren't any other grown Billys around. It also compelled people to think of him as a friend right away" (Vonnegut 46). Billy Pilgrim's name makes him accessible and familiar, in the plot and for the reader, and helps him maintain a symbolic innocence. In this way, Billy retains his childlike qualities and adheres to the idea that children, or babies, are the ones sent to war and not men or grown-ups. He is in a state of perpetual childhood, and the writing style of the novel, especially compared to the first and last chapters, is composed of short, childlike sentences. Billy Pilgrim's passive involvement in his life, in addition to the many allusions to children's tales and a sense of innocence, also support this interpretation of Billy Pilgrim as an innocent Everyman.

Other aspects of Billy Pilgrim's experience, personality, and attitude consist of symptoms commonly associated with shell shock or war trauma. His time traveling seems more like daydreaming or hallucinations or even mild epileptic fits. He first came unstuck in time during his military service in World War II (30, 43). As a result of his coming unstuck in time, "[h]e is in a constant state of stage fright" (23). Those around him notice that something is odd during his time-travel moments. His daughter constantly asks, "What are we going to do with you?" (29, 135). And "are you going to force us to put you where your mother is?" (29). Sometimes he closes his eyes just before he time travels (43, 58, 105) or feels dizzy (85), and when he was abducted by the Tralfamadorians, he felt paralyzed (75). Once, at a party, he had a strange expression on his face while watching a barbershop quartet, and Kilgore Trout stated, "You saw through a *time window*" (174). Montana Wildhack tells him, "you've been time-traveling again. I can always tell" (207). Billy Pilgrim constantly wanders through his life as if he were asleep or in a daze. According to studies mentioned in Ley's article on psychic trauma, some of the symptoms associated with shell shock or war-induced trauma include hallucinations, fainting spells or fits of unconsciousness, startled reactions to sudden noise, nightmares related to the trauma, loss of speech and melancholia that "in the extreme [gives] the appearance of a complete regression to the infantile state" (Leys 48). Other studies (Dohrenwend, Laufer, Merridale) also include hallucinations, feelings of demoralization, and feelings of guilt.

Billy Pilgrim's abduction to Tralfamadore has the feel of a hallucinatory experience or schizophrenic episode (75-77). The entire Tralfamadorian reality is in fact suspect. The pornography star kidnapped and placed in the intergalactic zoo with Billy, had, according to a magazine article that Billy Pilgrim sees, actually disappeared (204). The intergalactic zoo is a plot line in a Kilgore Trout novel (201), and the aliens look like the aliens in another Trout science fiction novel (108). Another hallucinatory experience occurred while Billy marched toward a POW camp: He began seeing St. Elmo's fire, "a sort of electronic radiance around the heads of his companions and captors" (63). When hearing the town's noon whistle, the siren "scared the hell out of him. He was expecting World War Three at any time" (57). He naps frequently (61) and weeps uncontrollably (61, 62, 197). He sleeps restlessly, kicking, yelling and whimpering (78-79), reliving the moments of his life over and over. He has relived his own death several times (23, 141). He continuously jumps from one moment to another, including all the moments in the war. The war episodes form the central moments around which all the other moments revolve. The war is a jumping-off and jumping-back point. This coincides with shell shock symptoms or disorders resulting from war-induced trauma (see Dohrenwend and Leys). The famous "so it goes" line reminds Billy Pilgrim that people do not really die, at least according to Tralfamadorian philosophy (26-27). This phrase becomes a means to trivialize death and make it unimportant, a matter-of-fact occurrence disassociated with the horrors that Billy has witnessed.

Throughout the novel "so it goes" follows each mentioning of a death. The Tralfamadorians teach that people do not die, "... when a person dies he only *appears* to die. He is still very much alive in the past, so it is very silly for people to cry at his funeral. All moments, past, present, and future always have existed, always will exist" (26–27). And further:

> When a Tralfamadorian sees a corpse, all he thinks is that the dead person is in bad condition in that particular moment, but that the same person is just fine in plenty of other moments. Now, when I myself hear that somebody is dead, I simply shrug and say what the Tralfamadorians say about dead people, which is "so it goes." (27)

And so it is that Billy Pilgrim can deny the reality of death. The pain of death does not touch him; he simply shrugs and says, "So it goes."

But the reader must ask if Billy Pilgrim is completely untouched by death and if the phrase "so it goes" is said in earnest. The phrase is repeated almost to the point of absurdity. It occurs more than seventy-five times in the novel. It appears in reference to death no matter if the death is that of a dog (139), Billy Pilgrim's wife's death (183), dead animals (157), death on television (200), murder (140), suicide (128), Christ (203), Dresden after the bombing (176-179), stale water on Billy's bedside table (101), the death of imaginary people in a novel (167), and even in reference to the death of the novel itself (205). Billy Pilgrim seems disingenuous, as if he protests too much about the insignificance of death or, at the very least, uses the phrase as a mask to protect himself from death's painful reality even though he may suffer due to his experiences. He constantly relives his war experiences, which are retold in a tragi-comic fashion. His reliving of the horrific moments directly violates the most important teaching that the Tralfamadorians have to offer earth: "That's one thing Earthlings might learn to do, if they tried hard enough: Ignore the awful times, and concentrate on the good ones" (117). It is the one thing that Billy Pilgrim does not do.

Instead of ignoring the awful times, the text attempts to domesticize the war horror, to minimize its impact through the repeated use of benign imagery and associations. The following comprise a sampling of the most commonly used, along with isolated examples. The phrase *nestled like spoons* in one instance describes the way Billy Pilgrim sleeps with his wife (126) and also how the prisoners were packed in the train to the POW camps (70). "Blue and ivory feet" is employed to describe Billy Pilgrim's cold feet (73, 75) and later the feet of the dead hobo (148). "Mustard gas and roses," or sometimes "roses and mustard gas," describes the author's alcohol-tinted breath (4), a drunk on the phone (73), and decomposed corpses (214). The color combination "orange and black" describes in one instance "a gaily striped tent in Billy's backyard" set up for his daughter's wedding (72) and, in an earlier instance, the markings on the transport trains for the POWs (69). "It was like the moon" refers to Dresden after the firebombing (179) and also to a ghetto burned down during a riot in Ilium (59). The full moon and moonlight are also prominent in the description of the night of Billy Pilgrim's extraterrestrial abduction (72-73). At times, the domestic imagery appears first, at other times the images originate with a nightmarish scene from the war. The strategy, in a way, backfires, reminding Billy Pilgrim of past "awful times" instead of lessening the impact of those horrors.

Other key points exist throughout the novel, indicating the existence of further cracks in or slippage of the death-protecting mask. These incidents demonstrate that death may cause more discomfort for Billy than the "so it goes" expression would indicate. When Billy first comes unstuck in time, he has just survived his baptismal experience during the Battle of the Bulge: "Billy survived but he was a dazed wanderer behind German lines" (32). After this experience, Billy wants to quit; his waking state and sleeping state were the same to him, as were standing or walking (34). Roland Weary, a fellow American soldier who takes it upon himself to keep Billy alive, recounts various methods and instruments of torture (34-38), but these descriptions do not move or horrify Billy, because he remembers "an extremely gruesome crucifix hanging on the wall of his little bedroom in Ilium" (38). His first time travel is to a terrifying moment when his father throws him into the deep end of a pool in order to teach him how to swim (43); to Billy "it was like an execution" (44).

Another sign that the "so it goes" refrain does not alleviate Billy's fear is that he does not want to talk about the war. He reluctantly tells Valencia about Edgar Derby's death and admits that sometimes the war was awful (121). His excuse for not wanting to tell Valencia about the war is that "[i]t would seem like a dream" and that "[o]ther people's dreams aren't very interesting, usually" (121). Billy's aversion to thinking about the war is especially clear when he admits that he might have a secret from himself: During his eighteenth-wedding-anniversary party, a barbershop quartet sings *That Old Gang of Mine* and "[u]nexpectedly, Billy found himself upset by the song and the occasion.... Billy had powerful psychosomatic responses to the changing chords. His mouth filled with the taste of lemonade, and his face became grotesque, as though he really were being stretched on the torture engine called the *rack*" (172-173). He realizes that "[h]e had supposed for years that he had no secrets from himself. Here was proof that he had a great big secret somewhere inside, and he could not imagine what it was" (173). Later, the secret is revealed and it is connected to his experiences after emerging from the newly firebombed Dresden. When he first saw the devastation, "[t]he guards drew together instinctively, rolled their eyes. They experimented with one expression and then another, said nothing, though their mouths were often open. They looked like a silent film of a barbershop quartet" (178). The barbershop quartet image later repeats itself during the plane crash that almost kills Billy (154-156). These two traumatic experiences still dwell within him and are no doubt the cause of his consternation during the wedding anniversary party. These traumatic episodes erode the death-denying "so it goes" refrain.

The final breaking point for Billy is not a single death or the accumulated pain of witnessing mass death but rather a single incident of suffering due to neglect. The neglect of innocent animals. After the firebombing, Billy was riding in a horse-drawn, coffin-shaped wagon through bombed-out Dresden. He wakes from a nap to the sound of a German couple speaking, "cooing" to the horses. Billy Pilgrim becomes curious and, after several attempts at different languages, the couple realizes that Billy Pilgrim speaks English, and so, "they at once scolded him in English for the condition of the horses. They made Billy get out of the wagon and come look at the horses. When Billy saw the condition of his means of transportation, he burst into tears. He hadn't cried about anything else in the war" (197).

Billy Pilgrim ceased to find any meaning in life because of his wartime experiences (101) and the "so it goes" tagline signifies that lack of meaning. Though in the same way that "so it goes" fails to insulate him from pain and loss due to death, it may also fail to keep life meaningless, and life may still hold some significance for Billy. Certain symptoms of pain, indications that Billy finds meaning and importance in some aspects of life, emerge here and there in his story. Some of these indicators have been alluded to earlier and include his weeping and general melancholia or malaise. He often feels sleepy. At one point after time traveling he opened his eyes to find himself in his optometry office with a patient who became uncomfortable with his silence. He was losing his sense of time, "[h]e had fallen asleep at work before. It had been funny at first. Now Billy was starting to get worried about it, about his mind in general. He tried to remember how old he was, couldn't. He tried to remember what year it was. He couldn't do that either" (56).

If life is meaningless, then these things should not matter to Billy Pilgrim. While Billy is in the hospital, the reader learns that his list-lessness is a ruse: "[a]ctually, Billy's outward listlessness was a screen. The listlessness concealed a mind that was fizzing and flashing thrilling-ly. It was preparing letters and lectures about the flying saucers, the negligibility of death and the true nature of time" (190). Billy wants to save humanity, "he was devoting himself to a calling much higher than mere business. He was doing nothing less now, he thought, than prescribing corrective lenses for Earthling souls" (29). When a boy is examined in the optometry office, Billy Pilgrim learns that the boy's father has died in the Vietnam War, and "[W]hile he examined the boy's eyes, Billy told him matter-of-factly about his adventures on Tralfamadore, assured the fatherless boy that his father was very much alive still in moments the boy would see again and again. 'Isn't that comforting?' Billy asked" (135). If Billy believed life was meaningless, he wouldn't find it necessary to try to tell the world about the Tralfa-madorians or to comfort a boy grieving the death of his father.

Billy Pilgrim suffers from shell shock or a type of post-traumatic-stress syndrome. Even though he claims to adhere to the famous poem: "God grant me the serenity to accept the things I cannot change, courage to change the things I can and wisdom always to tell the difference" (60, 209), and even though he acknowledges that one of the things he cannot change is the past, present, and future (60), he still engages in a campaign to "prescribe corrective lenses for Earthling souls." Though Billy Pilgrim wishes for the perfect epitaph, "Everything was Beautiful and Nothing Hurt," in reality he knows that everything was not beautiful and everything did hurt. That is the big secret that he keeps from himself.

Works Cited

Dohrenwend, Bruce P. "The Role of Adversity and Stress in Psychopathology: Some Evidence and Its Implications for Theory and Research." *Journal of Health and Social Behavior* 41.1 (2000): 1–19.

Hinchcliffe, Richard. "'Would'st thou be in a dream': John Bunyan's *The Pilgrim's Progress* and Kurt Vonnegut's *Slaughterhouse-Five*." *European Journal of American Culture* 30.2 (2002): 183-196.

Hume, Kathryn. "Vonnegut's Melancholy." *Philological Quarterly.* 77.2 (1998): 221–238.

Laufer, Robert S., M.S. Gallops and Ellen Frey-Wouters. "War Stress and Trauma: The Vietnam Veteran Experience." *Journal of Health and Social Behavior* 25.1 (1984): 65–85.

Leys, Ruth. "Death Masks: Kardiner and Ferenczi on Psychic Trauma." *Representations* 53 (1996): 44–73.

Merridale, Catherine. "The Collective Mind: Trauma and Shell-Shock in Twentieth-Century Russia." *Shell-Shock* Spec. issue of *Journal of Contemporary History* 35.1 (2000): 39–55.

Veix, Donald B. "Teaching a Censored Novel: *Slaughterhouse-Five*." *The English Journal* 64.7 (1975): 25–33.

Vonnegut, Kurt. *Slaughterhouse-Five*. 1966. New York: Dell-Laurel, 1991.

"Stopping by Woods on a Snowy Evening" (Robert Frost)

"The 'Death Wish' in 'Stopping by Woods'"
by James Armstrong, in *College English* (1964)

Introduction

Following John Ciardi's reading of symbolism in "Stopping by Woods on a Snowy Evening," in which Ciardi hypothesized "the dark and the snowfall symbolize a death-wish, however momentary," James Armstrong draws comparisons with another Frost poem, "The Onset," and also with other key literary works. Justifying Ciardi's controversial hypothesis, Armstrong concludes his argument by fanning out to Frost's universal vision, one that holds within its purview our fascination with death and dying.

Six years ago John Ciardi inadvertently unsettled a great many poetry-lovers with his analysis of Robert Frost's poem, "Stopping By Woods on a Snowy Evening" (*Saturday Review*, April 12, 1958). Mr. Ciardi's thesis was that practically all good poems are metaphorical, or symbolic, and that Frost's poem, in particular, "ends by suggesting meanings far beyond anything specifically referred to in the narrative."

Armstrong, James. "The 'Death Wish' in 'Stopping by Woods.'" *College English* Vol. 25, No. 6 (March 1964). 440–445.

His attempt to elucidate some of those meanings led him to propose that "the dark and the snowfall symbolize a death-wish, however momentary."

The response from readers was phenomenal. For weeks *SR*'s letters page was filled with denunciations of Mr. Ciardi's critical ability and with general protests against "probing, poking, and picking" at poems, as one reader put it. There were letters of appreciation and congratulation as well, but the anti-analysis and anti-Ciardi responses were clearly in the majority. Mr. Ciardi defended himself and the name of Criticism with grace and good humor in a short follow-up article, and the furor, after a few more sputters, gradually subsided.

The issue was far from dead, however, as I soon began to discover. Resentment was still smoldering among Frost's admirers. What surprised me most was that where I expected to find the most sympathy for Mr. Ciardi's position—among college English teachers—I found more often displeasure. It was not the process of analysis that they objected to, as I soon learned, but the suggestion that Frost's poem expressed a "death-wish." To find such a feeling in a poem by Robert Frost, of all people, was apparently to them literary Freudianism at its worst. I began to suspect that it was really this point of interpretation, rather than criticism in general, at which most *SR* readers had taken offense. When I heard Mr. Frost himself at a public lecture pooh-pooh the death-wish interpretation, to the obvious and audible delight of the audience, my suspicions were confirmed.

If we feel obligated to accept Frost's disavowal as the final word, then there is no more to be said; but we need not do so. Many a poet has publicly refused to admit in his work the presence of an intention or meaning that to any discerning reader is clearly there. It may be that he justly regards his poem as his best and final statement of the matter and dislikes having it diluted or distorted by paraphrase. Or it may be that he resents having his thoughts and feelings pried at by morbid admirers who are not satisfied with the exceptional frankness about himself with which he has already complimented them in his work. For example, for Frost to admit that his poem embodies a "death-wish" would inevitably have called forth from countless well-meaning and naive admirers the question, "But for goodness' sake—why?" Few men would willingly put themselves in the position of having to answer such a question.

What is it about the idea of a "death-wish" in a Frost poem that is so disturbing? Can the impulse itself—"that hunger for final rest and surrender that a man may feel," as Mr. Ciardi described it—be so unfamiliar to us? I find it hard to think so. And even those who have never recognized it in themselves can hardly pretend that it is uncommon in literature. More than one poet has "been half in love with easeful Death." Perhaps it is hard to believe that Robert Frost ever entertained the feeling, much less gave it public expression. Yet we have only to read his poems.

I think of one, for example, called "The Onset," which begins,

> Always the same, when on a fated night
> At last the gathered snow lets down as white
> As may be in dark woods, and with a song
> It shall not make again all winter long
> Of hissing on the yet uncovered ground,
> I almost stumble looking up and round,
> As one who overtaken by the end
> Gives up his errand, and lets death descend
> Upon him where he is, with nothing done
> To evil, no important triumph won,
> More than if life had never been begun. . . .

This is not so very different a poem, in setting and mood, from "Stopping By Woods"; and the poet says, "I almost stumble . . . , / As one who . . . / *Gives up* his errand, and *lets* death descend. . . ." The inclination, the temptation, to stop and rest is clearly there.

Nor is the association of death with dark, with winter, and with snow an unnatural or a novel one. Thomas Mann, to recall a famous instance, relies heavily on this traditional symbolic significance of snow in *The Magic Mountain*, particularly in the chapter called "Snow," in which Hans Castorp becomes lost in a mountain snowstorm while skiing. Like the speakers in Frost's poems, he recognizes the temptation and resists it.

The resistance, of course, is important. The "death-wish" is not so much a wish as a temptation, a brief flirtation with the possibility. Frost's final word is always an affirmation, a turning back from death to life ("But I have promises to keep . . .") and a postponement of the rendezvous with the dark woods and the snow.

Others have recognized the compelling attraction that the woods exercised upon Frost. Mr. J.M. Cox, writing in the *Virginia Quarterly Review* (Winter 1959), says, "Confronting these desert places of his landscape, Frost needs all the restraint at his command, for the dark woods possess a magnetic attraction drawing him spellbound into them." And in "Stopping By Woods," Mr. Cox sees "the powerful fascination the woods have upon the lonely traveler ..." who is "transfixed by the compelling invitation of the forest." Whether the whispered invitation comes from the darkness, the woods, the snow, or all three together, it is a strangely appealing one, and many men have heard it.

No one, perhaps, has heard it more clearly that the nineteenth-century English poet, Thomas Lovell Beddoes. The "death-wish"—the whispered invitation of death—is the theme of many of his poems. In "The Phantom-Wooer," there is not only a remarkable similarity of mood and theme to "Stopping By Woods," but a line occurring at a crucial point that is all but identical to a line in Frost's poem.

A "ghost" woos a lady as she sleeps. His identity is not specified, but his voice is the voice of "the little snakes of silver throat" that inhabit "mossy skulls" and whisper "die, oh! die." The poem gives us no alternative but to suppose that the voice comes from the sleeping lady's own subconscious mind. It is a persuasive voice, and a comforting one.

> Young soul put off your flesh, and come
> With me into the quiet tomb,
> Our bed is lovely, dark, and sweet;
> The earth will swing us, as she goes,
> Beneath our coverlid of snows,
> And the warm leaden sheet.

The "coverlid of snows" reveals a kinship at least of season with Frost's poem, but what really arrests the reader is that startling line: "Our bed is lovely, dark, and sweet...." Is it unreasonable to suppose that this line was running through the head of the poet who wrote "The woods are lovely, dark and deep ..."? Without insisting any further upon the likeness of the ideas embodied in the two poems, I will only point out that these two lines resemble each other not only in sound, but in tone and implication.

It is possible, of course, to dismiss this near-identity of line as mere coincidence, but it seems to me that to do so requires more audacity than to recognize the probability of a relationship. If we do recognize such a relationship, what does it mean? It means only that Robert Frost shared with the rest of us the common thoughts, fears, and dreams of humanity—something we knew all the time—and that he sometimes told us things about himself, and about ourselves, that we hadn't thought of before. It means, too, that a new interpretation of a familiar and favorite poem need not outrage us merely because it upsets our comfortable belief that we had it all figured out. The new idea ought to lead us instead to look at the poem again, and freshly, if we can. And if we are capable of being honest with the poem and with ourselves, we may see not only woods that are "lovely, dark and deep," but the promises that we must fulfill before we sleep.

❧ *Acknowledgments* ❧

Armstrong, James. "The 'Death Wish' in 'Stopping by Woods.'" *College English* Vol. 25, No. 6 (March 1964). 440–445. © National Council of Teachers of English.

Benstock, Bernard. "'The Dead.'" *James Joyce's Dubliners: Critical Essays*. Ed. Clive Hart. New York: Faber and Faber, 1969. Copyright 1969 by Faber and Faber. Reprinted by permission.

Bradley, A.C. "The 'Way of the Soul.'" *A Commentary on Tennyson's* In Memoriam. Third revised ed. London: MacMillan, 1929 (third edition, first published in 1910). 36–48.

Cowan, Louise. "Tragedy's Bloody Borders: *The Oresteia*." *The Tragic Abyss*. Ed. Glenn Arbery. Dallas: Dallas Institute Publications, Dallas Institute of Humanities and Culture, 2003. Copyright 2003 Dallas Institute Publications. Reprinted by permission.

Erskine, John. "The Theme of Death in *Paradise Lost*." *PMLA* Vol. 32, No. 4 (1917): 573–582.

Gass, William. "More Deaths Than One: *Chronicle of a Death Foretold*." *New York Magazine* Vol. 16, No. 15 (1983): 83–84. Copyright 1988 by William Gass. Reprinted by permission of the author.

Johnston, Arnold. "*Lord of the Flies*: Fable, Myth, and Fiction." From *Of Earth and Darkness: The Novels of William Golding*. St. Louis: University of Missouri Press, 1980. Copyright 1980 by the Curators of the University of Missouri. Reprinted by permission.

Krueger, Gretchen. "*Death Be Not Proud*: Children, Families and Cancer in Postwar America." *Bulletin of the History of Medicine* 78, (2004): 836–863. Copyright 2004 by the Johns Hopkins University Press. Reprinted with permission of The Johns Hopkins University Press.

Snyder, Susan. "*King Lear* and the Psychology of Dying." *Shakespeare Quarterly* Vol. 33, No. 4 (Winter 1982): 449–460. Copyright The Folger Shakespeare Library. Reprinted with permission.

Stewart, Garrett. "Lying as Dying in *Heart of Darkness*." *PMLA* Vol. 95, No. 3 (May 1980) 319–331. Copyright 1980 by Modern Language Association of America. Reprinted by permission.

Wyatt, David M. "Hemingway's Uncanny Beginnings." *The Georgia Review* (Summer 1977): 476–501. Copyright 1977 by *The Georgia Review*. Reprinted by permission of David M. Wyatt and *The Georgia Review*.

Index